ASIA
BETRAYED

How Churchill Sacrificed
the Far East
to Save England

John Bell Smithback

Asia Betrayed

By John Bell Smithback

ISBN-13: 978-988-8769-29-2

© 2017 John Bell Smithback

Cover design: Jason Wong

This book has been reset in 10pt Book Antiqua. Spellings and punctuations are left as in the original edition.

HISTORY / Asia

EB093

All rights reserved. No part of this book may be reproduced in material form, by any means, whether graphic, electronic, mechanical or other, including photocopying or information storage, in whole or in part. May not be used to prepare other publications without written permission from the publisher except in the case of brief quotations embodied in critical articles or reviews. For information contact info@earnshawbooks.com

Published by Earnshaw Books Ltd. (Hong Kong)

To Ching Yee,
whose parents 梁少初 & 唐明珠 lived it.

And my thanks to Graham Earnshaw,
a tough and demanding editor
who had the patience to see it through.

Contents

PART I   Malaya - Singapore - Hong Kong   1

PART II   The River Kwai   98

PART III   Hiroshima And Nagasaki   134

Epilogue   211

A Final Word - Connections   244

They Survived   252

Bibliography   258

PART I

MALAYA - SINGAPORE - HONG KONG

There are clear signs that Japan does not know which way to turn. Tojo is scratching his head. There are no signs that Japan is going to attack anyone.
Sir Chief Marshal Sir Robert Brooke-Popham
Commander-in-Chief Far East,
Singapore, December 5, 1941

IT WAS DECEMBER 1941 and Singapore stood as an intrepid symbol of the greatness of Britain's wandering lion. Even its name in Sanskrit—literally *Lion City*—seemed to attest to the might of the sprawling Empire that controlled it. To the north, Japan was rattling a mighty saber and the sounds it made created disquieting echoes that reached beyond Asia. But Japan was far away, and Singapore felt secure. In London, Prime Minister Winston Churchill had spoken proudly of Singapore as "that great bastion of Empire, the Gibraltar of the East," and he and the world seemed convinced that Singapore was, as he said, an invincible fortress.

Certainly, few within Britain's 140,000-strong military force and in her colonies doubted the truth of Churchill's words. They listened to his declarations and were persuaded that Japan would not risk national suicide in a bid to grab land on the Malay Peninsula.

The man in the street was listening too, and though he may have had apprehensions, he was prepared to accept those two eloquent tags of *impregnability* and *invincibility*. If he admitted to flashes of doubt about Singapore's ability to resist a Japanese attack, those wavering moments were promptly dismissed when the news assured him that Singapore was beyond the flying range of any Japanese bomber.

The men of Britain's army, navy and air force had been made aware of that too. "We think it unlikely that Japan will enter the war against Great Britain and the USA," Churchill assured his top admirals. "It is still more unlikely that they would attempt any serious land operations in Malaya."[1] In more recent weeks they were doubly assured when their commanders briefed them on recent medical findings that declared that Japanese pilots had remarkably weak eyesight which limited their ability to distinguish distant objects. That, of course, helped to explain why so many Japanese people wore eyeglasses. Of greater significance was a reported fresh discovery by a military medical team in London that the Japanese were unable to see in the dark.

And so, on that mild December night in 1941, the 550,000 citizens of Singapore went to bed believing that they were adequately protected, that their way of life was guarded, and that the probability of war was very low.

The events leading up to that momentous night had begun four-and-a-half years earlier with Japan's contrived excuse

---

1   Churchill to Alexander and Pound. Minute M.192/1 Public Records Office ADM 199/1932. 17 February 1941

for an invasion of China when it used the claim that one of its soldiers was missing and presumably being held captive to begin bombarding the Chinese at the Marco Polo Bridge near Beijing. Japan had already occupied Manchuria in 1932 after staging a phony bomb attack and had installed China's last Emperor, Henry Pu-yi, on an invented throne with a concocted title, effectively annexing China's three northeastern provinces. But in the dead of night on the seventh of July, 1937, Japanese troops at the Marco Polo Bridge launched a full-scale invasion of China in an undeclared war.

That date also marked the moment when a coalition of Japanese military and naval officers swept aside the civilian cabinet in Tokyo and took control of the government. Acting in the name of the Emperor of Japan, it established a unit named the *Cabinet Advisory Council to Conduct the Direction of the War*. Anyone who dared to voice disagreement with the Council or question the actions of the military—or anyone suspected of liberal tendencies of any kind—was subject to immediate arrest. In a word, Japan had ceased to be a constitutional government and had become a military dictatorship. And as the war with China advanced, Japan began to appear increasingly menacing to her Asian neighbors.

They had every reason to be alarmed. In the event of future hostilities with Japan, a horrifying example of what could be expected occurred after the fall of Nanking in December 1937. From that point on, there was a significant shift in Japanese thinking as it began waging a brutal campaign of national hate against the Chinese, and the appalling acts of violence that followed became part of a deliberate policy established by Lieutenant General Prince Yasuhiko Asaka, an uncle-in-law to Emperor Hirohito. Termed '*Sook Ching*' (meaning *purge through purification*), it was calculated to achieve two ends: to eliminate anyone considered anti-Japanese, and to show what awaited anyone who refused to willingly submit to Japanese domination.

Asaka's order was to kill all prisoners, and in less than six weeks perhaps as many as 350,000 civilians in the city were slaughtered. The exact number will never be known because the Japanese destroyed all records of their butchery. The event, downplayed or totally denied by some in Japan today, has become known as the Rape of Nanking, and it ranks as one of the worst massacres of the 20th century. To General Asaka, however, mass murder was, like bullets, bombs or poison gas, merely another weapon of war.

So, too, was rape, as his frenzied soldiers were allowed to go on a hysterical rampage savaging between 35-40,000 women, many of whom were subsequently killed. Those who escaped death were often forced into sexual slavery as 'Comfort Women' for Japanese soldiers.

Asaka's tactics achieved their desired result, and in Hangchow, Shanghai, Amoy, Canton—and wherever else the Japanese were to set their boots in Asia—the horrors of Nanking were repeated over and over again, though never on such a horrific scale. And in every instance, just as the periods of chaos peaked, Japanese leaders took control, established order, introduced food rationing, printed new money, policed the cities—and blamed the mayhem and carnage on the defeated white colonialists. All of which, they declared, proved that Japan's New Asian Order was right.

Over the next eight years of war, it became increasingly difficult to keep the many atrocities in perspective for, in the Japanese mind, any act of cruelty could be condoned. It was part of the *Bushido* code, a feudal military ethic which maintained that the Emperor of Japan was a divine being, that Japan was a divine country, and that both had a divine mission to fulfill. For soldier and citizen alike, *Bushido* taught that life was but a feather, a mere raindrop upon a vast sea. Glory was achieved by dying for the Emperor, and the death of an enemy mattered not at all.

By the beginning of 1940 Japan had, with the exception of the British Crown Colony of Hong Kong, seized every port on the Chinese coast. But a growing shortage of oil, rubber, tin and other minerals necessary to carry out a policy of expansionism distressed the planners in Japan and they instructed the military to study all aspects of a future move southwards toward the treasure troves of Malaya, Burma, Indochina and Indonesia. At the same time, the Japanese Navy General Staff was at work updating its Gradual Attrition Strategy, a well-developed plan of surveillance and air strikes against the future enemies of Japan.

While those plans were being drafted in Tokyo, Japanese troops that the world might have considered a threat to peace in Southeast Asia were clearly and openly dispatched to China. There, far removed from the prying eyes of unfriendly observers, a large portion of the Japanese land army in China began intensive training for combat in a tropical environment. That included learning the skills of jungle warfare, and in each soldier's hand was a copy of a secret manual entitled *Read This Alone And The War Can Be Won*.

Then, on the afternoon of June 22, 1940, the unforeseen occurred. Just as the military had completed its program of moving vast numbers of troops for jungle warfare training to the Chinese island of Hainan, a scant 155 miles (250 kilometers) off the coast of French Indochina, far away in Europe the French government gave up the fight and capitulated to the Nazis. For France, the war was over, and with the Germans occupying

Paris and controlling two-thirds of the nation, a government sympathetic to the German cause was allowed to move its seat of government south of the French capital to the spa town of Vichy. There, it became known as the Vichy French Government. In Tokyo, the Cabinet Advisory Council realized that Japan was in an extraordinary position to take advantage of a unique situation. The moment was ripe—almost divinely awarded—to make an incisive thrust. Without delay, the Council sent a daring message to the loose and uncoordinated Vichy Government still in the process of being constituted. Its message was a startling demand: because she was Germany's ally, Japan must be given free and unhindered access to all French naval and air bases in French Indochina.

The French collaborationist government, under the control of Marshal Pétain, one of France's great military heroes of the 1914-1918 war, acceded, and within sixty days of the French capitulation the Imperial Japanese Navy was moving south to take control of the magnificent French naval base at Cam Ranh Bay in Vietnam and Japanese troopships were steaming up the Saigon River with more than 30,000 troops aboard.

The soldiers had barely completed their jungle warfare courses in the tropical heat of Taiwan and Hainan when, without a single bullet being fired, they found themselves walking down the gangplanks of troopships to begin the occupation of Saigon.

With them came a crack battalion of engineers skilled in building roads, airports, landing strips, and military fortifications. Within a matter of weeks, new airfields had been completed and the first contingent of Japanese long-range attack bombers and Zero fighter planes began landing on soil that, only a few months earlier, had been the inviolable territory of a potential enemy, the French.

Virtually overnight, the astonishing surrender of the French—

and the new Vichy Government's swift cooperation—had given the Japanese fresh territory for its air force and a modern, well-equipped naval base 2,800 miles (4,500 kilometers) south of Tokyo to refuel, supply and repair her ships and submarines.

Of significance to Asia was the realization that the Japanese were then only 400 miles (700 kilometers) from Malaya and but 600 miles (1,000 kilometers) from the American air and naval bases in the Philippines.

It was at this point that Japan resolved to solidify her position as a world power. No sooner had the Imperial Navy moved ships into the ports of French Indochina and the Imperial Army positioned an occupation force in Vietnam than a representation was sent to Rome and Berlin to meet with Mussolini and Hitler, the dictators of Italy and Germany whose armies had conquered most of Europe and were at that very moment steamrolling across North Africa. At the conclusion of the meetings, the delegations from Japan, Italy and Germany signed a ten-year three-power agreement known as the Tripartite Pact that called for "the creation of conditions that will promote and serve the prosperity of all our peoples."

They, the fascists of the West and the militarists from the East, pledged to aid and support each other in the event that either of them became involved in a war *"with any country not yet at war with us"*.

The date was September 1940. Germany and Italy had subdued nearly every nation in Europe, and across the Mediterranean Sea they were in the process of adding Libya and Egypt to their long list of conquests. With the exception of China, Japan was not yet at war with any other nation. From the point of view of her military ambitions, however, it was vital to Japan's long-term plan that support be secured at the outset from the likely winners of the European conflict.

Six months later, a similar Japanese delegation visited Moscow where the two governments agreed "to respect each other's borders". With great ceremony, they solemnly confirmed their intentions by putting their signatures to a joint neutrality pact which declared that neither nation would become involved if one or the other of them became embroiled in a war.

These swift achievements, the acquisition of a non-involvement pact from the Russians on the one hand, while securing an agreement of collaboration with the Fascists in Germany and Italy on the other, preceded the start of the war in the Pacific by nearly a year.

Yet it was as if hardly anyone in Asia, Washington or London was even remotely aware that, in all but deed, war had already been declared.

In Washington, D.C., fresh estimates prepared by the United States Signal and Intelligence Unit suggested that Japan had, at that moment, approximately 300,000 men under arms in the Southern Region Army that stretched from Hainan Island in the north to French Indochina in the south.

Additionally, in the seas between Southeast Asia and the Japanese homeland sailed a mighty armada of ships that included ten modern aircraft carriers. Including the broad range of aircraft located on the ground and the bombers and fighters on the decks of those carriers, it was calculated in Washington that the Japanese Southern Military Region possessed a staggeringly huge naval air force that alone consisted of 2,274 first-class battle-ready bombers and fighter planes.

Strategically located halfway between the islands of Japan and the continent of Australia, the potentially rich—and certainly inviting in terms of available land, with a land mass nearly twice as big as the islands of Japan but with only twenty percent of Japan's population—the Philippine Islands had in effect been a United States colony since 1899 when, during the Spanish-American War, it had surrendered to a navel fleet from the United States under the command of Admiral Dewey.

In 1940 in its capital of Manila, a retired American general, Douglas MacArthur, was the senior US advisor to the Philippine Commonwealth government which, at that time, was actively seeking independence from the United States. In this position, and with his military experience to direct him, General MacArthur had written letter after letter to the US Army and Navy Departments in Washington warning them of the growing Japanese threat to Asian stability. In each of his letters he laid out what he considered to be the minimum military requirements necessary for the Philippines to resist a Japanese invasion, an invasion he considered extremely likely. "I have every confidence," he stated in the summer of 1941, "that we can defend this place with a force of 125,000 men."

Months passed, and the General's requests for reinforcements were systematically ignored. But on the day that the Japanese Imperial Army began disembarking in Saigon to begin its occupation of French Indochina—coincidentally, the same day the militarists in Tokyo had begun to call to active duty over one million army reservists—a joint Army-Navy board in Washington recommended to President Roosevelt that MacArthur be recalled to military service and be made the US Commander-in-Chief in the Far East.

At the same time, a formal message from the board was sent to MacArthur instructing him to strengthen the fortifications, and in particular to increase the defenses of the Bataan Peninsula and the island fortress of Corregidor in Manila Bay.

"In the unlikely event of a Japanese attack," the board said, "you must be prepared to fight a protracted siege that could last anywhere from one to six months."

In yet another peculiar development in the Far East equation, no one had bothered to notify General MacArthur of his recall to military duty. The first he learned of his presidential appointment was at his breakfast table when he read of it in a note buried at the bottom of a page in a Manila newspaper. After putting a telephone call through to Washington over civilian channels to confirm his appointment, MacArthur's first task was to set about surveying the situation he had inherited in the Philippines.

What he discovered could hardly have been surprising, for he had been warning Washington for ten years that Japan was dangerous, Asia was vulnerable, and that the Philippines was being ignored. Nonetheless, he reviewed the situation anew and grimly noted in his records that he was now the Commander-in-Chief of a garrison consisting of a newly-merged army of 17,000 American and Filipino troops armed with World War I vintage weapons and with no immediate prospect of receiving reinforcements or modern weapons from the United States.

For the defense of the Philippine skies, General MacArthur found that he had an air force consisting of thirty-four heavy bombers and fewer than one hundred fighters. Sooner than anyone in Manila realized, this pathetic few would be pitted against the might of the Japanese air armada.

An incalculable number of painstaking details, fused with a peculiar combination of unforeseen circumstances, go into the planning of a military adventure, and in the years that preceded those auspicious days when Japan was able to move untrammeled into French Indochina and secure an Axis endorsement of her ambitions, the thinkers and planners within the inner circle of the Imperial Japanese Military had worked late hours and held untold meetings to lay out detailed plans for Japan's eventual conquest of Southeast Asia.

Not just for the obvious military reasons, but also because of the enormous distances that lay between the Japanese homeland and the far-flung sectors in the east and south in time of war, the planners had maintained that the success of a future military campaign would depend upon three principal elements: Secrecy, Spurious Diplomacy, and Strategy. Spurious was the word they chose to describe diplomacy that was unauthentic.

Inside Japan, secrecy was not a major concern because the military was in firm control of one of the most closed societies on the face of the earth. But secrecy in the form of a completely indecipherable code was crucial. To that end, elaborate codes had been developed years earlier, and messages to and from Japanese embassies and missions abroad were framed in what the military planners believed to be the best diplomatic code ever devised. Under continual scrutiny and revision, it was judged to be totally secure.

It was reasoned, however, that because the code had been in use since 1921 — albeit with many improvements and constantly modified — it was essential to develop a new code solely for the use of the army and navy. The team selected to create the new code was composed of logicians and mathematicians who were graduates from the best schools in Japan, England and the US, including Oxford, Cambridge, Harvard, Yale and M.I.T.

When the result of their long and exacting hours of work was handed over to military intelligence, it was termed a remarkable achievement — a flexible, variable and absolutely unbreakable code. In honor of its greatness, it was given the name JN25. The J stood for Japan, the N for Navy.

With respect to the use of spurious diplomacy, this concept

had long been a built-in factor in Japanese military planning. Even before Japan's diplomats met with Germany and Italy to sign the Tripartite Pact, its military planners had concluded that for her generals and admirals to succeed in war, Japan must create an illusion of seeking peace. Therefore, while making plans for an all-out military offensive, it was concluded that diplomatic distractions would be essential. To achieve this in the lead-up to December 1941, it was decided that peace missions should be sent abroad — in particular to the United States — to affirm Japan's keen desire to remain neutral vis-à-vis the conflict raging in Europe and the Middle East.

Strategy — the last of the three elements necessary to insure the successful implementation of Japan's militaristic plans — decreed that nothing should be left to chance. Accordingly, a protracted plan was necessary, and to that end schemes were initiated to place well-trained Japanese 'eyes' within the enemy camp as quickly as possible. And long before any military action was taken, it was imperative that Japanese citizens living abroad be converted to a powerful new doctrine which the military planners had formulated. They termed it *The East Asian Co-Prosperity Sphere*.

In the beginning, the doctrine was little more than a vague propaganda abstraction. But as Japan swung its sword and began counting its victories in Korea, Formosa, Manchuria and China, the notion gained momentum. In a very short period of time the idea was to become a powerful creed that would motivate millions upon millions of her citizens to fight and die for Japan as a nation, and Japan as the supreme and masterful leader of all the Asian peoples.

The secondary title of the dogma, *An Asiatic Brotherhood of Asia for Asians*, revealed its full nature without any pretensions.

By way of its writings, its politics and its propaganda of

JOHN BELL SMITHBACK

Teutonic superiority, by 1940 the world was aware—or should have been aware—of German idiosyncrasies and of Adolf Hitler's racial assumptions; now, with its slogan of ASIA FOR THE ASIANS, the Japanese military had created a racial battle cry of its own.

In the months leading up to December 1941, this brotherhood philosophy had been introduced to Siamese officials during clandestine meetings to discuss the role of Siam (now called Thailand) in an Asia of the future. In the end, the conclaves netted Japan a beneficial agreement whereby it was guaranteed, during times of peace as well as during times of war, an abundant and constant supply of rice, coal, rubber, minerals and foodstuffs. In return, the Japanese awarded Siam vast areas of territory in Laos and Cambodia in what, until recently, had been French Indochina.

But more particularly—and of enormous military significance—it was agreed that in the event of hostilities, Japan would have unlimited freedom to position its troops on Siamese soil, to use Siamese airfields to shelter, to arm and repair its aircraft, and to have complete access to Siamese ports on the Gulf of Siam. These, of course, augmented the ports Japan had so recently acquired in Vietnam.

As an added inducement, Japan pledged that in the not-too-distant future it would build a railway through the dense and virtually impenetrable jungle to establish a permanent rail link between Bangkok and Rangoon, the capital of Burma. In time, the Japanese declared, this line would become part of a rail network that would extend to Delhi in the north of India and to the port of Bombay on the west coast.

At the time the Japanese presented their concept of a New Asian Order to those who ruled that peaceful land, the Siamese government had no alternative but to yield to the weight of Japanese pressure. Following years of border disputes and trade restrictions placed upon it by the major European powers, Siam had only recently—in 1926—gained autonomy. But even then, it was a kingdom governed by ministers because, following a series of coups and assassinations, its ten-year-old king was sent away to Europe to receive his education. He had only returned to Siam the year before, in November 1938.

As the planners in Tokyo explored every means of insuring the swift and efficient attainment of their militaristic goals, a hidden factor entered into their deliberations—and once again it seemed to them that they had uncovered another sign of a Divine Hand intervening in the affairs of their imperial nation.

The confirmation was this: since the early 1930s, deep concern in Japan over the rapid increase in her population—it was growing at the rate of over one million new citizens each year—had led her to adopt a national policy of encouraging Japanese citizens to emigrate. Many of those who had been persuaded to leave had gone east to the Hawaiian Islands and to the United States; some had ventured to the former German colonies in the South Pacific—the Marshalls, the Marianas, and the Caroline Islands, each one an island group strategically located in the lonely seas between Australia and Hawaii and which, after Germany's defeat in World War I, Japan had occupied as mandate territories. The occupation was formalized in 1920 when the islands were formally awarded to her by the League of Nations, the forerunner to the United Nations which vainly struggled to maintain world order between the two world wars. The irony was that in handing the territories over to Japan, the League was well aware that it was doing so because it lacked the means of dislodging the Japanese from them.

JOHN BELL SMITHBACK

Apart from those areas, a great many more Japanese emigrants had journeyed to the drowsy tropics of Southeast Asia where they became fishermen, shopkeepers and merchants. By the first months of 1940 the outflow of emigrants had become a strong current, but by then many of the new arrivals landing in Java, Sumatra and Borneo, in Manila, Hong Kong, Penang, Kuala Lumpur and Singapore, were anything but fishermen, merchants or traders. Many of them carried cameras, maps and notebooks. Their professions, ages and faces varied, but each and every one of them had a mission, and carried in their hearts and minds a resolute conviction: it was their steadfast belief that Asia was for Asians, and that they, the new Japanese immigrants, formed an elite vanguard destined to promulgate a divine objective. They were "The Silent Ones" who would one day make the Japanese ideal a reality.

At the furthermost tip of the Malay Peninsula, the verdant island of Singapore was a sleeping colossus, a giant in repose. While it napped, the Japanese residents of the island kept watch as they quietly and methodically prepared for the future. A formidable number of those who settled there had been among the first to leave Japan in the early years of mass emigration, and more than a few of them had elected to become fishermen. The fresh Japanese arrivals were eager to introduce themselves and to expound on their historic roots as they articulated a new vision for Japan and her people. Out of those contacts, covert fleets of small boats were formed, fleets that might one day be useful as landing craft to ferry men, munitions, and supplies from the mainland of Malaya to Singapore. Or even across the Straits of Malacca to Sumatra. If called upon, some of them would sail their vessels beyond the equator to the oil-rich areas of Java and Borneo.

Along the entire Malay Peninsula, from Alor Setar near the Thai border in the north to the furthest point in the south where the Sultan's Palace overlooks the island of Singapore at Johore Bharu, most towns and villages in Malaya had small one-man shops that sold cameras and film and which, some thought, displayed exceptional public-spiritedness because their Japanese owners gave such irresistible price reductions to process films and home movies for the foreign community. In particular, to members of the British military.

To the Japanese intelligence officials studying copies of the photographs and films in Tokyo, it was as good as having trained agents inside the military camps and air bases of the enemy. Even simple snapshots taken during an outing in the interior of Malaya or during a picnic in a forbidden military zone in Singapore contained information of inestimable value to trained eyes.

Near many of those camera stores were bicycle shops, also owned and operated by immigrants from Japan. And because they rented and repaired bicycles, they had a large number of them on hand. In retrospect, the number of bicycles available seemed greater than necessary — but only later did that thought occur to the people who lived in those towns and villages. Meanwhile, when an invasion came, the shops were prepared to supply an invading army with thousands upon thousands of sleek, well-maintained bicycles. And each bicycle shop was carefully referenced on new maps that were, at that very moment, being prepared thousands of miles away in the strategy rooms of the Imperial Military Headquarters in Japan.

More and more frequently, Japanese tourists, tradesmen and businessmen began taking long treks into the interior of the Malay Peninsula to hunt game, collect butterflies, search for unusual plants, and to make careful studies of the wildlife.

JOHN BELL SMITHBACK

From the dense jungle-thick valleys and the nearly inaccessible mountaintops, they studied the landscape, plotted the terrain, and drew finely detailed maps of every one of the interior regions. The results of their surveys were carried back to Tokyo where the data was incorporated in new maps containing vital information concerning paths and tracks through the jungle; of natural barriers, streams, bridges, rivers, marshes, clearings, beaches, sandbars — all that was essential to an invasion force in a strange and virtually uncharted alien land.

As they drew up their new maps in Tokyo, the only other maps at their disposal were the ones currently in use by the British Army, and they were all dated from the time of the last — and incomplete — British Ordnance Survey in 1915.

Less athletic, perhaps, but equally active Japanese citizens stood on the shore at Butterworth overlooking the harbor at Penang in Malaya, or at Clifford Pier in Singapore, looking out at the shipping channel and the league of ocean vessels at anchor in the two harbors. From where they watched, they could observe the military and civilian airplanes flying past, and in a very short time the arrival and departure schedule of every ship and plane into every port and airfield in Singapore and Malaya had been logged, many compiled by entire families sitting on the grass enjoying what appeared to be a long and pleasant picnic.

At the airports, an increasing number of Japanese students and male tourists dressed in dark business suits booked return flights to all points of the compass, but they showed a particular interest in Java, Malaya, the Philippines and Sumatra.

Only later, when fellow passengers exchanged information, did any of them reflect on the almost obsessive curiosity these tourists and students had displayed, and how they were constantly taking photographs from the windows of the planes.

The impression stayed with them, they said, because it didn't appear that the tourists were photographing anything of particular interest: just pictures of the coastlines and the harbors, of oil storage depots, of refineries, factories, shipyards and docks.

While the tourists and students were capturing images of oil depots and naval installations from the air, immigrants who had found work as laborers and construction workers were methodically being converted to the concept of a New Asian Order. In their spare time, they began contributing their diminutive share to the future of Japan by stockpiling bricks and nails, scraps of steel, building girders, tree trunks and other obstructive materials that could, before or during a battle, be strewn on the roads and railway tracks to stop an enemy advance or slow his retreat.

The sites where these objects were concealed were carefully charted, and information about them was sent to Tokyo to be marked on the new maps that were being prepared by military cartographers with painstaking accuracy.

At about the same time that Japan had been getting anxious about its growing population, the health authorities in British Singapore had become alarmed by the increasing number of cases of venereal disease that were being reported by the city's physicians. They put their concern on paper and submitted it to the government. When the information was brought to the attention of the Governor, he appointed a special committee to look into the situation. Logically enough, the committee was called the Venereal Commission, and when the commissioners concluded their study and reported their findings, the government was shocked: apparently 66% of the citizens of Singapore were infected with a contagious venereal disease for which, in those pre-penicillin, pre-antibiotic days, there was no known cure.

The health officials concluded their report by declaring that, by themselves, syphilis and gonorrhea were menacing the very existence of the Colony.

Stunned, the Governor issued an immediate decree closing all known brothels. Immediately after receiving their copies of the Commission's report, army and navy commanders issued grave warnings to all military personnel and, painting with a wide brush, made it a punishable offense for members of the military to be found in dalliance with 'any lady of questionable virtue.'

As though to prove the adage that all is fair in love and war, a number of newly arrived Japanese businessmen were quick to purchase many of the closed brothels and, virtually overnight, found themselves in the service industry performing as hotel operators. The advantages were many, including the welcome ability to overhear stories exchanged by guests coming and going from all points of the globe—most especially, the conversations of engineers and civilians who had business dealings with governments and military officials in all quarters of Southeast Asia.

Almost as a bonus, they found themselves in the bizarre position of having in their possession the keys to many of the hotel rooms in Singapore and, as a consequence, surreptitious access to an untold number of suitcases containing receipts, inventories, plans, maps and documents of inestimable value to Colonel Masanobu Tsuji and his hand-picked team in Tokyo who were, at that exact moment, preparing a campaign of action against Malaya and Singapore.

There was one hotel among the many that remained very private. Situated in an attractive and peaceful location looking out over the beautiful Pasir Panjang hills, it had hurriedly been converted into a luxurious clubhouse and retreat—for

Japanese people only. By coincidence—and if a person had been so inclined—from the upper windows of the hotel he could look out at the slow and deliberate work being carried on by a contingent of British military engineers and their subordinates as they set about building and strengthening a number of ground fortifications for the possible defense of Singapore Island.

If someone had indeed been watching, one wonders if he would have been able to observe that those dealing with the defense projects on the island appeared to toil with almost dispassionate interest? Or if, from those same windows, he could perceive that the men on the job seemed to have their thoughts not on their work but on their families and homes in England, another island, but one that seemed, in terms of time, distance and reality, so far away that it could have belonged to another world?

England, another island in another place where for more than a year the people had been shaken and numbed by constant day and night air attacks by the German Luftwaffe; a place where thousands upon thousands of homes had been flattened by bombs, its factories destroyed, its cities reduced to piles of brick and ash, and its population demoralized. Coffee, tea, sugar, coal, petrol, shoes, clothing and more were rationed in that England they had left behind, and one and a half million people there were homeless or living in emergency shelters. Families were separated, their men away at war, their children transported out of the cities to the countryside where they were assigned beds in the homes of strangers until an indefinite day in the indefinite future when, if ever, they could return to their homes. Forty-three thousand people were dead, and the nation had run out of coffins to bury them.

Devastated, many stoic citizens were living in their basements or in underground subway stations to escape the intense bombing attacks when as many as a thousand German bombers at a time roamed the British skies from the Channel to Scotland, bombing almost at will. Entire blocks burned, and row upon row of houses trembled and collapsed from the shockwaves of exploding bombs.

Living often without running water, without gas, and on meager rations, by the summer of 1941, England had become almost totally dependent upon food imported from the United States.

By contrast, in the tranquil green paradise of Singapore no bombs were falling and there was no immediate threat of invasion by an enemy. Serenity reigned, and in that world of calm, one sensed no crisis. Under the circumstances, very few people in the civil or military services felt any urgency to complete the building of still more military defenses. However, over a period of time, most of the wives and children of civil servants, businessmen and members of the military were, in fact, removed to Australia "as a precautionary measure". Yet they had hardly arrived before the women began stirring up a commotion by writing letters to newspapers and to officialdom from Canberra to London complaining that they had been sent away from their places beside their men unjustly. It wasn't long before the women found leaders who began circulating petitions claiming that they were innocent victims of "government war hysteria", and they loudly demanded military transportation so they could rejoin their husbands in Singapore, Malaya and Hong Kong. Like a great many others, they sincerely believed that Japan would never dare attack Great Britain.

A government-provided caveat influenced their thinking, the contents of which had been formulated in London and passed along with virtually every official report. It went like this: in the event that Japan was foolish enough to do so, if she was really and truly hell-bent on creating mischief, there was only one way for an enemy to approach Singapore, and that was to come at the island straight on from the sea.

In the clubs and bars, around the swimming pools and at dinners and formal functions, opinions were frequently voiced that adding to the existing defenses of the island was a colossal waste of money. Beyond that, it was an absurd way of consuming everyone's time. As proof, the skeptics pointed to the facts: in the months leading up to those final days of 1941, Singapore had been converted into a military stronghold of men, munitions and equipment at a cost, in today's terms, of something in the neighborhood of 120 million dollars. Earlier, when Winston Churchill was Chancellor of the Exchequer, he had fully agreed with the skeptics, figuring that Singapore's sheer distance from Tokyo made Singapore invulnerable to an attack by Japan. Consequently, he shaved 60 million dollars from the building of the naval base, though he gave approval for the installation of the huge fifteen-inch naval guns. They had been installed onshore to point menacingly out over Singapore harbor, and several additional sites were being prepared to put still more of the huge guns into position in thick bunkers of steel-fortified concrete. Once that work was completed, Singapore would be fully transformed into a fixed battleship seventeen miles wide and thirty-one miles long.

Then, even with the defense and reinforcement efforts in full swing, an astonishing thing happened: someone in London had come to the conclusion that the Malay Peninsula was perfectly secure and, to the amazement of Singapore Command, the best-trained and the most seasoned officers and men were ordered out of Singapore and Malaya. In what appeared to be a mad dash, they were taken to the waterfront, put aboard ships and transported to India where they were to undergo training for warfare in the Libyan desert. Untested troops, in the shape of the just-formed 27th Australian Brigade and 22nd Indian Brigade, were dispatched to Singapore to take their place. From Britain came one anti-tank and three artillery regiments. Canada, too, had been asked to provide support troops, and she responded by sending two battalions of young recruits—the Royal Rifles from Quebec and the Winnipeg Grenadiers—who had been undergoing training in the cool autumn climate of Newfoundland in eastern Canada. Through a bureaucratic blunder, the soldiers were sent to Hong Kong and their baggage and gear to Manila in the Philippines. Sapped of all energy after weeks spent on rough seas, many of them disembarked in the tropical heat of Hong Kong wearing their woolen winter uniforms. And nearly all of them were seasick.

From London, Winston Churchill issued a message designed to assure skeptics that the situation was stable, declaring that, beyond its newly-established bases in Indochina and Siam, there would be no further Japanese advances in Southeast Asia.

To add weight to his words, Churchill stated that he was sending a considerable number of new Hurricane fighter planes to the Royal Air Force in Malaya and Singapore. Furthermore, in a statement with the two-fold purpose of offering assurance to the world—as well as conveying a strong message to Japan— he announced that he had already dispatched two of Britain's fastest and "virtually unsinkable" battleships, the *HMS Repulse* and the newly-commissioned *HMS Prince of Wales* to the region. Somewhat earlier, Churchill told President Roosevelt it would "help prevent the spread of war" if he were to send the US Navy on a "courtesy visit" to Singapore. Such a measure, Churchill said, would demonstrate to Japan that, although Britain was wincing under ceaseless bombing attacks from the Germans at home, she had no intention of abandoning a single inch of soil in her Far East possessions. Citing the deep isolationist mood prevailing in the United States, Roosevelt vetoed the suggestion.

The rejection did not prevent Churchill from issuing a sober admonition to the military planners in Japan: any attack on United States territory, he said, would constitute an attack on an ally. As a consequence, he stressed, Japan would have to reckon on confronting the fearsome might of Great Britain.

On the day that Winston Churchill was giving his forward assurances of Britain's commitment to the protection of Asia and pledging to defend Hong Kong, Burma, Malaya and Singapore to the full in the event of a Japanese attack, the situation that existed in the European theater could only be described as perilous. Across the whole of North Africa, General Erwin Rommel's Afrika Corps had the British Imperial Army in full retreat. In Libya, Tobruk was encircled; in Egypt, the Germans were racing across the sands toward Alexandria. Once in control of it, Cairo and the Suez Canal—the all-important waterway to Asia and the Far East—was surely fated to fall into German hands.

In the North Atlantic, German submarines had established a blockade that was so effective in restricting ships from moving goods and supplies from the United States to Great Britain that the British Isles were on the verge of being cut off. In point of fact, since the first days of the war in September 1939, German submarines had sent well over one thousand ships to the bottom of the sea.[2]

---

2   The blockade failed, but at a tremendous cost. By the end of the war, and with the loss of 783 U-boats, the Germans had sunk 3,500 merchant ships and 175 warships.

JOHN BELL SMITHBACK

In the east of Europe, and along a battlefront more than two thousand miles long, a Nazi army comprised of two hundred divisions and more than three million men had shocked the world by invading the Soviet Union. So swift and unexpected was the move that in a little over three months, more than two million of the Soviet Union's soldiers — approximately 50% of the entire Soviet Army — had been overwhelmed and captured.

Within that short span of time, elements of the German army were in the suburbs of Moscow, just 25 miles from the city center. At one point, a fast-moving German tank unit succeeded in moving beyond the outskirts and began shelling the city, disrupting a meeting that Stalin was holding with his advisors in his underground bunker in the Kremlin. To the south of Moscow, the German army was sweeping across the Ukraine at the rate of twelve miles a day, and the important cities of Leningrad and Sevastopol were under siege.

The Russian army had become so desperate, it had taken to sending sword-swinging, horse-mounted Cossack cavalry divisions against the steel and cannon of German Panzer tanks.

At that same time, in bombed-out Britain, an Intelligence officer had just delivered a serious new report to the Prime Minister: in preparation for an invasion of Britain, the Germans had assembled an estimated eight hundred landing craft in the harbors of northern France and along the North Sea, each one capable of carrying eight to ten tanks.

In sharp contrast to the bold words he had just relayed to Japan and the assurances he had delivered to the people of Southeast Asia, Churchill wrote a dire message to President Roosevelt in Washington: "We must expect that as soon as Hitler stabilizes the Russian front he will begin to gather perhaps 50 or 60 divisions in the West for the invasion of the British Isles."

It was at that precise moment that Stalin cabled Winston Churchill requesting urgent help: "The position of the Soviet forces along the entire front remains tense," he warned. To save Russia, he would need at least thirty divisions of British combat troops, plus fighter planes, bombers, tanks, canon and ammunition.

That was the somber world situation in the months leading up to December 1941, and in London and Washington there were more than a few who were certain that the Soviet Union would soon be compelled to sue for peace. And on both sides of the Atlantic, there were influential groups—some within Churchill's own government—who were beginning to accept the inevitability of a negotiated settlement with Hitler. They were regarded as appeasers, though in actual fact a growing number of diplomats, politicians, advisors and military men in Great Britain and the United States—including the US President, Franklin D. Roosevelt—had begun to assert in private that the European situation was so gloomy that Russia and the British Isles could very probably be written off by the summer of 1942.

An overview of the situation made it clear that little deliberation was required to come to that painful conclusion. And in their minds, the men, ships, tanks, planes and munitions that would be required under the Churchill plan to fight a possible Asian war were, by any reasonable assessment, more desperately needed in the Libyan Desert to repel the relentless onslaught of the Axis war machine. To many, it would be better to send the supplies and armaments to the Eastern Front to save Russia.

Of equal significance, thousands upon thousands of men and the bulk of their military supplies and hardware were required to remain confined to defensive positions in the Home Islands of Britain in readiness for an impending invasion coming from across the Channel.

In the opinion of his detractors, Churchill's ambitious plan for Asia, as publicly described, amounted to little more than bravado meant to scare Japan—and in their minds there wasn't one chance in a million of any of his grandiose schemes being actuated.

The detractors may have had some reason to believe that Churchill had been reading their minds when, soon after his speech promising aid to Asia, an undisclosed number of ships laden with munitions, military supplies and four squadrons of RAF fighter planes destined for Singapore were suddenly, while at sea in the Indian Ocean, diverted back toward Africa. Destination: Libya.

Incongruously, what few battle-ready Royal Air Force airplanes there were at Kai Tak Field in Hong Kong—the most obvious British front-line target in the event of a Japanese attack—were unexpectedly ordered to be flown away to Singapore. This inexplicable move left Hong Kong virtually defenseless with little more than a symbolic air force consisting of four Vickers Wildebeest torpedo bombers for use against naval targets, and three ancient Walrus amphibian airplanes that were used to study the weather. The latter possessed no armaments whatsoever. At the same time the RAF was relocating airplanes, the Royal Navy's 4th Submarine Flotilla began shifting its entire fleet of fifteen submarines, five heavy cruisers and the aircraft carrier *HMS Eagle* from Hong Kong to Singapore.[3] What's more, and as ludicrous as it may seem, "for security reasons" all ammunition and shells for the few large artillery cannon in the Hong Kong

---

3   *Eastern Fortress: A Military History of Hong Kong, 1840–1970*, by Kwong Chi Man, Tsoi Yiu Lun. Page 75

military garrison were transported out of the Colony and sent several hundred miles away. To Manila, in the Philippines.

Such peculiar developments did not seem to distress Major G. F. Eliot, a British officer in Hong Kong, who wrote an unofficial report on the situation: "As we approach a showdown, it seems likely that Japan will choose to fight. But it will be a hopeless fight for Japan, and one which can hardly be long continued. The presence of a powerful naval force at Singapore was the one thing needed to close the gate of hope in the face of Japanese ambitions, and the Japanese are now neatly trapped in a naval pincers between Singapore and Sourabaya (Surabaja, Indonesia) on one hand, and Hong Kong and Manila as advance bases, and Hawaii and its outlying islands on the other. This is the golden moment, the opportunity which will never recur again, and for once it does appear that the democracies have seized the initiative and are going to exploit it to the full."[4]

In the planning rooms of the War Department in Washington, D.C., decoded translations of up-to-the-minute messages of almost every Japanese cable of diplomatic or military origin were marked TOP SECRET and locked in the safes of a select few civilian and military planners who comprised the president's inner group of advisors. By this time, little could be concealed from the British and United States Signal and Intelligence code breaking units that operated in stealth on Stonecutters Island in Hong Kong, at Kahuku Point on the Hawaiian island of Oahu, at Bletchley Park in England, in the dark tunnels at Monkey Point on the island of Corregidor in the Philippines, at Kranji in Singapore, and in rooms 3416 and 3418 at the Munitions

---

4   The Winnipeg Tribune, November 17, 1941, page 6

Building on Constitution Avenue in Washington, D.C. As early as August 1939, the new 'unbreakable' code which the Japanese referred to as NJ25 had been broken by British codebreakers. When deciphered by US Signal and Intelligence, they chose a rather more prosaic name for it. They called it Code Purple.

Earlier still, in 1921 British and US Intelligence units had not only succeeded in breaking the less refined Soviet and French codes, they had also cracked the Japanese diplomatic code *gaimushoo*, which the Japanese continued to believe was invincible. Developed using a radically different Morse code system in Japanese, a language the Tokyo cryptologists considered "impregnable", by 1927 the call signs and radio frequencies of every major Japanese ship had been logged and their home bases recorded. Perhaps because it provided them with so much incalculably valuable information, the code breakers referred to that cipher as code magic.

The following year, and again in 1934 when it was updated, the code breakers were reading that and nearly every message sent in the Japanese Navy's new General Operational Code. So effective were they that during the entire turbulent period from August 1940 to November 1941 they had accurately decoded 223 of 227 messages, most of them several pages long, sent via MAGIC from Tokyo to its diplomatic corps in Washington.

Similar achievements had been realized by American and British cryptologists eavesdropping on Japanese Foreign Ministry codes in other parts of the world, and in particular in areas much closer to Tokyo. The US Navy station at Pearl Harbor was considered first-class in its capability and efficiency.

One notable example of that station's eavesdropping success became apparent when, within a matter of hours after Japan had made its agreement with the French Vichy government to move its troops into Indochina and establish a military region headquarters in Saigon, United States Intelligence experts reading decoded PURPLE and MAGIC intercepts were able to write a full and complete review of the tense situation in Southeast Asia and present it immediately to President Roosevelt via the President's Joint Army-Navy Board. Based on that report, on July 26, 1941 the President of the United States decided that from that day onward all Japanese assets and credits in the United States would be frozen and American firms with trade connections with Japan were forbidden to export any oil, iron, scrap metal, tin or rubber to it. Trade in a number of other commodities, including textiles and cotton, was also halted, and at the specific request of President Roosevelt, Britain followed suit.

Though under a ruthless Nazi occupation in Europe, the Netherlands was still the third largest empire in the world, and 10,000 miles from the torment within its home borders it had an ad hoc government in Asia with imposing army and navy units still in control of its vast resources in Java and Indonesia. At the request of the United States, the Netherlands, too, declared similar trade embargoes against Japan.

In a further step to isolate Japan, the Panama Canal — a United States territorial possession and guarded by United States military forces — was abruptly closed to all Japanese shipping.

In Washington, President Roosevelt knew full well the consequences of a Nazi victory over the Soviet Union and Britain. At the same time, a strong and almost irrational isolationist mood within the United States had succeeded in tying his hands. On the surface, Roosevelt seemed incapable of acting to assist Britain in her battle, for within the US Congress there was a great deal of resentment toward Europe and European politics. This feeling was shared by a loud minority within the United States, even as Britain's cities were being devastated by German air raids. One of the largest of the anti-war groups with a paid-up membership of 800,000 was the America First Committee (AFC), formed at Yale University in September 1940, just three days before the start of the London Blitz. Early supporters included student and future president Gerald Ford, future Peace Corps director Sargent Shriver, and future president John F. Kennedy who, upon joining, contributed $100 and sent a note saying "What you all are doing is vital." The Committee soon joined with the 135,000-strong Keep America Out Of War Committee founded by the six-time presidential candidate for the Socialist Party of America, Norman Thomas. The membership of the AFC, headed by the Chairman of Sears, Roebuck and Company, General Robert E. Wood, included prominent senators from both the Republican and Democratic parties, as well as a long list of celebrities, starting with the aviation hero Charles A. Lindbergh, the poet e. e. cummings, architect Frank Lloyd Wright, author Gore Vidal, actress Lillian Gish, newspaper publishers Joseph M. Patterson of the *New York Daily News*, Colonel Robert R. McCormick of the *Chicago Tribune*, and Hollywood film producer Walt Disney. The AFC did not trust Franklin D. Roosevelt, saying he was not telling the American people the truth, and though they supported strong measures against Japan, they strongly opposed Roosevelt's Lend-Lease Bill that was to provide food, oil and other necessary supplies to Great Britain. Its four basic principles were:

* The United States must build an impregnable defense for America.
* No foreign power, nor group of powers, can successfully attack a prepared America.
* American democracy can be preserved only by keeping out of the European war.

* "Aid short of war" (Lend Lease) weakens national defense at home and threatens to involve America in war abroad.

The Committee was particularly distrustful of Roosevelt after his mid-August 1941 meetings with Churchill aboard ships off Newfoundland, during which the two secretly agreed to a number of post-war goals: in particular the disarmament of aggressor nations, the abandonment of the use of military force, and a restoration of self-government to those deprived of it. Quickly termed the Atlantic Charter, the AFC saw it as one of Roosevelt's clandestine maneuvers to get the United States involved in Churchill's war. While no signed version of the Charter existed, nothing about Japan was mentioned in the communiqués following the conference and the AFC was certain the two leaders had come to a covert understanding about Asia as well as Europe.[5]

The opposition of such people was so forceful and persistent that when Franklin D. Roosevelt ran for an unprecedented third term of office in 1940 his adversaries branded him "a war-monger" because of his many attempts to supply Britain with war materials as she stood alone against the Nazi war machine. He won the election, but to do so he had to bow to pressure from the conservative bloc by declaring again and again in his campaign speeches that "no American boy shall fight in a foreign war," and "our boys are not going to be sent to foreign shores to fight a war... *except in case of attack.*"

In reality, Roosevelt's appeasing words did not tally with the facts as he knew them. Just eight short months before Pearl Harbor, in April 1941, a Gallop Poll result had shown that three-

---

5   Years later, a copy of the Charter was found among Churchill's papers. It was signed by Roosevelt and himself — though *both* signatures were in Churchill's handwriting.

quarters of the American people favored going to war if it was certain that there was no other way to defeat Germany.

Perhaps it was because of that poll that Roosevelt sent his valued friend and special administrative advisor, Harry Hopkins, to London to deliver a private message to the Prime Minister: *"The President is determined that we shall win this war together. Make no mistake about it: he has sent me here to tell you that at all costs and by all means he will carry you through."*[6]

During that meeting at sea off Newfoundland, and contrary to reports made available to the press at the time, Roosevelt and Churchill spent nearly all their time in secret discussions on the coming war. Lord Halifax, the British Ambassador to Washington, summarized the Conference in his confidential dispatches in this way: *"Strategy against the Axis was planned in the full expectation that the United States would inevitably be drawn into the war."*[7]

Twelve months earlier, American and British staffs conducted full-scale strategy talks in Washington to lay the groundwork for the Conference. After two months, both sides agreed that should the war spread to the Pacific, priority would be given to the European theater, and in March 1941 a contingent of United States military officers visited Britain to begin selecting locations for American airfields and naval bases.[8]

Seven days after returning from the Conference, Roosevelt signed into law a bill permitting the Army to keep all its men in the service an additional eighteen months.

In time, Roosevelt would conduct a poll of his own to seek answers to difficult questions. On November 7, 1941 — one month

---

6   The statement attributed to Harry Hopkins is cited in the *New York Times*, January 26, 1950.
7   Hachey, Thomas E. Confidential dispatches: *Analysis of America by the British Ambassador, 1939-1945.*
8   Ibid.

to the day before Pearl Harbor—Roosevelt asked members of his Cabinet if the United States should go to war against the Japanese if they committed aggression against the British or the Dutch possessions in the Pacific. The Cabinet said yes, the United States should absolutely go to war. And, they added, the country would support such a move.

Three weeks later, the President asked the full Cabinet if they would agree to go to war if Japan attacked Malaya and Singapore. The Cabinet again said yes—but they suggested that Roosevelt should push negotiations further by speaking personally to Emperor Hirohito.

Instead, Roosevelt asked his Secretary of State to send a message to the Japanese government asking for some evidence of goodwill.

That was the exceptionally awkward political situation within the United States, and the very threatening military situation abroad, when, in July 1941, President Roosevelt concluded that the only way to curb the Japanese and contain their expansionist aims was to place a firm trade embargo on the nation.

In Japan, the military planners were inflamed. Some of them—and in particular General Hideki Tojo, the blunt and traditional samurai militarist who would soon push Prince Konoye out as Japan's Premier and, with the backing of the army, take his place—cried out for immediate military action, saying that the United States and her allies had declared war on Japan in every way but in name. "The United States has delivered us an ultimatum," he bristled.

Other voices within the Cabinet pleaded for caution. There was great doubt about the shifting military situation in the far north along the Siberian border where, despite her neutrality pact with Russia, Japan had committed a strong military force with the option of invading Russia "if the fitting moment presented itself."

As a member of the German-Italian Axis Alliance, some planners thought it might be the right time for Japan to attack Russia and increase her territorial gains in the north. But before that situation was settled, Japan must be prudent, they said. Above all, she must use extreme care in assessing her next moves.

To stall for time while the militarists evaluated their position and weighed the immediate effects of the quarantine placed on Japan by the United States and her allies, the military suggested to Emperor Hirohito that Prince Fumimaro Konoye, Japan's Prime Minister, propose a meeting with President Roosevelt to discuss the lifting of the trade embargoes.

Konoye agreed, suggesting a meeting in Hawaii. But even as the messages of that proposal were being sent to the US representatives at its embassy in Tokyo, the Tojo-led faction within Japan's military chose that precise moment to summon more than one million reservists to active duty. And on that same day, plans were also announced in Tokyo to melt down every temple bell, gate, fence and metal object in the country to make more guns. Each citizen in the nation was asked to come forward and donate anything he or she possessed that was made of metal.

The cause of the militarists was now in place and ready to become the Great Cause of the nation. Henceforth, every man, woman and child in Japan would be called upon to make his or her personal contribution.

It is very unlikely that President Franklin D. Roosevelt ever heard of, or read, Major Eliot's report from Hong Kong, the one in which he declared that the Japanese were neatly trapped in a naval pincers and that the Allies had been presented with a golden moment that should be exploited to the full. Nonetheless,

Roosevelt must have shared some of the Major's sentiments, for on July 9, 1941, shortly before he called for the trade embargo against Japan, he sent a memo to his Secretary of War, Henry L. Stimson, "to prepare a mobilization plan that would be needed to ensure the defeat of our potential enemies."

The project was turned over to one of America's top military planners, General Albert C. Wedemeyer, who immediately formed a joint Army-Navy study board. As Roosevelt had often proclaimed he would not send American boys to a foreign war, the last thing he wanted was to let the American public know that he was asking the military to draw up plans for war. Hence the project was termed the Secret Victory Program. Working around the clock, on September 25, Wedemeyer submitted to the President a 147-page document that stated that what Winston Churchill and Franklin D. Roosevelt had told the people of Malaya, Singapore, Hong Kong, the Dutch East Indies, Burma and the Philippine Islands would never happen: that war with Japan was not only probable, it was inevitable.

What's more, the report laid out a course of action which was to become US policy the moment Japan made its decision to launch an attack. The essence of the program was this: In the minds of the Army-Navy planners in Washington, Europe would occupy the principal role in their strategy. Regardless of whatever actions transpired in the Far East, Asia would have to wait. The report made that quite clear: *"Due to the situation in England and Russia, any military measures against Japan will have to be defensive in nature until after victory has been achieved in Europe. Additionally, in the event of a two-ocean war, the United States will direct its primary energies in an offensive effort in the direction of*

Africa and Europe."⁹

Amazingly, a copy of this clandestine United States Victory Program report was picked up by German code experts working in Switzerland, for information relating to it was found in the files of the German High Command in Berlin after the war. Honoring its pledge to aid a confederate, there is every reason to believe that as soon as the Germans received this momentous piece of information it was instantly transmitted to its new Japanese ally.

And in what is probably one of the more bizarre turns in the intelligence war, that same information undoubtedly went full-circle around the world — from Switzerland to Berlin to Tokyo — only to be picked up in the end by a group of startled US Signal and Intelligence code breakers working in Asia and Hawaii. They would have copied it as they received it and sent it on to Washington.

At that same point in time, as he reviewed the up-to-the-minute Code Purple intelligence summaries that landed on his desk in the White House, President Roosevelt was wholly aware of the recent military developments within Japan and of the reluctance of her military planners to confront the huge Soviet Siberian Army.

He knew, too, of the military call-up of one million reservists, the melting down of the temple bells, and of the measures Japan was taking in response to the trade embargoes he had announced. Assessing the reports, Roosevelt's reaction to the Konoye request for a special meeting to discuss trade issues was

---

9   In a sensational development, on December 5, 1941 the entire contents of the Victory Program were disclosed on the front pages of the *Chicago Tribune* and the *Washington Post*, under the byline of Chester Manley.
http://www.general-wedemeyer.com/victoryplan1.html#_ftn4 ;
http://www.history.army.mil/books/wwii/csppp/ch11.htm

to send a tersely-worded message to Tokyo stating that he had no intention of discussing anything with Prince Konoye.

Instead, the President of the United States chose that moment to instruct his Chief of Staff, George C. Marshall, to contact the Philippines and immediately recall General Douglas MacArthur to active military duty. What they failed to do was to notify MacArthur of their decision.

What President Roosevelt didn't know, of course, was that his blunt refusal to meet with Prince Konoye provoked an immediate meeting of the Cabinet Advisory Council in Tokyo. The meeting was relatively brief, and the Council came to a rapid decision: Japan's assistance in confronting Russia to aid Germany by opening a two-front war was unnecessary to Japan's immediate interests. Instead, Japan would carry out a plan that had been under continual review for the past two years: She would attack the United States at Pearl Harbor, destroy the bulk of the US Fleet at anchor there, and rapidly follow through with land, sea and air attacks on all British, Dutch and American territories in the Southeast Asian sphere. For Japan, a nation created by the gods, ruled by a god and looked over by the gods, it was time to go to war.

If we are to believe subsequent reports relating to Japan and her belligerent intentions during that period, this astonishing information never reached the US or British Intelligence Units operating in Hawaii, Ceylon, Hong Kong, Singapore, China or the Philippines, units that previously — and for at least a year prior to the Cabinet Advisory Council's decision — had proved so masterful in cracking nearly every Japanese coded message transmitted to its military and diplomatic offices throughout the world.

Instead, this decision to go to war, this vital information that presumably was not intercepted by US or British intelligence experts anywhere in the world—and which, apparently, did not reach the desk of the President of the United States or find its way into the hands of Prime Minister Winston Churchill—ended up, in August 1941, three months before Pearl Harbor, on the desk of Marshal Joseph Stalin in war-torn Moscow.

The person responsible for delivering this extraordinary intelligence report to Stalin was a notorious double agent and Communist spy posing as a Nazi newspaperman in Tokyo. His name was Richard Sorge.

When the histories of wars are written, they usually deal with large battles and grand exploits. But when the definitive history of the war between Japan and the Western Allies is written, it will also have to explore in depth the role played by a congenial, womanizing, hard-drinking party-goer who supplied Russia with information so secret it wasn't even known to most of the officers within the Japanese military and intelligence community. A man with a brilliant mind, fluent in more than half-a-dozen languages, a man with a Ph.D. in philosophy and political science from the University of Hamburg, a man whom Hitler listened to and believed to be a tried-and-true Nazi, Richard Sorge was probably one of the top spies of all time.

Born in Russia of a German father and a Russian mother who returned to Germany when he was a child of three, Sorge served in the German army during World War I where he was twice wounded. He was discharged after losing three fingers from shrapnel, and at the end of the war was awarded the Iron Cross, one of Germany's highest military honors. One of his war wounds left him with a noticeable limp. After completing university studies in Berlin in 1924, he went to Moscow where, at the age of 28, he was recruited into the Soviet Secret Service. Five years later, he was back in Germany associating with top Nazi officials and quietly gaining credentials from several prestigious German magazines to act as their foreign correspondent. Joining the staff of the *Frankfurter Zeitung*, he was soon representing the newspaper in Tokyo, where his jovial wit and natural brilliance so charmed the German Ambassador—who found no reason to doubt Sorge's allegiance to the Nazi cause as, night after night, they drank toasts to a succession of Nazi victories across Europe—that he soon asked the brilliant newspaperman to assist him in the editing of a few cables that he was about to send to Germany. It wasn't long before the Ambassador, Eugen Ott, was giving Sorge secret messages to write in diplomatic code for transmission to Berlin.

A hard drinker with a love for women, it was at this same time that one of the ladies, a left-wing American journalist working for a German newspaper, introduced Sorge to Hotzumi Ozaki, one of Japan's most famous journalists. Through his Moscow contacts, Sorge would soon discover that Ozaki was, in fact, a clandestine member of the outlawed Communist Party of Japan. After the two became friendly and Sorge had shown a sympathetic interest in Ozaki's politics, the journalist was appointed an advisor to the Japanese Prime Minister, Fumimaro Konoe.

Sorge can be excused if, to himself, he paused in his busy career to express amazement at his good fortune and to congratulate himself on his success: In the space of two short years in Japan he had been given, almost as a gift, the top-secret German diplomatic code that gave him access to virtually every piece of intelligence information in the code room at the German Embassy in Tokyo. And to add to that remarkable achievement, with amazing ease his friendship with Ozaki had given him admission to almost all the information passing through the various offices of Japan's

Prime Minister. Yet more success was to follow.

In the spring of 1941, with Russia still at peace with the Germans because of the secret non-aggression pact that Hitler had signed with Stalin a year earlier—a move that Hitler had initiated to keep Russia behind its frontiers and out of the European war—Richard Sorge was at the German Embassy when an envoy from the Ministry of War arrived from Berlin. The Ambassador invited Sorge to join them for dinner that evening, and it was during dessert that the envoy, glancing suspiciously around the room, announced in a muted voice the purpose of his visit: he was on a mission to personally deliver information so secret and so vital that the German High Command would not risk sending it to Tokyo in code.

The secret, he said, leaning across the dinner table and assuming a conspiratorial tone, was that Hitler had been quietly assessing Russian defenses along his eastern borders; that they had been found to be astonishingly weak; and against the advice and judgment of his best generals he was going to break his non-aggression pact with a quick and hard-hitting attack against Russia that would prove his own generals shamefully wrong. He was absolutely certain his surprise attack would lead to the total collapse of Russia before the first snows of winter. Asking the Ambassador and Sorge to lift their wine glasses in a salute, he declared that the operation would henceforth be referred to in their cables only by its code name, *Barbarossa,* and the date for *Barbarossa,* he said, was set for sometime in the early hours of the morning between the 20th and 22nd of June 1941.

Late that night, the German Ambassador called upon Sorge to encode and send several routine diplomatic messages to Berlin. The following day, Sorge dutifully transmitted the same diplomatic information to the Secret Service in Moscow—but along with it he sent an urgent message marked to the immediate attention of Marshal Joseph Stalin.

The message contained the details and the commencement date for *Barbarossa*.

With the conviction that Germany would respect its non-aggression treaty, the Russians had moved between two and three million men to stand guard against the Japanese along the Siberian / Manchurian border. That meant that Russia's long borders in the west were vastly undermanned, but Stalin was firmly convinced that if an attack were to come, it would not come from Germany but from Japan.

With that thought foremost in his mind — and even though he was well aware that his undercover agent in Tokyo was a man quite literally with a direct line to Hitler and the information on Hitler's desk — when the startling message from Richard Sorge arrived in Moscow, Stalin was not prepared to believe it. A coded message was relayed to Sorge that night: "What is Japan going to do in Siberia?"

To Stalin's complete dismay, Sorge had been right. On June 22, Hitler struck and *Operation Barbarossa* became a non-stop nightmare that rolled virtually unchecked up to the very gates of Moscow.

Three months after sending his warning on *Barbarossa* and Hitler's treachery, in the middle of an August night in 1941, Richard Sorge received the information that Stalin had so desperately wanted. The journalist Ozaki came to Sorge with the details of a secret meeting that had just been held by the Cabinet Advisory Council to discuss the overall picture of the war in China and Europe, and in particular of Japan's situation vis-à-vis the trade embargoes and credit freezes imposed on her by the president of the United States.

The Council had been pragmatic: Germany did not need Japan to defeat Russia, but Japan herself had been pushed to the edge of a precipice by Roosevelt's trade embargo and was on the verge of a cataclysmic disaster if she did not act swiftly and decisively.

To begin, the Council declared that all Japanese troops stationed along the Manchurian-Siberian border would be moved south to prepare for massive and concurrent land and sea attacks against the enemy in Hong Kong, Guam and Wake Islands, Malaya, Thailand, Singapore and the Philippines. Furthermore, the US Pacific Fleet would be carefully monitored in its home port of Pearl Harbor in Hawaii, and at the right moment it would be destroyed in a single monumental air attack, preferably on a Sunday morning when the fleet was at anchor in the shallow waters of the harbor and the majority of its sailors were on shore or on weekend leave away from their ships.

The details of the sea attacks would be worked out by the Admiral of the Imperial Navy, Isoroku Yamamoto; the particulars of the amphibious landings in Malaya and Siam would be dealt with by General Tomoyuki Yamashita.

In the interim, and as a continuation of Japan's overall war strategy, diplomatic gestures toward an agreement with the United States and its European allies were to be resumed. Admiral Nomura and a special peace envoy would go to Washington to engage the United States in discussions concerning the lifting of the US trade barriers, the unfreezing of credits, and the reopening of normal trade links with the United States and the Netherland East Indies. In what would appear to be a conciliatory gesture, a conference with the Americans was to be proposed to sort out mutual difficulties.

This, Sorge learned, was Japan's swift response to Roosevelt for his refusal to meet with Prince Konoye to open up a dialogue concerning the lifting of trade embargoes.

Later, in the silence of his radio room on his personal yacht rising and falling with the tide in Tokyo Bay, one can only speculate what Richard Sorge's mood was or what his thoughts were as he carefully transcribed this phenomenal information into code and transmitted it to the NKVD in Moscow. Fully aware of the scope of the revelations that had fallen into his hands, he must surely have sensed that he was writing his name into history.

Far removed from the gentle waves of Tokyo Bay, and deep within the confines of a concrete bunker inside the Kremlin walls, the muffled sounds of exploding shells could be heard as Joseph Stalin was handed the decoded message from Richard Sorge. Not far from his desk, German tanks were pressing hard in the suburbs of Moscow to force shut the only open rail line leading out of the city. Stalin's generals had ordered it to be kept open "at all costs" as a last-minute escape route for the government leaders when, as seemed increasingly likely, they would be forced to flee the city.

Ironically, that sole open route out of Moscow was the Trans-Siberian Railway line leading east, and it was in the east that the balance of what remained of the Soviet Army was tied down along the Manchurian-Siberian border waiting for the moment that Japan might strike.

As Stalin finished reading the message from Sorge, he leaned back in his chair and picked up a telephone to summon his military chiefs to an urgent meeting. Based solely on the information that had been supplied by Sorge, an immediate withdrawal of nearly all Russian troops in the east was ordered, and 15 infantry divisions, 3 cavalry divisions, 1,700 tanks, and 1,500 aircraft moved from the Soviet Far East to the European front to beat back the Nazi onslaught. It would be those reinforcements that would turn the tide in the Battle of Moscow.

In yet another of the war's ironic twists, the Soviet troops who were returned from the northern borders to confront the Nazis journeyed back via that single open railway line. And because of it, they were able to launch their first counter-offensive against the German army on December 6, 1941 – the day before the Japanese attack on Pearl Harbor.

Undeniably, the message that was received in Moscow that day marked the turning point of the entire war, not just for Russia but for the world. Yet all these years later, history hardly recognizes that two men acting in concert, a German Soviet spy named Richard Sorge and a politically-minded Japanese newspaperman named Hotzumi Ozaki, were responsible for saving Russia from destruction at the hands of the Germans. Further, that these two men were responsible for the reprieve of Great Britain and the eventual defeat of Nazi Germany. And because Soviet Russia and Great Britain were saved from defeat, the United States was not left to carry on a solitary fight against the armies of Germany and Japan that had mutually planned to fight their respective ways east and west to meet, by their joint calculations, in the north of India in the autumn of 1942.

Looking at the entire undertaking, it seems perfectly reasonable to conclude that the spying activities of Richard Sorge and Hotzumi Ozaki hastened the end of the war by many years. And yet, if Sorge had indeed allowed vanity to enter his pragmatic mind that night in Tokyo Bay and permitted himself to suppose he was writing his name into the history books, he was badly mistaken. In almost all of those books, his and Ozaki's names have been engulfed and forgotten in the flood of events that they helped to perpetrate, events that were soon to become known as the Pacific War.

Paradoxically, as far as his fruitful spying activities were concerned, Richard Sorge had sent his final message. The following night, he and Ozaki were arrested on suspicion of espionage. From evidence readily obtained at his home and in the radio room aboard Sorge's yacht, the two men were convicted of spying for a foreign power. Hoping he would be considered valuable enough to the Soviets that he would figure in a trade of spies, he waited for Stalin to make the arrangements. The Japanese appeared to be waiting as well, but to Stalin Sorge represented an embarrassing mistake and he was ignored. Three years after his arrest, on November 7, 1944, he and Ozaki were hanged at Sugamo Prison. Richard Sorge was 49.

It was at this point, with Japan's Cabinet Advisory Council on the verge of deciding to declare war on Great Britain, the Netherlands and the United States and to occupy their territories in Southeast Asia, that the ten-year exodus of Japanese citizens intended to ease the population problem in the Home Islands was abruptly reversed.

As the militarists and the diplomats in Tokyo became increasingly involved in meetings day and night to draw up plans for offensive military action, Japanese citizens living in Southeast Asia were told that their duties had been skillfully performed and the moment had come for them to return home. All those who had cooperated with the visionaries championing the concept of a New Asian Order and had lent their support by sketching maps, noting ship and air movements, observing military constructions sites, or simply storing logs, bricks and scraps of construction steel in marked locations along the roads and railways throughout Asia, were instructed to return to the land of their birth. Momentous days were in the offing, they were told, and every last one of Japan's citizens would be required to make his contribution in the Divine Adventure.

Ignored, overlooked, or treated with apparent indifference by everyone except those Japanese who were returning home, were the articles that began appearing in Asia's leading newspapers in September and the final months of 1941: "JAPANESE PEOPLE BEING ORGANIZED FOR WAR," one newspaper proclaimed in a story that was transmitted around the world via the wire services.[10] The report, from Rangoon, Burma, announced that the Japanese Consul-General had advised all Japanese firms in Burma to close down at once and evacuate all Japanese workers *"at the earliest possible moment."*

In Singapore, the English newspapers contributed their own reports. "It has been learned from reliable sources here," said one, "that at least one Japanese firm has been ordered to wind up its affairs and return to Japan. Furthermore, all the Japanese iron mines in Malaya will cease operation very soon. By the end of the year, most small Japanese shops in Singapore and Malaya will be closed up and their owners and employees will have returned to Japan."

Dating from a time that corresponded with the meeting of Japan's Cabinet Advisory Council in August, more and more newspapers throughout Asia began featuring reports on the evacuation. *The East Indies Daily News* headlined EXODUS FROM BATAVIA, and JAPANESE EVACUEES LEAVING NETHERLANDS EAST INDIES.

The *South China Morning Post* reported JAPANESE IN HONG KONG GOING, and in Penang and Ipoh, the *Malaya Times*, the

---

10   South China Morning Post, November 7, 1941

Straits Echo, and the *Perak Shimbun* reported ALL JAPANESE LEAVING SINGAPORE.

There were similar stories daily in the Singapore *Straits Times* and the *Singapore Free Press*. In the Philippines, the *Manila Tribune* headline read MORE THAN ONE THOUSAND JAPANESE ABOUT TO LEAVE MANILA.

From Indonesia, an account stated that "the Japanese steamer *Takachiho Maru* had arrived in Batavia [now Jakarta] from Singapore to take on board more than 600 Japanese residents from East Java."

Within the week, another report stated that "over one thousand more Japanese evacuees from several parts of the Netherlands East Indies would be leaving for Japan on another ship, the *Takaiho Maru*."

In Singapore, a bold headline in the *Straits Times* read: "JAPANESE WANT TO GO," and the article stated: "More than 1,000 Japanese have applied for shipping passage back to Japan this week. It is understood that another Japanese evacuation ship will call on Singapore very soon."

A separate article recorded that "450 more Japanese have left Singapore and many hundreds more will soon do likewise."

The following day, the same newspaper, the *Straits Times*, devoted considerable space to a story from Manila with the headline, THE GREAT EXODUS TO JAPAN: "It was stated by the Philippine Census Bureau that 8,000 Japanese have left the Philippines within the past months owing to the Far Eastern situation."

In a continuation of the saga, story after story went out over the news wires giving accounts of the situation in neighboring Hong Kong. Picking up the story, the *Manila Bulletin* reported:

"Acting on instructions, a large number of Japanese left the Colony today, most of them making for Canton via Macau.

Untold others sailed direct to Japan on the *Shirogane Maru*. Only about 50 Japanese remain in the Colony, and this number will probably be further reduced in the next few days. The Japanese Consulate General declined to grant an interview yesterday."

In the middle of the following week, the report proved accurate when the *South China Morning Post* reported: "Thirteen Japanese residents left for Canton yesterday morning, while several others boarded riverboats for Macau. This leaves only about 30 Japanese in the Colony."

Vying for attention on the same pages were concurrent accounts of recent Japanese military activities in the region:

"SOUTHWARD MOVE. It has been reported that 20 Japanese transports and some warships left Chungshan and Bocca Tigris simultaneously for the south. Their destination is presumed to be French Indochina. The transports took a few thousand troops. Ten other transports are off Tongkawan in Chungshan (China) waiting to take more troops away."

And the reports continued: JAPANESE MASSING PLANES IN FORMOSA (Taiwan). NEW MOVEMENTS OF JAPANESE WARSHIPS AND TRANSPORTS HAVE BEEN SIGHTED IN THE CANTON RIVER DELTA.

Mincing no words, Singapore's *Straits Times* went directly to the point:

JAPAN SAID TO BE WAITING FOR THE RIGHT TIME.

Meanwhile, across the Pacific an editorial in the October 27 edition of the *Chicago Daily Tribune*, a staunch Republican Midwestern newspaper, assured American readers that "She (Japan) cannot attack us. That is a military impossibility. Even our base at Hawaii is beyond the effective striking power of her fleet."

Two years earlier, in March 1938, the United States military forces in Hawaii had, at the direction of the Naval and War Departments in Washington, organized practice maneuvers to test the security of its defenses in the Hawaiian Islands. The Naval Command in Honolulu organized its forces into two separate battle units, one of which was designated the Blue Unit assigned to represent a joint Army-Navy group in the defense of the Hawaiian Islands and the US naval fleet. The second, the Red Unit, was to represent a potential enemy — presumably Japan. With a fleet of warships and the *USS Saratoga* aircraft carrier, the Red Unit was instructed to go to sea and attempt to attack Pearl Harbor in a mock bombing raid.

Accordingly, the Red Unit sailed north and planned its mission. In distant waters beyond the reach of the Blue Unit's observation planes, the attack force waited patiently until the weather turned foul and the seas became heavy. In the interim, all ship-to-ship communications were halted, the airplanes remained on the carrier's deck to avoid being picked up by the embryonic radar system installed on a mountain top on Oahu Island, and the group waited until the storm finally swept down on Honolulu.

Then, at what he considered to be the right moment, the fleet's enterprising admiral launched a surprise attack on Honolulu. In the mock raid, the enemy attack unit sank most of the ships of the United States Pacific Fleet as they "sat like ducks" at anchor in Pearl Harbor.

The Hawaiian defense unit had been caught completely off guard, and if the attack had been real, the United States would have suffered the worst naval defeat in its brief but imposing history.

Shortly after the exercise, a detailed report of it — the manner in which the attack was executed, the way in which the defense forces responded, and the results achieved by the Red attack group—was published by the US Department of the Navy. The public report was given prominence at the time and was widely circulated to spur the Hawaiian naval and military commanders to take immediate protective measures to prevent a real attack from achieving similar results.

That had not been the first airborne attack on Pearl Harbor. Ten years earlier, maintaining that "Japan had always started operations by attacking before a declaration of war," Rear Admiral Harry Yarnell designed an attack plan utilizing carrier aviation. Taking the *Saratoga* and *Lexington* to a point northeast of Hawaii, he waited until dawn on the morning of February 7, 1928, a quiet Sunday, to launch 152 planes. They took Hawaii by complete surprise, the planes first attacking the airfields and then the many ships anchored along battleship row. Dropping sacks of white flour, they completely "destroyed" the airfields without a single plane getting into the air. Turning their attention to the battleships, they dropped enough bags of flour to achieve what Yarnell said was a complete surprise victory. All his planes returned to their carriers safely.

Not so, cried the Army and Navy brass. They weren't having any of that victory talk. In the first instance they said Yarnell had cheated. He had attacked the ships at dawn on a Sunday morning, a time they thought to be totally inappropriate. Furthermore, his attack vector was from the north-northeast. Lastly, the Navy argued that low-level precision bombing of battleships at anchor was totally unrealistic since "everyone knew that Asians lacked sufficient hand-eye coordination to engage in that kind of precision bombing".[11]

---

[11] Edwyn Gray. *Operation Pacific: The Royal Navy's War Against Japan, 1941- 1945*. Naval Institute Press, Annapolis, Maryland 1989 http://www.military.com/navy/pearl-harbor-first-attack.html

Admiral Isoroku Yamamoto, newly-appointed Commander-in-Chief of Japan's Combined Imperial Fleet, read the United States Navy's reports of the two attacks on Pearl Harbor many times over. For more than thirty years Japan had been contemplating a war with the United States, and Yamamoto was well aware of a plan of attack envisioned by the Naval General Staff. But Yamamoto was disturbed. The General Staff plan was to draw the US Fleet into Japanese Home waters where, owing to Japan's superior naval capability, it would be thoroughly decimated by her battleships and submarines. At that point it was assumed that the US would be forced to sue for peace, and the conditions drawn up would be solely on Japan's terms.

But Yamamoto was deeply concerned: the plan had been drafted in 1907 addressing only ship-to-ship and submarine engagements. Everything about it was unquestionably obsolete as much about the navy, its ships and naval warfare tactics had changed, and in particular the coordinated use of land-based bombers and aircraft carrier attack planes, both at land and at sea. Aware of that, to bring about change and update its naval warfare methods, Japan had formally requested the service of a naval expert from Great Britain. After the defeat of Germany in World War I, in an attempt to regulate the size of the world's navies and thus reduce the risk of a future conflict, the United States determined that Japan should maintain a sixty-percent ratio of capital ship tonnage compared to the tonnage allowed the US and Britain's Royal Navy. Voicing Japan's strong disapproval, and at least on one occasion threatening to walk out of the negotiations, Admiral Tomosaburo Kato finally relented and put his name to the Washington Naval Treaty of 1922. It was shortly afterwards that Japan appealed to Great Britain for the loan of a naval expert to assist it in the rebuilding of its fleet within the terms of the Treaty. They had a particular person in mind, an English nobleman, a war hero and an ace pilot of World War I who had recently been advising the British Royal Navy on the construction of—and the use of—aircraft carriers. He was a visionary who realized the importance of carriers and warplanes to a modern naval fleet, and after turning down a number of Japan's supplications, Britain finally relented and sent them Baron Sir William Francis Forbes-Sempill.

Much to Britain's later lament, for the next twenty years this man was to remain Japan's foremost naval advisor. It was he, Lord Sempill, who would help develop Yamamoto's aircraft carriers and demonstrate how they could be used in time of war.

In that same year, 1922, a Japanese Naval Attaché in London named Oka Arata recruited another British air ace who, like Sempill, was a pioneer in naval air warfare and the use of torpedo bombers flying from aircraft carriers. Awarded the Distinguished Service Cross for serving "with great distinction" in World War I, Squadron Leader Frederick Joseph Rutland was won over after a tour to Manchuria. Initially paid to advise on carrier landing and takeoff training, he was soon given the codenamed *Shinkawa* (New River) and the equivalent of three million pounds to open an import-export business in London's fashionable Regent Street. The business was a cover for Oka's espionage operation in Britain. Finding himself suddenly rich, Rutland resigned his commission and left the navy, though due to his fame and his flamboyant personality he continued to have access to virtually all of Britain's top secret military information and intelligence reports, all of which were passed on to Oka's twenty-one member naval spy team working out of the Japanese Embassy in London.

Eleven years later, Rutland was offered a salary of £150,000 a year (approximately $600,000 in today's terms) to move to Los Angeles, California to open import/export offices there and in

Honolulu, Hawaii. With a tax-free wage paid through a special account with the Mitsubishi Company, Squadron Leader Rutland packed up and moved to Hollywood.

Reviewing the two earlier US Navy reports, plus the latest intelligence information provided by Sempill and Rutland, Yamamoto was convinced that the time was ripe for the Imperial Japanese Navy to follow the same path as the Red Unit and sink the United States Fleet at Pearl Harbor. Asking for a secret meeting with the naval board, Yamamoto presented the mock attack reports and said that he was prepared to catch the United States Fleet at Pearl Harbor, and, in the same manner, destroy it.

The board seemed reluctant to act, and Yamamoto was uncharacteristically enraged. "If I am not allowed to fulfill my destiny as a naval officer, I will have to offer my resignation," he proclaimed.

Alarmed at the prospect of losing its best admiral, the board made a proposal: "At this time, Japan is not ready," they said, "but continue with your preparations in haste for an attack on Hawaii at a future date."

Precisely two years later, Admiral Yamamoto was in Japan's Inland Sea secretly gathering together Mobile Air Unit One (*Kido Butai*). Consisting of six aircraft carriers and an attendant battle fleet of two battleships, three cruisers, nine destroyers, eight tankers, twenty-three submarines, four midget submarines and 414 dive bombers, fighters and torpedo planes, his fleet was at that moment the single most powerful naval force the world had ever known. Code named AI, with Admiral Chuichi Nagumo in command, the carrier force had spent the past several months practicing bombing attacks on imitation battleships, cruisers, and aircraft carriers in a mock-up harbor that closely resembled

JOHN BELL SMITHBACK

Pearl Harbor. The Japanese Imperial Navy had judged that the time had come, and when Yamamoto's and Nagumo's ships were in position, they sailed northeast from Hitokappu Bay in Japan's Kurile Islands, cut off all but semaphore communication between ships, and hoped, somewhere north of Midway Island and near the International Date Line, to encounter bad weather.

Six thousand miles to the south a convoy of twenty-five troop transports escorted by five cruisers, seven destroyers, a number of minesweepers, assault ships and submarine chasers was steaming westward through the Gulf of Siam toward Malaya's Kra Isthmus. To the east, an invasion force consisting of troop carriers, two destroyer squadrons and a cruiser division sailed from Palau and the Ryukyu Islands toward the southern shores of the Philippine Islands. To its north, five light cruisers, twenty-nine destroyers, two seaplane tenders, the aircraft carrier *Ryūjū*, plus minesweepers, torpedo boats and troop transports, along with the combined support of 541 planes, left Taiwan and made for the northern shores of the Philippines. Out of Hainan came two cruisers, twelve destroyers and eighteen transports carrying 26,400 troops, while under the cover of darkness the I-121 and I-122 submarines rose to the surface off Singapore and began laying a line of minefields. Along the eastern coast of Malaya, two surface vessels were putting down a line of one thousand mines across the entrance to the Gulf of Siam.

The Japanese invasion master plan, possibly the most complex and ambitious ever undertaken, had been launched, and by land, sea and air Japan was on the move toward objectives situated along a perimeter of more than 6,500 miles.

In Singapore, the Royal Navy's deterrent consisted of the *Prince of Wales* (the *Repulse* had just left port, aiming to make a friendly visit to Australia), one veteran battle-cruiser, a handful of destroyers, and three old cruisers stood ready "to protect Britain's vast and valuable interests in Asia, Australasia and the Pacific Islands. Never before had so few been asked to defend so much!"[12]

Nearly six thousand miles away, Lieutenant General Hiroshi Oshima, Japan's Ambassador to Berlin, a man greatly respected by Hitler and at one time described as being "more Nazi than the Nazis," received an urgent message from Tokyo via the diplomatic code MAGIC which the American code breakers had been eavesdropping on for twenty years.

General Oshima was instructed to inform Hitler that 'THERE IS EXTREME DANGER THAT WAR MAY SUDDENLY BREAK OUT BETWEEN THE ANGLO-SAXON POWERS AND JAPAN THROUGH SOME CLASH OF ARMS.'

At that moment, General Yamashita was, as the newspapers in Singapore, Manila and Hong Kong faithfully reported, engaged in transferring his huge army south. In an effort to assure the world that Japan's intentions were entirely peaceful, the Tokyo newspapers reported that "a modest concentration of troops" was being sent to relieve those who had spent the past year in the tropical heat of French Indochina.

What the newspapers could not report, of course, was that the troops were part of a multi-pronged attack that was about to engage Japan in a war with the Netherlands, Great Britain and the United States. As the soldiers boarded the ships they were pressed together in cramped quarters above and below decks, and as they sailed south into the warm tropical breezes of the South China Sea, each man was handed a newly-printed manual

---
12 Ibid.

and told to memorize every sentence and know every word. It was titled *"Kore Wo Yomeba Katsu"* — If You Read This Booklet, Then Victory.

The manual was, in fact, a comprehensive guidebook that furnished each soldier with the basic facts, both on a military and non-military level, about the countries in which he would soon be fighting. He was instructed how to move quickly and efficiently through the jungle, and how, if he became separated from his unit, he could live off the land. The manual told him what natural foods he would be able to find to eat, and it warned him about things he shouldn't eat. He was told how to find pure water, avoid malaria, and treat his own wounds.

But apart from being a survival guide, in a chapter entitled "Asiatic Brotherhood", the manual was as much a lesson in history as a guide to the future:

Today as you read this, a hundred million Asians are being tyrannized by three hundred thousand white men. If we exclude India, one hundred million are oppressed by less than three hundred thousand. Once you set foot in the enemy's territories you will see for yourself just what oppression by the white man means. Money squeezed from the blood of Asians maintains these small white minorities in their luxurious mode of life — or disappears to their respective home countries. These white people may expect, from the moment of their birth, from the time they issue from their mother's wombs, to be allotted a score or so natives as their personal slaves. Therefore, the present war is a struggle between races and we must achieve the satisfaction of our just demands with no thought of leniency to the Europeans unless they be the Germans and the Italians. That is God's will. At stake in the present war, without doubt, is the future prosperity or decline of the Japanese Empire.

December 7, 1941
TO FIELD MARSHAL GENERAL AUCHINLECK (commander of British forces in the Middle East): MOST SECRET. For Yourself Alone:

President has now definitely said that the United States will regard it as a hostile act if Japan invades Siam, Malaya, Burma or the East Indies, and he is warning Japanese this week, probably Wednesday. We and the Dutch are conforming. This is an immense relief as I long dreaded being at war with Japan without or before the United States. Now I think it is all right.

Winston Churchill

TO THE PRIME MINISTER OF THAILAND, Field Marshal Plaek Phibunsongkhram:
There is a possibility of imminent Japanese invasion of your country. If you are attacked, defend yourself. The preservation of the full independence and sovereignty of Thailand is a British interest and we shall regard an attack on you as an attack on ourselves.

Winston Churchill
December 7, 1941[13]

A light rain was blowing against their faces as the large ships eased slowly through the calm, dark waters of the Gulf of Siam until the black horizon of the sea slowly merged with a flat, black shore. Then their engines stopped. The eerie silence engulfed them so suddenly that it at first gripped them with alarm. But the soft sound of the waves slapping against the hulls seemed to reassure them, and the many weeks of rehearsal came into play and they automatically followed each other over the sides of the ships into landing boats. The muffled sounds of bodies

---

13 House of Commons, *Hansard*

dropping into the small boats sounded unusually loud, too loud. Time seemed to be standing still, and the rocking motion of the small boats made them uncomfortable. They bent their heads low and focused their eyes on the menacing shore, waiting for the first flashes of fire from the guns they knew were waiting in concealed bunkers to catch them in a murderous crossfire. Then they heard the strange sound of sand grating and scratching against the bottoms of their boats. Whispering voices hissed close by. Their officers were impatient, and they suddenly leapt from the boats as a single unit and ran through ankle-deep water until they reached the soft, wet sand of the shore. They fell onto their bellies in the morning twilight and scanned the trees ahead of them. Their chests pounded with excitement and fear as they waited for the first bursts of enemy gunfire.

They were just north of the Siam-Malayan border on the nearly deserted eastern coast of the Malay Peninsula near the village of Pattani, and the war between Japan and the Allied forces of the United States, Great Britain and the Netherlands had begun.

No bombs fell, not one shot was fired. The only discomfort experienced by the thousands of men struggling to get ashore that morning was that most of them got their feet wet.

Far to the south, Singapore Island looked beautiful and magical. The bright lights of the harbor sparkled brilliantly in the clearness of the night as the bombers and their fighter escorts flew in a direct line due south toward the naval base. From their altitude, the pilots could see a slim grey streak on the horizon as the sun prepared to break above the sea into a serene morning sky. They glanced up often to survey the ebony sky for signs of enemy aircraft that might have scrambled from the Singapore RAF base, or from one of the smaller landing fields that were scattered along the length of the Malay Peninsula. In their preflight briefing they had been told that there was no chance that they would be met by any of the new Hurricane fighters that Winston Churchill had promised he would send to Singapore. But in the improbable event that they had been fooled or their information was incorrect, they kept their eyes peeled for telltale signs of exhaust flame traces from enemy planes. At least for the moment, all they had for company were the stars.

A total of 81 Mitsubishi G3M bombers had taken off from Thu Dau Mot, one of the newly-established Japanese air bases in southern Indochina, but 65 of them had reversed course and returned after encountering bad weather over the South China Sea. The 16 remaining bombers lumbered on. Knowing that Singapore had recently been reinforced with anti-aircraft guns, the crews scanned the horizon and waited for the flash of exploding shells in their flight path. No flashes appeared, and they fidgeted in their seats with nervous excitement, leaned slightly forward, the sounds of the engines pounding in their ears, and then they began their gradual descent.

Guided by the lights on the ground, they peered ahead to locate their targets. Night upon night in the ones that preceded this one they had flown practice missions over mock targets of Singapore until some pilots said they could have flown it with their eyes closed. But this bombing run was different because it was real, and their minds were racing so fast that they had to tell themselves to stay composed.

Out at sea, a special attack squadron with armor-piercing bombs searched the dark waters off the Malay Peninsula for the *HMS Prince of Wales* and the *HMS Repulse* which had arrived in Singapore from Manila that very week. It was impossible to know where they might be concealed in the murky darkness below, but soon the sun would be up, and when the new day broke, the ships would be found and their primed armor-piercing bombs would be ready for them.

In the stillness of the night, with only the mellow sound of unseen crickets communicating in the grass, a guard on watch at the Singapore Naval Base heard the growing drone of planes approaching steadily from the north. He felt a sense of relief knowing that the sounds came from the new planes that Winston Churchill had promised to send to reinforce Singapore's RAF base. He yawned and glanced at his watch. It was almost 4:00 o'clock in the morning, and it was Monday, the 8th of December, 1941.

At that same moment, as Japanese bombers were moving into position in the skies over Singapore, thousands of Japanese troops with tanks and motorized equipment were going ashore on Thailand's Kra Isthmus. The troops that were spilling onto the unattended beaches were on the shores of a friendly nation with whom Japan had recently signed a mutual assistance agreement. However, their concern was that they were in an extremely vulnerable position. It had been a risky adventure to land so many men on an exposed beach, and they perceived that it would have taken but a small effort on the part of the British forces across the border in Malaya to move up to intercept them and force them back into the sea before they had an opportunity to unload their equipment and regroup their men.

Yet when Singapore Command learned that the Japanese had landed an enormous force on the narrowest and most vulnerable part of the Malay Peninsula, and knowing it was in the process of supplying that force with provisions from a host of transport ships, it decided to do nothing. Thailand, after all, was a neutral nation.

Of more pressing concern was the information that a landing was taking place at Kota Bharu in Malaya, but while awaiting details from the front lines, the Singapore Command hesitated. Caught by surprise, the Indian troops of the 3/17 Dogra Regiment protecting a newly-constructed RAF airbase fought fiercely with the invaders. Quickly realizing they were fighting a losing battle, the RAF ground staff set fire to the buildings and destroyed their equipment before climbing into lorries to evacuate the base without waiting for orders.

In Singapore there were fears within the Command that the attack was a diversion. To those huddling in the underground operations room at Fort Canning, that seemed a reasonable assumption because Kota Bharu was, after all, almost four hundred miles to the north. If an attack was to come, they reasoned, it would undoubtedly have to be at a place closer to Singapore. Studying their maps, they decided to wait for a clearer picture to emerge.

In the meanwhile, orders were sent out instructing all troops up-country to withdraw from the Thai-Malaysian border area and to draw up new defensive positions somewhere to the south. No attack orders were issued: move back, dig in and wait for reinforcements. That was their one and only command.

At such a moment, time was clearly of the essence. But even when the first Japanese tanks led a task force across the border into Malaya, no one in the Singapore Command seemed to comprehend the seriousness of the situation. Once again, along the entire front the British and Empire forces were told to withdraw and regroup, and by the very nature of that uncoordinated backward movement the front line units facing the Japanese became more and more out of touch. Before the afternoon of the first day they were exhausted from such activity, and in most instances they hadn't even been fighting the enemy.

Communications had become so disrupted and there were so many orders and counter-orders to the forward command positions that the situation could only deteriorate — which it did. It appeared that the only ones who knew what they were doing were the Japanese. Their officers were continually consulting their newly-made maps of the Peninsula, and in the villages they pointed out the now-deserted bicycle shops to their subordinates. The doors were easily broken open, and within hours of landing in a hostile nation, the Japanese Imperial Army was riding south toward Singapore on neat and clean new bicycles.

One hour and thirty-five minutes after the Japanese invasion of Malaya and the sudden outbreak of war between Great Britain and Japan, 414 dive bombers, fighters and torpedo planes from the decks of six aircraft carriers under the command of Vice Admiral Chuichi Nagamo's Air Fleet One swept out of the bright dawn skies over the United States Pacific Fleet sitting at anchor in Pearl Harbor. Piloted by Japan's most experienced airmen in planes equipped with special armor-piercing bombs and newly-designed shallow water torpedoes, *Operation Al* was underway. Based almost entirely on intelligence provided by military attachés working as naval assistants for the Japanese Consulate in Honolulu, the naval planners in Tokyo had provided a plan that proved nearly faultless.

In two waves, the pilots left the decks of the carriers, and each time one of them returned the pilots and the crews of the ships cheered and rejoiced at their remarkable achievement. Behind them, acrid black smoke rose thousands of feet into the clear blue sky over Pearl Harbor. Huge ships that had been considered the core of the US Pacific Fleet blazed, exploded, and rolled over onto their sides in the shallow bay. Though Admiral Nagamo's pilots did not have an absolute figure, they would eventually learn that eighteen ships, including the battleships *Arizona, California, Maryland, Nevada, Oklahoma, Pennsylvania, Tennessee* and *West Virginia* had been sunk, and 347 airplanes were destroyed or damaged. The huge ships had been moored side by side in what was known as Battleship Row, and the majority of the United States warplanes — 188 of which were totally destroyed in the first few minutes — had been lined up wing-tip to wing-tip in perfect ranks on their airstrips.

"Like giant silver ducks in a shooting gallery," one of the grinning Japanese airmen was to recount after returning to his carrier.

Copied straight from the pages of the published United States Naval account of its own war games staged two years earlier, the Japanese Navy had scored a brilliant victory. And though far from being dead, the US Pacific Fleet was badly wounded.

But even in victory, something troubled Admiral Nagamo. During the accelerated debriefing sessions held with the jubilant pilots who had led the attacks, and reviewing with his staff the hurriedly-processed photographs of the burning and sinking ships in the oil-slick waters of Pearl Harbor, it puzzled Admiral Nagamo that not one of the stricken ships was a modern vessel. The ships he had journeyed so far to destroy, and those his pilots had risked their lives to send to the bottom of the sea, were mostly of World War I vintage, all more than twenty years old. In terms of modern naval warfare, they were fundamentally outdated.

Where were the newer warships his intelligence reports had told him would be at anchor in Pearl Harbor that morning? And in particular, where were the vastly important aircraft carriers? Where was the *USS Enterprise*, the flagship carrier of the US Pacific Fleet? Where were its sister carriers, the *USS Lexington* and the *USS Saratoga*, both loaded to their flight decks with modern American fighter planes and bombers? Not one of those all-important warships had even been sighted! Why?

As he paced the bridge of his command ship, Admiral Nagamo pondered the situation. He voiced his thoughts to an aide: The attack on Pearl Harbor had been delayed because of heavy seas, therefore his bombers and torpedo planes had approached Hawaii approximately two hours *after* Japanese planes in the Southern Region had dropped their first bombs on Singapore.

It was a disquieting thought, and he continued pacing the bridge of his ship, weighing and balancing the specifics even as the last of his torpedo bombers circled overhead and landed on the decks of his carriers amid the rapturous cheers of their crews.

But above their jubilant shouts, a single vexing thought haunted him: Something wasn't right. Was it likely that United States intelligence had discovered the presence of his fleet? Was it possible that the United States Navy had dispersed the major ships of its Pacific Fleet to the open seas before his planes had an opportunity to reach Pearl Harbor?

Such thoughts were daunting, and yet in the Admiral's calculating mind he could find no other answer. It followed, then, that his attack on Pearl Harbor had not been the surprise it was meant to be. His strike force was 6,200 miles from Japan, and if the enemy knew its position he was at immediate risk of being ambushed and losing his own fleet to enemy ships and aircraft.

The Admiral stopped pacing and scanned the skies to the south. Then, against the protestations of his buoyant squadron leaders who cried out for a once-in-a-lifetime opportunity to return with a third wave of planes to sink the remaining ships at Pearl Harbor and destroy the US military infrastructure, the dry-dock facilities, the submarine base and the all-important oil storage tanks, he ordered his armada to change course and increase its speed to accelerate out of the range of US bombers and torpedo planes.

He had decided to take his fleet as rapidly as possible back to the safety of Japanese waters.

Throughout Asia and the entire Pacific region, the forces of the Japanese Empire were attacking, though presumably because of the logistical problems involved in such a massive operation and human confusion over the time differential from one area of attack to another, there were in some cases substantial intervals between them. Certainly there was an excessive time lapse between the first amphibious landings at Kota Bharu in Malaya and the attacks on Hong Kong. Perhaps if all sides in the conflict had looked at the schedule of events in Greenwich Mean Time rather than in local or Tokyo time, the sequence of those major attacks would have been easier to put into perspective:

MALAY LANDINGS	00.25 local time, Dec 8	16:55 GMT, Dec 7, 1941
PEARL HARBOR	07:55 local time, Dec 7	18:25 GMT, Dec 7, 1941
		[1:30 hours later]
SHANGHAI	04:20 local time, Dec 8	19:50 GMT, Dec 7, 1941
		[2:55 hours later]
PHILIPPINES	05:00 local time, Dec 8	21:00 GMT Dec 7, 1941
(First air raid on Batan)		[4:05 hours later]
HONG KONG	08:00 local time, Dec 8	23:30 GMT Dec 7, 1941
		[6:35 hours later]

The Japanese bombing of Singapore and the invasion of Malaya began at least one hour and thirty-five minutes *before* Admiral Nagamo's aircraft bombed Pearl Harbor. And the attacks on Clark Field in the Philippines and Kai Tak at Hong Kong came, respectively, 4:05 and 6:35 hours *afterwards*.

JOHN BELL SMITHBACK

At a time when United States and British intelligence agencies prided themselves on their ability to eavesdrop on enemy—as well as friendly—communications virtually anywhere in the world, it is exceedingly hard to imagine that soon after 16:55 GMT on the morning of December 7, 1941, some word of the astounding Japanese attacks on Malaya and Singapore was not immediately dispatched to other parts of the world. Even signals from the weakest radio transmitter would have been sufficient to inform listeners or ham radio operators somewhere that the Japanese Empire had made an audacious move and was on a wild march throughout the whole of Southeast Asia.

Yet the haunting suspicion that raced through Admiral Nagamo's mind in the choppy seas north of Pearl Harbor could very well have been real, for it is almost inconceivable that no one in Hawaii or Washington or London had the slightest idea that for the past three weeks a powerful Japanese armada had been bearing down on Pearl Harbor with the objective of unleashing a colossal strike that would cause massive—and possibly irreparable—damage to the United States Pacific Fleet. One that in the end would cost the lives of 2,403 Americans, 1,177 of them sleeping sailors who were entombed inside the *USS Arizona*, a mighty battleship now capsized in the shallow waters of Pearl Harbor.

Another peculiar thing happened in the Philippines. According to the plan, in the event of a Japanese attack—code named *War Plan Orange*—General MacArthur was to respond by immediately sending his B-17 bombers to destroy Japanese airfields on Formosa (Taiwan). Yet as soon as his staff informed him of the Japanese attack at Pearl Harbor, General MacArthur retreated to his suite at the Manila Hotel and for ten hours refused to respond to knocks on his door or to answer telephone calls. There were 91 fighter planes and 34 B-17 bombers lined up in perfect rows on the runways at Clark Field when Japanese attack planes swept down from the skies, and nearly all of them were destroyed. The 14 bombers that survived were hurriedly flown to Australia.

Years after the fact, some writers and historians said that MacArthur seemed to freeze when told of the Japanese attack on Pearl Harbor. Some members of his staff said that when receiving word at 4am in the morning, he sat on his bed, appearing gray and exhausted, and reached for his Bible. Some speculated that the general suffered a nervous breakdown. Whatever the case, it was only when Japanese troops were landing on the beaches of Luzon that MacArthur finally exited his rooms to take charge of operations.

But if Hawaii didn't have information about the timing of the Japanese moves, elsewhere in Asia reports that the Japanese Imperial forces were set to spring appeared to have been known in several quarters many hours *before* the moves took place because 26 hours before the Pearl Harbor attack, merchant sailors and officers in Hong Kong were hurriedly summoned back to their ships, and 32 out of 36 major vessels left Hong Kong to sail away to safe seas well ahead of the Japanese assault. Additionally, some time between the hours of 2:30 and 3:00 that Saturday morning, at the very moment that the fleet of merchant ships was hurrying out of the harbor, Madame Sun Yet-sen, widow of the Republic of China's first president, along with the head of the London *Times* newspaper bureau and a number of other notables who had been visiting Hong Kong, were hurriedly piling their luggage outside their doors at the Hong Kong Hotel and desperately summoning help to get them to a boat that was waiting to take them across the harbor to the airport. When someone asked them why they were leaving in such a mad rush, they replied that he "had to be a dumb mutt" not to know that the Japanese were going to attack Hong Kong at any moment.

Madame Sun Yet-sen, along with the Chinese Finance Minister Kung Hsiang-hsi and 275 others, were, in 16 sorties piloted by eight American flyers, flown from Kai Tak Airport to Chiang Kai-shek's northwest capital of Chungking (Chongqing). And while they got clean away, the "dumb mutt" didn't: he spent the next three years and eight months being beaten and nearly starved to death by Japanese guards behind barbed wire in a prisoner of war camp. If he had read the Hong Kong Government Gazette issued three days earlier, he might have considered packing his bags too. For in an edition labeled *Extraordinary Issue*, it was reported that "Authority for the removal of the Head Office of The Hong Kong Bank from the Colony is granted by a Special Order of His Excellency, the Governor."

It was the Hong Kong Bank that issued and regulated all the Colony's currency. In other words, Hong Kong's banker was fleeing.

In Singapore and Malaya, the story was the same. Twenty-four hours before the Japanese attack, Singapore radio issued a series of bulletins commanding all naval personnel to report to their ships and bases immediately. A similar call went out to RAF personnel, and the next call was to command all military personnel to return to their bases urgently. Naval patrols walked the streets rounding up sailors and merchant crewmen, sending them back to their ships. At the Cathay Cinema, the long-awaited showing of the film *Major Barbara* with Rex Harrison was suddenly interrupted and foot-high letters appeared on the screen telling all military personnel to return to their bases immediately. The same thing occurred in cinemas in Kuala Lumpur, Penang, and elsewhere throughout Malaya. Seamen from merchant ships were rounded up on shore and taken by motor launch to their anchored ships and, just as it was in Hong Kong, most of the ships that left port at that time were spared the wrath of Japanese bombs.

The "dumb mutt" in Hong Kong was John Stericker, an executive of ZBW, at that time Hong Kong's only radio station. In his words, "Somebody knew. Who knew? Were our intelligence reports better than those of the Americans? Between Hong Kong and Singapore's certainty and Pearl Harbor's uncertainty, there was time to get every ship at Pearl Harbor to sea. What a difference that would have made!"[14]

Perhaps somebody did know. Perhaps somebody knew more than has ever been revealed. Just look at the facts:

* Just before the Japanese struck, the Hurricane fighters that had been destined for Singapore were abruptly sent somewhere else.

* Just before the pre-dawn landing of Japanese divisions on the beach at Kota Bharu, the experienced troops that could have best defended Malaya and Singapore — and possibly saved them from Japanese conquest — had been inexplicably ordered to India.

* Just before the bombs began to fall, Churchill's authorization for a fleet of fast torpedo boats for the defense of Singapore was rescinded.

* Just days before the sudden attack on Kai Tak Airfield, virtually all RAF combat planes stationed in Hong Kong were suddenly flown away.

* Just before the first enemy troops crossed from China into Hong Kong, the munitions and supplies from Canada that were meant for Hong Kong's defenders were mysteriously sidetracked to the Philippines.

---

14   John Stericker, *A Tear For The Dragon*.

* Just before hostilities began, nearly all merchant and naval ships were ordered out of the harbors of Singapore and Hong Kong.

* Just before the attack, the 15 vessels of the Royal Navy's 4th Submarine Flotilla were transferred to Singapore.

*Along with the ships, the naval headquarters and its vice-admiral relocated in Singapore.

* Just before the start of the war, the official bank of Hong Kong, the one that printed and controlled its currency, had been spirited out of the Colony.

* Just before the war began, just about every Japanese civilian who had been living in Southeast Asia had left, all returning to Japan.

* Three days prior to the invasion of Hong Kong, the Japanese-language *Hong Kong News* ceased publication.

* Just before the air and land attack in the early hours of Monday, December 8, 1941, most of Hong Kong's artillery shells were shipped out of the Territory and put in storage in Manila.

* In the days leading up to the Japanese surprise attack, virtually every important British government official in Hong Kong, from the Governor down to the Director of Public Works, was transferred out of the Crown Colony, most of them called back to England.

It seemed, all of it, part of a planned withdrawal that came immediately after the face-to-face meeting between Winston Churchill and President Roosevelt aboard a warship in the Atlantic Ocean in August, and at 7:30 a.m. on Monday, December 8, 1941 [Sunday, December 7 GMT], when the Japanese bombs began falling on Kai Tak Airport, Hong Kong was in the hands of a new Governor, a new Colonial Secretary who had arrived from Ceylon less than 12 hours earlier, a new Commander of the Royal Air Force, who arrived five days earlier, a new Financial

Secretary, a new Commander of the Army, and a new Director of Public Works.

The longest-serving senior official in Hong Kong had been there only one month.

All a coincidence? It seems very unlikely, and when the Japanese attack came, the battle for Hong Kong was fought by 14,000 ill-equipped, untested Commonwealth troops — British, Canadian, Indian — and its Volunteer Defense Corps, a 2,200 man militia made up of mostly overseas civilian businessmen, traders, merchants, lawyers, bankers and brokers who knew little or nothing about fighting a war. Some of them, armed with nothing more than pistols and World War I rifles, marched out to confront the cannon and mortars of 52,000 battle-experienced Japanese warriors of the Japanese 38th Division.

Like John Stericker, many of those who survived the 17-day battle for Hong Kong, only to spend the next three years and eight months in a Japanese prisoner of war camp, never gave up wondering: *"Somebody knew. Who knew?"*

Their officers? Or was it someone at the top?

Like many others, he had his fears and suspicions. But to give a name to a person, to fully acknowledge that he was a victim of someone's treachery, would mean accepting that he was thought of as little more than a person of no value. And to pursue that line of thinking would mean concluding that he, and everyone else in the Far East, had become expendable.

In Malaya, even as war raged in the north of the country and it became apparent that the situation was becoming ever more critical, the military command in Singapore refused to accept that their Bastion of Empire was being threatened. To them, the enemy was engaged in a futile jungle action hundreds of miles to the north, and there wasn't the faintest doubt in any of their minds that it was a physical impossibility for an army to threaten Singapore from the north.

As though they were making an effort to prove them wrong, by day and by night the Japanese bombers continued to harass them, guided by the smoke at noon and by the lights of the city at night. There was no liaison between the military and the civilian administration, so nobody gave orders to turn off any of Singapore's lights—not even the lights at the huge naval base and shipyard. Worse, no one knew how to locate the switches that *would* turn them off.

To complete the confusion, it wasn't certain who was supposed to turn on Singapore's air raid sirens to signal the approach of the Japanese bombers.

The special Japanese attack squadron with armor-piercing bombs that had gone to Singapore in search of the *HMS Prince of Wales* and the *HMS Repulse* failed to find their quarry the first day, and they failed again the next. But on the third day of the war, a flight of 84 Mitsubishi torpedo attack bombers found them hiding in the waters off the Malayan eastern coast. The two major battleships, that had only recently come so far, were quickly and almost effortlessly sent to the bottom of the South China Sea. Churchill and the world were shocked.[15]

As Britain mourned the loss of two of its largest battleships and one of her most admired admirals, Tom Phillips, the Royal Navy—that had proclaimed the two ships unsinkable—finally began to question the confidential medical findings which

---

15 Churchill to Stalin on November 4: "With the object of keeping Japan quiet we are sending our latest battleship, Prince of Wales, which can catch and kill any Japanese ship, into the Indian Ocean, and we are building up a powerful battle squadron there."

ASIA BETRAYED

reported that Japanese pilots had remarkably weak eyesight.[16]

The type of torpedo used to sink the two ships had been invented by an Englishman. The individuals who trained the Japanese Imperial Navy in the aerial use of them were the British traitors Frederick Rutland and the Lord William Forbes-Sempill.

Between the disorganized and disconnected battlefronts in Malaya and the command officers in their bunker at Fort Canning in Singapore, communications had became so disrupted that civilian telephone lines had to be used to send and receive orders. In those days before direct dialing, long distance telephone calls had to go through a central telephone exchange. And because the number of lines was limited, all calls were restricted to exactly three minutes. Three minutes and no more. Worse, there was but one phone line linking the north of Malaya to the south.

In one of those believe-it-or-not situations that occur when no one seems to know what is happening or what his or her role is, the civilian telephone operators in Singapore handling the calls to the northern reaches of Malaya severed them in the middle of conversations after briskly announcing that time was up, the callers' three minutes had expired.

On the island of Singapore the situation had become appalling. Ugly clouds of black oily smoke rolled into the skies over the beautiful green island, and when a light rain fell, the oil dripped from the skies and clung to the trees, the plants, the grass. From everything.

Like crazed hornets, Japanese fighter planes circled low overhead, and when they no longer seemed to have bombs or obvious targets, the pilots came in low over the rooftops, pushed

---

16   A moment-by-moment account of this monumental air-sea battle can be found in Edwyn Gray's *Operation Pacific: The Royal Navy's War Against Japan, 1941-1945*

back the canopies of their cockpits and began dropping hand grenades on the thousands of refugees milling in the oily rubble that littered the streets.

The city water reservoirs had been so badly bombed that the gutters and storm drains of the city were flooded as the overflowing water spilled into them. Firemen who had risked their lives to turn out to douse the thousands of blazes stood looking at the flames with slack hoses. There was no water pressure in the hydrants.

Bombs that fell on the underground storm drains ruptured them and sent decomposing bodies into the streets because the dead had been buried in one of Singapore's few remaining burial grounds — the storm drains which had been designed to protect the city from monsoon floods. The acrid stench of death and the promise of disease filled the air, and the carcasses of mules and dogs befouled the streets and canals. Abandoned vehicles of all types blazed and exploded like a network of firecrackers every time another bomb or grenade was dropped onto the debris.

The hospitals were treating more than two thousand casualties a day, and the carefully manicured green lawn of the Singapore General Hospital had to be ripped open and made into enormous pits where the dead were placed in shallow graves and covered with lime.

To add to everyone's despair, beyond the green edge of the city and the soft sandy shores at the water's edge, Singapore itself had become the final beach. Beyond it was the sea. There was no way out.

Meanwhile, the Singapore military command was waiting for the main thrust that they were confident would come from the direction of the sea, and despite the falling bombs they were determined to see that Singapore would continue to function in a civilized atmosphere unaffected by war. The golf, bridge and tennis clubs held their regular meetings, and people tried to make light of the unfriendly disturbances going on about them. At the Alhambra Cinema, queues formed to see the much talked-about new film, *Ziegfeld Girl*. Newspapers continued to publish abbreviated editions, their editors expressing regret about the inconvenience but proclaiming optimistically that events were about to change and the unfortunate circumstances would soon pass. It was only a matter of time, they declared, before everyone would be able to rejoice.

At the Adelphi Hotel, Riller's Band tuned their instruments to play slow and romantic favorites for the evening dance. That was by design, for the orchestra was under strict instructions to play slow tunes "so the dancers would not perspire unnecessarily and embarrassingly."

"There is no cause for alarm," a British officer stressed to several anxious-looking Australian newcomers while leaning against the bar at the Raffles Hotel. He wasn't talking about Riller's Band and the lingering threat of perspiration: he was talking about Malaya's geography. "Singapore is a fortress without equal in the world, and Malaya is the easiest country in the world to defend," he explained. "There are only two rail lines and one major road running from north to south. If it comes to it, all we have to do is to defend those and the country will remain ours. As for the rest, the entire country is nothing more than thick, impenetrable jungle. There isn't an army in the world capable of marching through it. An enemy must attack Singapore here, from the sea, and that would be sheer suicide because the sea is completely protected by our fifteen-inch naval guns."

If the apprehensive Australian officers were assured, those

fighting in the jungles to the north of Singapore were not. For the most part, they were unseasoned soldiers, totally unprepared for the events that were so rapidly engulfing them. Their units were undermanned, understaffed, out-gunned and out-maneuvered. The trained men, those who knew about jungles and jungle fighting, had been transferred to India weeks earlier, and everything that could possibly be wrong with an army was wrong with this one. In the burning heat of the day and in the chilling silence of the night, it stumbled and groped within a nightmare of fear, depression and confusion. "Fall back and reorganize, fall back and reorganize," came their orders, and under the rubber and mangrove trees they fought and bled and died.

The only thing real to them was that they had suddenly and without warning become involved in an uncontrolled and unprecedented nightmare. Fighting by day and withdrawing by night, they were totally exhausted. Even when they did receive orders to stop and make a stand, the Japanese deftly got on their bicycles and moved around them through what everyone had described as an impenetrable jungle. By the time the defending soldiers finished digging their positions and getting their guns in place, the enemy was already ten or more miles behind them on its relentless trek south to Singapore.

That does not mean that the British, Indian, New Zealand and Australian soldiers did not fight. Many brave men died in bewildering scenes of individual and collective heroism. The casualty list of men who fought against the odds within the claustrophobic jungle in battles they couldn't understand, of men who fought valiantly and well against the odds of ignorance and incompetency, is heartbreakingly long. It was a battle that would not stand still for a single instant, and their velour could not hope to compensate for the preponderance of inefficiency, neglect, bureaucracy, bumbledom, guff and red tape that had tumbled out of London for years—and which had suddenly become their inheritance.

From the very beginning, their campaign had been destined to become a battle of futility, and the men fighting in Malaya's tough, humid and alien environment breathed the earthy, leguminous smells of the jungle and found that their withdrawal was nearing the feverous pitch of a retreat. The battle had reached that irreversible position where each man was thinking in terms of personal survival. And because he had been led to believe it, he thought it was the island of Singapore that would save him.

In their minds, they had every reason to think that once they reached the island of Singapore they would be safe. Yet when they finally got there, they were dazed. In less than six weeks they had walked, crawled, run and fought the entire length of the Malay Peninsula, and when they staggered across the narrow causeway that links Singapore to Malaya they stumbled onto a burning island already crowded with over a million refugees moving around like automatons. Some of the troops who reached the presumed safety of the island had rifles, many did not. Along with the men and women and children of all races, they cowered in the rubble of the buildings as the Japanese planes circled repeatedly overhead and dropped their bombs and then their grenades.

Blitz is a German word meaning 'lightning'. The speed with which the German army stormed through Europe was said to be as fast as lightning, so the word blitz was soon used to describe any war conducted with great speed and force. The battle of Malaya had become precisely that: a blitz. But it was a blitz with a difference, for the Japanese army was riding bicycles. And to the soldiers who heard the convoys of them moving down the roads at twilight or in the dead of night, the sound of the bicycle tires was the only sound they heard. It had become a frightening sound. The roads seemed to hiss. In the minds of the concealed soldiers who had spent the day fighting an enemy that had been in front of them, they knew they had again been bypassed and they would have to spend that night and the next day fighting their way back to their own lines. Psychologically, Malaya had become a demoralizing nightmare.

By the time his blitz on bicycle wheels had moved within sight of Singapore Island, General Yamashita had earned, from his soldiers and his superiors, a distinctive title—The Tiger of Malaya. Sooner than any of the planners had expected, he had reached the furthermost point of the Malay Peninsula at Johore Bharu where he ordered his troops to put their large guns and mortars in place and await further orders to attack.

A large body of water separated Singapore from the mainland, and he needed time to evaluate the situation. The strait was blue and beautiful, but it was a barrier as well as a threat. He had unexpectedly moved so fast that he had overstretched his lines of supply by nearly three hundred miles. He had suffered far fewer casualties than he or the strategists in Tokyo had believed possible, and now that he stood looking across the waters at Singapore, he still commanded a fighting force of 30,000 battle-hardened soldiers. But they were fatigued, weary from their tireless rush south. And most worrisome of all, they were now short of bullets.

Staring across the Johore-Singapore Causeway, General Yamashita surmised that there were still between 100,000 to 150,000 British, Australian, New Zealand, Indian and Commonwealth soldiers in the jungles and the green hills of Singapore. And he assumed from the way the previous battles had gone that the soldiers were under orders to retire to Singapore with the intention of luring his army into a deadly trap.

Now, standing on a hill in the shade of the Sultan's Palace and looking out at the lush green island, he debated whether or not he should cease his advance and wait for reinforcements. He removed his cap to fan himself. Drops of sweat oozed from his forehead. Should he wait? Or should he take one more risk and send scouting patrols across the water to probe the island's defenses?

As he studied his maps and considered his next course of action, he summoned his ordnance officer. In the event that it seemed possible for him to take his army across the water and land on Singapore Island, he wanted an exact accounting of the amount of ammunition remaining in his scarce supply.

His ordnance supply officer appeared and bowed deeply. He was virtually in tears as he recited the painful news to his general: Supplies were too low to continue fighting any longer at full strength. If every man was given ammunition, each one would be able to receive only two bullets.

General Yamashita praised the officer, stared once more across the obstructing blue waterway, and then told the officer to distribute the remaining bullets, two each to every man. "The last one," he declared, "is for himself."

This was a reference to the Japanese Soldier's Code which stated that, to avoid the despicable humiliation of being captured in battle, the soldier must always use his last bullet to kill himself. Then, having made the decision, General Yamashita directed the ordnance officer to have his gunners break into the remaining stock of artillery and mortar shells and begin shooting at the city at will. Borrowing a page from Attila, leader of the Ostrogoths who sacked Rome in 546 by first cutting its water supply, he stressed that his gunners aim first at Singapore's reservoirs.

The weary soldiers who had survived the battles in the jungles and had crossed the causeway into Singapore found that they had entered another hell, and they were stunned.

They had staggered out of the north and into the presumed safety of the island at the very moment that Yamashita's artillery and mortar shells began indiscriminately pounding the city. Destruction, death and disaster was everywhere.

At the Singapore Naval Base, abrupt new explosions thundered as demolition teams began blowing it up. And then, late at night on February 10, the remaining forces of His Majesty's Royal Navy along with the Supreme British Commander for the Southwest Pacific Region, General Archibald Wavell, sailed out to sea in search of a safer port. In his dash to leave the burning city, Wavell slipped on the Singapore dock and broke two bones in his back.

Nearby, at one of the few remaining docks, one of the commanding generals of Singapore "quietly, voluntarily and without permission" (as the report was to read after the war) slipped onto a boat and made his way to the safety of Australia.

Behind him, hundreds upon hundreds of survivors of the fighting began to desert their units, and small evacuation efforts were made but with little success. Almost all of the boats had already been commandeered and taken to sea by the deserters who had preceded them. In many instances, it may have been fortunate that their attempts were thwarted, for Japanese observation planes had reported the previous exodus of small boats and it had been decided at the highest level that retreat and evacuation would not be tolerated. There would be no more survivors from Singapore, they declared, and Japanese patrol ships were dispatched to wait just beyond the horizon for any floating vessel whose occupants were attempting to flee.

"Singapore will not be another Dunkirk," they said, referring to the evacuation of nearly 350,000 British and Allied troops from the beaches of France in the last days of May in 1940 as they fled the Nazi war machine sweeping across Europe.

At the huge naval base, ciphered messages from the outside world continued streaming in, but no one knew whether relief was coming or not because the only man who could decode the messages had already fled: he had taken a boat to Java, carrying with him the only known copy of the code book. The naval base—which, after all, was one of the prime reasons for the Empire troops being there in the first place—consisted of docks and repair yards to service and supply the British Fleet. In addition, five enormous naval guns of the type that are normally found on the navy's largest battleships had been installed. Shells for such guns are so huge it takes several men using special equipment to load them. The barrels out of which a shell leaves such a gun measure fifteen inches in diameter, and each shell weighs 1,938 pounds. They are massive and frightening weapons capable of blowing an entire ship out of the water, and the effect of such shelling on an army of men would be dreadful to contemplate. General Yamashita knew their danger, but he also knew that the huge weapons on the island had been strategically placed to shoot in but one direction, and that was outward toward an empty sea. As such, the lethal weapons that had cost so much money and served to give Singapore its title as *The Invincible Fortress* waited for an enemy attack that would never come.

It had been sixty-five days and nearly five hundred miles of combat since he put his troops ashore at Kota Bharu, and with the prize of Singapore Island now before him, General Yamashita pulled his exhausted body up the deserted stairway of the Sultan's Palace. His boots squeaked and his long samurai sword clanged on the steps in the eerie silence. From the top of the Sultan's Palace, he gazed across the thousand-yard causeway separating the island from the Malayan mainland. Ignoring the advice of his subordinates who feared that enemy sharpshooters would be lurking in the dense foliage across the waterway, he wanted to review the situation of his adversary and to collect his thoughts. He knew that the rout imposed on them by his advancing troops had been so swift that many of the defenders had simply thrown away their weapons and given up the war. The tons of foodstuffs, munitions and military equipment they left behind became known as Winston's Supplies, and much of it had sustained his soldiers on their march south. Now, staring across the causeway in the heat of the morning sun, he suddenly sucked in his breath and blinked in disbelief.

Expecting a strong and determined struggle from a besieged garrison, he saw instead a naked island. There were no signs of the expected fortifications, there was no barbed wire, there were no trenches, no gun emplacements—nothing at all to offer military resistance. And in bold disregard of all reason, even the vital man-made causeway with the only highway and railway link leading to and from Singapore Island was exposed and virtually undamaged. As far as he could tell, even that had no apparent defenses set up for deployment against his troops.

Raising a hand to shield his eyes, he wiped perspiration from his forehead and scowled. Like the fleeing army he had been pursuing, he, too, had come to believe many of the British accounts about Singapore being a fortress bristling with armaments. Furthermore, he had access to detailed intelligence reports that correctly measured the combined forces of Commonwealth troops at close to 200,000 men.

A tough and battle-tried warrior, he was unexpectedly

confused. Carefully scanning the island once again to confirm his observations, he went down the wide staircase and summoned his aides to a conference in a bare room within the empty palace. His supply lines were over-extended, and though his men were weary, they were skilled hunters set and determined to make the final kill. But Yamashita sensed that something was wrong, and suspecting an enemy trap he ordered his commanders to hold up their assault on the island until he was able to assess the peculiar situation. It was February 1942, and the day was Friday the 13th.

Across the causeway, and beyond General Yamashita's view, a British Army captain hurriedly approached the Singapore Golf Club to locate someone in charge. He had been ordered by one of his superiors to obtain permission before digging up the greens and chopping down the banana trees to sink trenches and set up defenses to obstruct the Japanese advance.

A fatigued man badly in need of a shave sat alone inside the clubhouse fanning himself. He seemed surprised to have a visitor, and while apologizing for his appearance he offered the captain a glass of warm gin. But the captain was in a hurry. The Japanese were less than two miles from the golf links, he cried, and he needed immediate written permission to begin digging up the manicured lawns and greens.

The lone individual straightened his back and expressed shock at such a suggestion. He was a long-standing member of the club, he said, and he was there to preserve its propriety. He had the further task of keeping it from being overrun by the thousands of refugees who were wandering around homeless in the streets of Singapore. He had no authority, he declared, to grant permission to such a request. He suggested that the British Army wait three or four days to put the proposal before the club's officers at a special meeting that was scheduled later in the week. They would most certainly refuse him, he said decisively, but they would be the ones to speak to about things like that.

In desperation, the officer decided that he would act without approval and he drove away frantically through the rubble-strewn streets to the Army Ordnance Office to request a vehicle, workers, shovels, and some barbed wire. A bomb crater blocked his way, and swinging the car door open he leapt out and ran the rest of the way to the Depot.

A carefully lettered sign on the locked gate told him that the Ordnance Depot was closed. It was the start of the Lunar New Year, and a legal holiday. Happy Year of the Horse!

Three, perhaps four miles away, smartly dressed waiters in the dining room of Raffles Hotel were busy spreading the tables in clean white linen, polishing the silver to a spotless shine and arranging the crystal for the usual evening dinner. At the far corner of the room a dance band was softly tuning its instruments and preparing to play for the diners. Occasionally, an enemy shell could be heard whining low overhead and the windows rattled when it landed. But for the first time in over a month the sounds had abated and the guests said it was an encouraging sign that the British Army had, as they knew it would, halted the Japanese advance.

At the bar, military staff officers in their formal dress uniforms awaiting the evening dinner bent their elbows in a heated debate concerning their missions, complaining that there was nothing for them to do in Singapore but "sit, drink and crap". Those from the Singapore Command insisted that they were only there to fight to save the giant naval base. Those from London maintained that the objective of the Army was to protect Singapore Island, and that included defending the naval base. The field officers frowned at that and claimed they were under the impression that they were there to defend the entire Malayan Peninsula. The Australian officers who had only recently been dispatched to Singapore listened to the arguments and were confused.

At about the same time that Yamashita had been studying the island through binoculars, General A.E. Percival, the Commander-in-Chief of the British Army in Singapore, was ordering his driver to bring a car to his headquarters so he could take a drive through the burning streets. An indecisive man directed by too many advisors, General Percival looked out his car window at the once-beautiful city that seemed to have been reduced to rubble at every turn. Beyond the palm-lined boulevards of the residential areas, the streets of the city had been turned into a tragic sight. The wharfs burned out of control along the water's edge, and inside his car the general could hear the muffled explosions as naval demolition teams began the task of blowing up the huge naval base. He had ordered their destruction as a precaution. Dense clouds of oily smoke rose high above the city and a form of miserable black grease rained down from the skies. The stench of death was everywhere.

As his car turned a corner, something caught Percival's eye and he ordered his driver to stop. On a wall, one of his disillusioned warriors had scribbled a message in chalk or paint:

England for the English, Australia for the Australians – but Malaya for any son- of-a-bitch who wants it!

The General slowly rolled up his window and ordered his driver to turn the car around and drive back to his headquarters.

Two days later, on the 15th of February 1942, General Percival walked with his aides through the rubble of the streets to an arranged rendezvous at Singapore's partially-wrecked Ford motorcar factory. He was on his way to discuss surrender and evacuation terms with General Yamashita. One of Percival's aides carried aloft the Union Jack from British Army Command Headquarters. Another carried a white cloth that appeared to be bigger than the flag. In the same way that the aqueduct of ancient Rome had been severed by the Goths to starve the city of water, the reservoirs of Singapore had been breeched and there was no more fresh water. Fearing for the well-being of his soldiers and for Singapore's civilian population, Percival had asked the Japanese for a temporary ceasefire.

Now, sitting across from him at a makeshift table, General Yamashita was savoring the moment. His men had no more ammunition and the enemy was making an appeal to an army without bullets. He had no time to waste on negotiations and he offered General Percival no terms. He was there to accept Percival's surrender, he barked, and it was to be immediate and unconditional. When Percival wavered, Yamashita hit the table with his fist. "Surrender immediately or face the consequences!" he shouted.

Involuntarily, Percival lifted a hand to his breast pocket and felt a letter given to him by General Wavell just before he hurried to catch a boat leaving the island. For whatever reason, Percival had slipped it into his pocket when setting off to meet Yamashita, and now, being ordered to put his name to a surrender document, Wavell's words raged in his brain:

It is certain that our troops in Singapore heavily outnumber any Japanese who have crossed the Straits. We must destroy them. Our whole fighting reputation is at stake, as well as the honor of the B.E.F. It would be disgraceful if we yield our boasted fortress of Singapore to inferior forces.

There must be no question of surrender. Every unit must fight it out to the end in close contact with the enemy. Please see that the above is brought to the notice of our senior officers and to our troops. I look to you and your men to fight it out to the end to prove the fighting spirit that won the empire, and still insists to defend it. Your gallant stand is serving a purpose and must be continued to the limits of endurance.

There must be no thought of sparing troops, or the civilian population, and no mercy must be shown in shape or form. Commanders and senior officers must lead their men, and if necessary die with them.

Wavell[17]

"Sign!" Yamashita shouted a second time, and a pen was thrust toward him.

Head bowed, blinking back tears, Percival signed, and in less than thirty minutes he had turned over to General Yamashita's weary, hungry, ill-equipped and nearly unarmed army the whole of Singapore and his army of 138,708 men to the force of 23,000 Japanese who had crossed the Johore Strait to the island.

Yamashita, the Tiger of Malaya, had out-bluffed Percival. In the seventy-day campaign the British and Commonwealth armies had lost a total of 138,708 men to the Japanese. Japanese casualties throughout the entire Malayan offensive totaled 3,507 dead and 6,160 wounded. The lopsided ratio was 14 to 1.

Only when he was a prisoner of war would General Percival learn that at the moment of his surrender Yamashita's army was out of food, it had no more ammunition, and if the battle for Singapore had continued for even another three or four more days, Yamashita and every last one of his loyal soldiers would have proved their allegiance to their Emperor by committing suicide.

---

17   https://www.cofepow.org.uk/armed-forces-stories-list/general-wavells-letter

That night, General Yamashita drank a silent toast and bowed toward his Emperor in far-off Tokyo. What he had feared to dream had become a reality: the Japanese had inflicted the greatest Asiatic defeat on a European power since the fierce horsemen of Genghis Khan had whipped out of the steppes of the East and threatened Vienna seven centuries earlier. It was the first time a British Crown Colony had surrendered to an invading force, and Britain's Impregnable Fortress had a new name: *Shonan*. Meaning Bright South.

Alone with his thoughts, Yamashita stretched out on the floor and went to sleep as he had always done, with his head facing northeast in the direction of the Emperor.

On another island at another time, Winston S. Churchill would sit in the stillness in front of a pleasing fire in his warm and comfortable study, look down at his large desk and turn over page upon page as he searched through his wartime files to compile his memoirs.

He would see in his notes that on the day the first bombs fell on Pearl Harbor and Singapore, his Foreign Secretary Anthony Eden had sailed from the Scapa Flow naval base in northern Scotland to meet Joseph Stalin in Moscow. Eden had complained of having a cold, but he was on an important mission: he had been instructed by Churchill to try to persuade Stalin to get Russian participation by declaring war on Japan.

From his notes, Churchill would see what he had cabled Eden: "Today the U.S. has sustained a major disaster at Hawaii and it now has only two battleships in the Pacific against ten Japanese. Hope you are better. We are having a jolly time here!"

As former First Lord of the Admiralty and a man with considerable knowledge about naval affairs, at that point he might have referred to additional notes he had concerning the true size of the United States Fleet at that time, and he would have been able to confirm that the US had seven regular aircraft carriers and England had three. And as he very well knew when he sent his message to Eden, the joint US-British Fleet was not as weak as the press had reported it to be. What's more, at the time of the attack on Pearl Harbor, shipyards throughout the United States were about to launch a wide range of new warships of every type, the scale of which would dwarf anything Japan and her Axis allies were capable of putting to sea.

As his recounting of events was written well after the defeat of Japan, Churchill would have observed from his notes that, on December 7, 1941, the missing aircraft carriers that had disturbed Admiral Nagamo and frustrated Japanese attempts to neutralize the United States Pacific Fleet in one swift surprise blow had been nowhere near Pearl Harbor.

The mighty flagship of the United States carrier fleet, the *USS Enterprise*, had been two hundred miles to the south on its way back to Hawaii after a quick visit to a United States military installation at Wake Island.

At that same time, the carrier *USS Lexington* and a large fleet of modern vessels and submarines had been almost close enough to Nagamo's task force to have been monitoring it as it prepared to pounce on Pearl Harbor. It had been in the same high seas approximately six hundred miles northwest of Hawaii journeying back to its home port after a mission to the US military base at Midway Island.

Of the ships that were caught at anchor and sunk at Pearl Harbor that day, all except the *Arizona* were re-floated, and all but the *Oklahoma* — which was scrapped — rejoined the US Pacific Fleet soon after the Japanese attack. The battleships *Maryland*, *Pennsylvania* and *Tennessee* were repaired without any great difficulty.

Significantly, it was five months to the day after Nagamo's attack on Pearl Harbor that several of the repaired ships took part in the first US-Japanese sea battle in what has been called the Battle of the Coral Sea. In that battle, the US Pacific Fleet destroyed more than 100,000 tons of Japanese ships. More importantly, exactly one month later it decimated Admiral Nagamo's entire fleet and turned the tide of the Pacific War in another mammoth sea battle fought between planes from opposing aircraft carriers in the Battle of Midway.

Nagamo's worst fears were realized, and after only six months of war his once-powerful naval force was on the defensive, a position it would maintain throughout the remainder of the war.

At the time those sea battles were raging, Churchill had talked to his cabinet. "It was a blessing to us that Japan attacked the United States and brought America wholeheartedly and unitedly into this war," he said, though he went on to acknowledge that both he and the United States had been wrong about the Japanese for they had not rated Japan's military capacity very highly. Though not unexpected, the loss of Singapore was part of the price he paid for that erroneous assessment.

Returning to the messages he had written to his Foreign Secretary, Anthony Eden, during the first days of the war in December 1941, Churchill would see he had written a particularly sad note about a sad event: "We have lost the battleships *Prince of Wales* and *Repulse* today. On the other hand, accession of the US makes amends for it all. The situation is changing day to day in our favor."

The word accession is defined as 'the act of becoming joined', or the act by which one nation becomes party to an agreement already in force'. Was Churchill saying that he and Roosevelt had already agreed to unite in war against Britain's foes? That would certainly appear to be the case, for after his meeting with Roosevelt at sea in August 1941, Churchill had returned to England to tell his cabinet, on August 19, "that Roosevelt had said he would wage war but not declare it, and he would become more and more provocative."[18]

He went even further, telling the cabinet that Roosevelt had talked to him about looking for a naval incident which would serve to bring America into the war.

Thumbing through his papers and making notes for his memoirs, he would also have been able to review the numerous messages he had sent to Hong Kong, the Pearl of the Orient, that bleak December in 1941. During the unavailing struggle in which Hong Kong fought a losing battle against overwhelming odds, he had sent many cables that encouraged the Hong Kong's defenders to stand firm, to carry on the good fight. Reinforcements were surely on the way, he had said. The Chinese army of Chiang Kai-shek was rushing to counter-attack the Japanese from behind and help relieve the beleaguered colony, he had wired.

Yet he would also know that he wrote those cables simply to hearten the population and stimulate the Empire, the British Army, and the Hong Kong Volunteer Forces fighting the Japanese. In truth, he knew that no reinforcements would be coming and the Chinese, insofar as he was aware, were unable to offer any aid whatsoever.

Perhaps in reviewing those notes he might have observed that

---

18 Full text of "*Roosevelt To Churchill Americans Will Provoke Military Incident With Germany To Start War British War Cabinet 19 August 1941*"
https://archive.org/stream/RooseveltToChurchillAmericansWillProvokeMilitaryIncidentWithGermanyToStartWarBri/Roosevelt%20to%20Churchill%20Americans%20will%20provoke%20military%20incident%20with%20Germany%20to%20start%20war%20British%20War%20Cabinet%2019%20August%201941_djvu.txt

when Hong Kong fell on Christmas Day after seventeen days of intense, heroic but futile fighting, he had failed to make a single mention of that day or that occasion in any of his diaries or memoirs. He was then in the United States, having gone to Washington to discuss strategy with President Roosevelt. While at sea, however, in a letter to his wife he expressed his view about the colony's situation: "Hong Kong seems on the verge of surrender after only a fortnight's struggle. But the entry of the United States into the war is worth all the losses in the East many times over. Still, these losses are very painful to endure and will be very hard to repair."[19]

That same day he hand-delivered a letter to President Roosevelt:

"We must expect to be deprived one by one of our possessions and strong points in the Pacific, and that the enemy will establish himself fairly easily in one after the other, mopping up the local garrisons. It is of the utmost importance, therefore, that the enemy should not acquire large gains cheaply; that he should be compelled to nourish all his conquests and be kept extended, and kept burning up all his resources. The resources of Japan are a wasting factor. They were at their maximum strength on the day of the Pearl Harbor attack. Our policy should be to make them maintain the largest number of troops in their conquests overseas and to keep them as busy as possible. It is, therefore, right and necessary to fight them at every point where we have a chance, so as to keep him burning and extended. Our joint program may be late, but it will all come along."[20]

The following day he sent an urgent communiqué to Hong

---

19 Churchill Papers, 20 December
20 Churchill, The Grand Alliance, page 579

Kong's Governor, Sir Mark Young:

> *Winston Churchill, 10 Downing Street*
> *SECRET*
> *We are greatly concerned to hear of the landings on Hong Kong Island which have been affected by the Japanese. We cannot judge from here the conditions which rendered these landings possible or prevented effective counter-attacks upon the intruders. There must, however, be no thought of surrender. Every part of the island must be fought and the enemy resisted with the utmost stubbornness.*
>
> *The enemy should be compelled to expend the utmost life and equipment. There must be vigorous fighting in the inner defenses and, if the need be, from house to house. Every day that you are able to maintain your resistance you and your men can win the lasting honor which we are sure will be your due.*
>
> *The eyes of the world are upon you. We expect you to resist to the end. The honor of the Empire is in your hands.*[21]

A note from between the pages of one of his files would drop to the floor and Winston Churchill would lean his portly frame forward to retrieve it. He would adjust his glasses on the end of his nose and look at the page. The note would have been out of place in his files for it was dated a couple of months before the bombs fell on Pearl Harbor and Japanese troops began their invasion of Malaya. The note would have been written at a time when the German Air Force was continuing to batter Britain from the skies, when German submarines had sunk over 900 ships bringing supplies and armaments to Britain, and at a time when German troops were massing in France as final preparations were being made to cross the Channel to invade Britain.

---

21 Churchill papers 20/50

JOHN BELL SMITHBACK

Reading the page, he would have smiled. The subject of the message was something that was close to his heart. It was marked THOROUGHBRED HORSE-RACING, and it was addressed to the attention of his Home Secretary:

"If anything were done which threatened to terminate horse-racing in time of war in Britain, or that would ruin the bloodstock (of thoroughbred horses), it would be necessary that the whole matter should be thrashed out in Cabinet first."

Reflecting on these events, a poem written by an anonymous author in Hong Kong is haunting. It was written before the Japanese invasion, and it appeared in a local English newspaper's letters column a few short days before the bombs and shells began to fall and the whole of the world was rearranged. It is unknowable if the writer survived the war or lived through years of captivity in a Japanese prisoner of war camp, but hopefully he did. It is difficult to know, since 10% of Hong Kong's defenders died in battle and 20% of the prisoners of war interned in Japanese camps did not live to witness the end of the war or to experience freedom again. But all these years later, one man's poem opens a window to show, in some small way, the mood and contradictions of the times.[22]

HONG KONG, 1941
Almond eyes a-twinkle
in the dance's sway,
Blood and Tears and Sweat
ten thousand miles away.

Bold and urgent captions

---

22 Letters, the South China Morning Post, November 17, 1941

stare across the street,
"Pacific Crisis Looming;
Russians in retreat."

Brightly floats the music
on the midnight air,
"If you were Ginger Rogers
... and I were Fred Astaire."
L.

How hopeful and contrasting those words seem when put next to those spoken by President Roosevelt's Secretary of War, Henry L. Stimson, at a private meeting in Washington between Stimson, President Roosevelt and Prime Minister Winston Churchill shortly after the fall of Hong Kong.

During the meeting in the White House they discussed future cooperation in the war against Germany and Italy and, at Churchill's suggestion, the possibility of a joint operation to land troops in North Africa was reviewed. When the situation in Asia was brought up, Roosevelt and Stimson became somber and told Churchill they had assured General MacArthur and the people of the Philippines that every vessel available was bearing down on them with reinforcements. But man-to-man, and in the quiet of the presidential study in the White House, they told him that the United States had already concluded that it would have to write off the Philippines as a lost cause.

In fact, four months before the Japanese bombed Pearl Harbor and sent troops ashore in Hong Kong, Wake, Guam and Malaya, on August 20, 1941 a joint US Army-Navy board had reaffirmed War Plan Orange. Orange was the military codeword for Japan, and the conclusion of the board was that the Philippines would have to be yielded to Japan until the war against Hitler had been won. That was not something that was going to be accomplished quickly, and there was the possibility it wouldn't be accomplished at all. Until that war had been decided, however, the one in Asia would have to wait.

Having spoken to the people of Asia in the same way and under the same circumstances, Churchill must have known exactly how Roosevelt and Stimson felt, for there was a long and serious pause in their conversation. Finally, as he cleared his throat and lit a cigar, Secretary of State Stimson broke the awkward silence.

"There are times," Stimson said, "when men have to die."[23]

---

23 Marconi M. Dioso, *The Times When Men Must Die: The Story of the Destruction of the Philippine Army During the Early Months of World War II in the Pacific*, December 1941-May 1942, Dorrance Publishing Company, Inc.

PART II

THE RIVER KWAI

The Japanese had mainly human flesh for tools, but flesh was cheap... with a plentiful supply of native flesh -- Burmese, Thais, Malays, Chinese, Tamils and Javanese -- more than sixty thousand of them, all beaten, starved, overworked. And when broken, thrown carelessly on that broken human rubbish heap, the Railway of Death.

British POW Ernest Gordon

I hate the sight of the Rising Sun flag! The red I see is the red of prisoners' blood, the white is the white of their bones.

Nagase Takashi, English translator with
the Kempeitai at the River Kwai

ON THE FURTHEST AND MOST REMOTE corner of Singapore Island stood Changi Jail and Selarang Barracks, a cluster of former British military barracks that, when first constructed in the 1920s, had been designed to accommodate less than a thousand men. That might have caused a problem, for though the Japanese military planners had mapped a near-perfect military operation, no thought had been given to the housing or feeding of prisoners.

JOHN BELL SMITHBACK

The Japanese soldier could not conceive of capitulation. He was trained to believe that he was on a holy mission and that to surrender was not just dishonorable but would be a cowardly stain forever linked to the family name. His obedience was blind and absolute, and his last bullet was always saved for himself. Furthermore, it would have been sheer fantasy to think that the British military commander in Singapore could be tricked into surrendering 138,000 armed, capable, perfectly healthy fighting men to General Yamashita's small army.

But surrender they did, and when assessing the housing situation, Yamashita's engineers came up with a workable solution. Unlike the frustrated British captain, they had no problem whatsoever with the ordnance office when they wanted something. Nor was the depot closed for a holiday when Yamashita had demands to be met. At his command, victorious soldiers broke open the gates of the depot and located roll upon roll of the precious barbed wire that had remained piled high to the ceilings in the warehouses throughout the many days of his assault. With the wire in their possession, Yamashita's men constructed a fence around Changi Jail twelve feet high. Then they built gates, added towers, and in the end proceeded to march more than fifty-three thousand captives inside. That, Yamashita reflected, was more men than he had in his entire army the day it landed on the beaches of northern Malaya.

Next, on the orders of his subalterns, the streets of Singapore were swept clean of the dreaded foreigners from the West and they, too, were taken to Changi Prison, instantly transforming it into one of the most congested prisoner of war camps on record.

Days earlier, as a Japanese force racing down the island was about to enter the Alexandra Hospital grounds, Lieutenant William E.J. Weston, the man in charge of the reception area, slipped on a

Red Cross armband and, taking up a white sheet, went down the back steps to surrender the hospital. He was immediately bayoneted to death by the charging soldiers, and Japanese troops of the 18th Division rushed into the wards and operating theatres where they bayoneted a total of 250 patients and staff members. In a horrific frenzy, they removed 400 patients and staff and locked them in a room where many were to die from suffocation. When a shell burst nearby, a door was blown open. A number of men staggered out seeking fresh air, only to be mowed down by Japanese machine-gun fire. The following day the survivors were taken out in small groups with their hands tied behind their backs and shot, their bodies hurled into a mass grave freshly dug in the spacious hospital lawn. Several of those murdered that day were survivors from the ill-fated HMS *Prince of Wales* and HMS *Repulse*.

At the Singa General Hospital where the wards were stuffed with the dead and dying on beds, under beds, between beds and in the corridors, the civilian doctors and nurses—medical personnel who would soon be badly needed in the prisoner of war camps and other prisons—were marched to a shore looking out toward Sentosa Island and forced to wade into the warm sea. When they had gone in up to their necks, hidden machine guns appeared and a command was given to open fire. None were allowed to survive. Yamashita's army, high on *shabu* (crystal methamphetamine) and drunk with victory, had run amuck. Those who survived the hospital slaughter were piled into wheelbarrows and onto hawker's carts and pushed through the streets to Changi Prison.

When the civilian population hiding in the rubble began moving about to forage and conduct business, one by one and in groups they were picked up by the military police and taken to their Orchard Road headquarters to be tortured and grilled. Within a week, five thousand Chinese thought to be insufficiently pro-Japanese were dead, nearly all of them beheaded. Women and girls of all ages found it wise to disguise themselves as men to avoid being raped. *Sook Ching,* General Asaka's 'purge through purification', was being employed in Singapore as well.

In large print, the *Asahi Shimbun* declared that with the fall of Singapore the war had been decided. In an interview, Hideo Ohira, Chief of the Press Division of Imperial Headquarters, said: "To seize Singapore Island in as little time as three days was only possible with our Imperial Army. Japan is the sun that shines for world peace. Those who bathe in the sun will grow, and those who resist it shall have no alternative but to go to ruin. Both the United States and Britain should contemplate the 3,000 years of scorching Japanese history."

At Changi Jail, those who weren't immediately put on work details building roads, unloading ships, clearing up war rubble in the streets or constructing new runways at the airport, spent hours lined up under a hot sun on parade fields and made to bow again and again in the direction of the Imperial Palace in Tokyo. They had offended the Japanese sense of honor by surrendering, and with the understanding that treating them harshly would cure the native population of any respect they might have for their colonial masters, Prime Minister Tojo had ordered that all prisoners be treated tyrannically. They were commanded to briskly salute every Japanese soldier in passing, and if the soldier thought the salute was lame or half-hearted he was free to hit the prisoner with his rifle and kick him when he was down. From their very first day of captivity, it was difficult to know what offended the guards: it might be two or three men sharing a joke, or it could be someone who happened to smile at the exact moment a guard was looking in his direction. No one was safe, and tall men in particular believed they were being singled out for sudden attacks by the shorter Japanese guards and their Korean conscripts. But of one thing everyone was certain: there were no guidelines and there was no protection from the unexpected blow, the slap in the face, or the sharp kick, all of which become more and more frequent.

Except for those on work details, everyday life inside the overcrowded prison became dull and monotonous. For the most part, the Japanese soon left them to their own devices, allowing the officers of the various nationalities to maintain a certain military regimen. Some officers continued to think they should be deferred to, to be saluted, to have separate living accommodations, to have aides and assistants, and even be allowed to carry swagger sticks. But their wishes were met with resistance by soldiers who had grown cynical of officialdom and weary of military incompetence. Army Leadership was defined as 'the process of influencing people by providing purpose, direction, and motivation while operating to accomplish a mission.' They had seen little of that, and remembering the flight of their leaders and the humiliation they experienced when told to lay down their arms, they dusted off a popular World War I phrase that seemed not to have lost its relevance: An army of lions led by asses.

"We can change things," one officer said, "if we can keep their minds busy," and he approached his jailers with a suggestion: Give these men books and they will remain model prisoners.

For once, the Japanese listened, and within the week trucks arrived carrying more than 200,000 books to be shoveled off at the officer's feet. The Japanese had emptied the shelves of the Singapore and Raffles College libraries, and after a number of tables had been constructed and the books sorted, Changi Prison Library opened its doors. It was a small but important step in the right direction.

Time moved slowly in Changi, but in early May it was learned that several thousand prisoners were to be transported "up country". Rumor had it that they were needed to work on a railway, and A-Group, under the command of Brigadier General A. L. Varley, was quickly formed. It consisted of three thousand Australians, many of them volunteers who were hoping for something better than the near-impossible living conditions they were experiencing in Changi Prison. Among them was Major Jim Jacobs, formerly the officer in charge of the A.I.F. Malayan Concert Party. Another was Bandmaster Norman Whittaker from the 2/18th Infantry Battalion's Brass Band. Carrying their musical instruments, they marched out of the Changi gate and made their way to the Singapore docks where they boarded a ship that would take them to Burma.

A second unit numbering between five and six thousand prisoners, F-Group, was formed to go north to Thailand where, the Japanese said, food would be more plentiful and living conditions more comfortable. Once again there were any number of eager volunteers, and off they went to a parade field where each man was handed two balls of cooked rice and one bottle of water. Then, with knapsacks containing a few of their personal effects, they marched across Singapore to the central train station where they were crammed into small metal boxcars and the doors slammed shut and locked. From there, the train began a slow trek across Singapore Island, over the damaged causeway that General Percival had neglected to have fully destroyed, past the Sultan's Palace on the high hill at Johore Bahru, through the shadowed groves of rubber trees, and up the long green peninsula of Malaya.

There were thirty to forty men nearly baking alive inside each of the narrow railway cars, and as the train stopped and started they peered out through small holes at the familiar landscape and felt a horrible sickness in their stomachs when they saw their abandoned equipment still standing deserted alongside the railway tracks. It was a scene to be repeated the entire length of Malaya, and to see it was like looking at the world from within a dream. Except that what they were seeing and experiencing was not a dream: it was a nightmare that filled each man's eyes with tears. Voices from within kept crying out for an opportunity to return, to return, to return...

To go back to that terrible reality and be allowed to continue the fight, to wage battle with the enemy again and, if it happened, to die a much quicker death in that unfinished mêlée.

Day and night it is hot, always hot, in Malaya and Thailand. The temperature rarely goes lower than 77 F (25 degrees Celsius) and usually hovers around 95 F (35 degrees C), and for five burning days and four sweltering nights the train creaked slowly through the palm groves and rubber plantations, moving the length of Malaya and into Thailand to a small market village west of Bangkok called Ban Pong. It was there that the rail line ended, and it was there that a Japanese major, speaking near-perfect English with an American accent—a Columbia University graduate with a diploma in Economics—assembled his charges into a loose formation after allowing them to rub the sweat from their bodies with wood ash and sand that lay in heaps beside the rail line. Ban Pong was as poor a village as any they had ever seen, with piles of bamboo and attap palm leaves stacked beside the track. There was no water apart from the muddy puddles left in the roads by the monsoon rains, but water to drink was readily available at a price from the village's enterprising residents. The earth was black, the houses little more than attap shacks. Numerous mangy dogs wandered among them limping and scratching fleas, and the smell of the place was appalling. Within minutes, any thought they might have entertained about being moved to a comfortable living place vanished, and from that moment on they would never again believe anything the Japanese told them.

The Japanese major with the degree from Columbia wasn't interested in what any of them were thinking. Seemingly enjoying his role as an orator, he kept them standing in the hot sun instructing them in the way to bow before every Japanese soldier, no matter his rank. Taught from birth that the Yamato race was unequalled, he required the prisoners to acknowledge that they, as sons of Nippon, were there on a divine mission representing the Emperor. And the Emperor, the major declared, was a god. Or perhaps even God himself.

Lecture over, the prisoners were given tools and moved into the jungle to clear a space and build living quarters for themselves, long structures fitted together with bamboo posts covered with palm leaves. Two long sleeping platforms made of split bamboo were to run the length of each hut, the floors nothing but the bare earth. They quickly learned to slash, cut and tie bamboo, but no sooner had they constructed the Ban Pong camp than they were told they would be moved to make room for more of their kind about to arrive from Changi Jail.

With their picks, their shovels and their blistered hands, they were loaded with supplies and turned over to a group of Japanese and Korean guards who led them on an uninterrupted forty-five mile (seventy-three kilometer) march that ended on the shore of a wide, muddy river. They were at Kanchanaburi, an ancient crossroads village on the banks of the Khwae Noi. Exhausted, hungry, in pain, they fell to the ground. All they could see on the opposite side of the river was a dense and forbidding jungle. They slept that night on the ground where they had fallen.

At the first light of dawn they were shouted awake and assembled in loose groups on the shore to await barges that would take them up river. As they stood waiting, another Japanese officer mounted a box. They were pioneers, he said. Trailblazers who would be building a historic railway that would extend through the jungle of Thailand to the border of Burma. In due course, it would reach Rangoon.

From news reports heard on a clandestine radio hidden in one of the men's canteens, the prisoners already knew the Burmese capital was in the hands of the Japanese. Under savage attack and in danger of being surrounded, the beleaguered British forces had pulled back to safer ground in India.

When the officer climbed down from the box, they stood alone with their thoughts, staring at the impending darkness of the jungle across the slow-moving river.

After being transported a short distance up river, they pressed forward into that forbidding darkness, the soft muddy road soon becoming a trail, and the trail becoming a path. They no longer walked three or four abreast, they walked in pairs, and then in a single column with bayonet-fixed guards leading the way and bringing up the rear, jostling and slamming stragglers, constantly shouting and barking orders as they were prodded along like a herd of unruly farm animals. Fighting off a horde of stinging insects, they slashed and cut their way through the thick undergrowth, eventually being stopped and told to cut a wide clearing in the jungle and construct a camp of forty bamboo huts. The camp would be called Chunkai, a headquarters base camp for the guards, the *Kempeitai* and a staff that would transfer supplies forward to a projected series of camps.

JOHN BELL SMITHBACK

Once built, the "pioneers" were marched on to make room for H-Group, and when that group moved on, another came. Then another. Contingent after contingent of exhausted men exiting the cattle cars at Ban Pong, marching to Kanchanaburi, being towed in barges up the muddy Khwae Noi, each group following a path hacked through the jungle by F-Group. With each one, the trails would be widened and extended, and in the end sixty thousand men from Britain, Wales, Scotland, Ireland, Australia, Canada, New Zealand, the United States and Holland would make that journey, followed in turn by nearly 200,000 Malays and Thais, Tamils, Indians, Chinese, Indonesians and Javanese, men, women and children. Entire families uprooted from their homes, their villages, their countries, and transported into the dense undergrowth to join the prisoners of war in the building of a historic railway.

The Japanese had names for them. Those from Indonesia and Malaya were *romusha,* meaning laborers. The European prisoners were called *maruta.* Logs.

Following the defeat of General Macarthur's combined United States-Filipino force at Corregidor in the Philippines in May 1942, the victorious Japanese army force-marched the survivors 66 miles (106 kilometers) along the Bataan Peninsula to a concentration camp close to Manila. The infamous trek became known throughout the world as The Bataan Death March.

The march from the end of a railway line at Ban Pong to the shore of a jungle river at Kanchanaburi was 45 miles (73 kilometers), but the Japanese and Koreans who convoyed the men of the defeated army didn't think it necessary to count the number of prisoners who died making the trek. Years later, some Japanese suggested to the world that fewer than three hundred of them died, mostly from illness. The prisoners, however, calculated that more than 3,000 of their friends and comrades failed to finish that forced journey. Exhausted, demoralized, half-starved and dehydrated from the non-stop journey in the hot rail cars, their strength sapped by the heat and humidity, they collapsed in droves along the path as the procession of defeated men inched its way ever deeper into the dense jungle. The guards who pushed, shoved and beat them along had no time to listen to their complaints, their cries of anguish, or to hear excuses from the sick and injured. To them, they were in charge of a company of dishonored cowards. Such men were less than human, as any man would be who committed the inexcusable sin of surrendering to a foreign army in time of war. As a direct consequence of General Percival's decision to hoist the white flag of surrender, those being herded into Thailand were debased creatures who had forfeited all rights to be treated as human beings. Moreover, from the standpoint of the officers controlling the march, there were many more of these dishonorable and disgraceful men — these logs — available. And not just from Changi Jail in Singapore, but from any of the camps and prisons that were scattered throughout Malaya and Thailand.

Additionally, the Japanese who were pressing them on had been bloodied in combat, and many of their comrades and friends had been killed by these foreign devils. That made it easier to detest them. But most of all, each and every one of them knew by heart the lines written in their Soldier's Manual. The words had been drilled into them: *"This war is a struggle between races and we must achieve the satisfaction of our just demands with no thought of leniency to the Europeans..."*

In Singapore, upon seeing his first American prisoners, one of the Japanese reporters had written, "I gaze upon the men of that arrogant nation which sought to treat our motherland with unwarranted contempt and I feel I am watching dirty water running from a nation whose origins were mongrel, and whose pride has been lost."[24]

The soldiers who died during the appalling death march into Thailand that summer of 1942 were kicked, beaten and bayoneted where they fell by spiteful Japanese soldiers and Korean guards who had been nurtured by those words, and by the unyielding Bushido Code which dictated that life was nothing more than a droplet of water from a melting snowflake upon the sea, and the life of an enemy soldier — particularly that of a soldier who had quit fighting in the midst of battle — mattered nothing. Many of them could recite stanza upon stanza from ancient texts and poems that attested to that.

Deep in the dense Thai jungle, the 'logs' from the jails of Singapore were marched to the edge of a muddy river that, to them and to most of the world at that time, was nameless. They built a cluster of barracks, each one to house more than two hundred men, and each man having to himself no more space than could be found in a narrow grave. When work on their housing was completed, in violation of all international covenants governing the treatment of prisoners in time of war, they were ordered to pick up the tools that had been given them in Ban Pong and were forced to cut a swath through the jungle to prepare the land for a railway. At the river, thousands more were being shown a way of constructing a five-story high bridge of logs spanning the river.

The rules of the camp were posted on a bulletin board near the Japanese quarters:

NOTICE
1. It shall be forbid to plot to kill the commandant. (Penalty: to

---

24 Max Hastings and others, *Beheaded at whim and worked to death: Japan's repugnant treatment of Allied PoWs*. Last updated on 18 September 2007 by Daily Mail, UK

shoot-ted to death and life imprison!)
2. It shall be forbid to steal of Japanese army. (Penalty: the heavy punish, with life not assured!)
3. It shall be forbid to not take care for health. (All prisoners shall take care of their own health! Lack of health is a most shamful deed)

There was another notice posted near an open trench that served as a latrine:

DEVOTION UNTIL DEATH IS GOOD.

According to the best Japanese calculations made in Tokyo, a railway line 258 miles (415 kilometers) long linking Siam (as Thailand was then called) to Burma would take approximately six years of diligent labor. And because of the conditions and because of diseases endemic to men working in the heat and the perilous conditions of the jungle, the entire endeavor was likely to cost them dearly in terms of human life.

Several years earlier, a British mapping team had surveyed the same area and had submitted a detailed report to London stating that such a scheme, the building of a rail line linking Thailand and Burma, was a human impossibility.

The war was moving fast, however, and with a need to transport troops and supplies to Burma to dislodge the British from India, General Hisaichi Terauchi, Commander of the Southern Expeditionary Army Group based in Singapore, asked Tokyo for authorization to use prisoners of war as laborers. When permission was granted, that changed things and the Japanese engineers in Bangkok recalculated. Miraculously, they discovered that it would be possible to construct the entire railway in just eighteen months.

By the time that information had sifted down to the staff officers on the site at Kanchanaburi, it was decided that the time required to build a railway and the necessary bridges could be compressed even more.

Meeting in the shade of the trees, the engineers and various officers in charge of the prisoners spread out their maps, paced back and forth along the shore of the murky river, stared repeatedly off toward the blue haze of the mountains in the west, and then studied their maps once again.

The only major engineering feat that could be compared with this one had been the building of the Panama Canal, one of the officers informed them. And that, he said disparagingly, had been an American achievement. A mere fifty miles long, it had taken them—and the French before them—thirty-five years to construct.

The officers and engineers grouped under the trees sucked in their breaths, nodded their heads knowingly, gazed once again at their maps—and then decided that in view of the importance of this project to winning the war for Japan, they could complete the new railway line in a mere twelve months.

There was only one way of achieving that goal and that was with the huge labor force at their disposal. As soon as Tokyo approved the new building schedule, the Japanese military set out to achieve its objective using the dazed captives from Changi Prison as the "flesh" necessary to get the Imperial job done. And in Tokyo as well as in the jungles of Thailand, flesh was cheap. By all accounts at the River Kwai—the name by which the muddy river would forever after be known—counting the number of prisoners from Changi Jail, plus the Chinese, Thai, Malayan, Indian, Tamil, and Indonesians, they had more people than in some of Japan's larger cities. As one of the engineers was to remark, they had virtually the same number of "pioneers" in Thailand as there were people living in Nagasaki.

To accelerate the construction process, the Japanese and Korean guards swung sharpened bamboo staves. They kicked, prodded, slapped, and drove the men ceaselessly, from dawn to nearly dark, shouting *kurro, kurro, kurro,* – hurry up – or using the single word of English that many of them seemed to know: Speedo! Speedo! Speedo! Apparently the word had a pleasing sound for they used it often, barking, crying, screaming, shouting, swinging their sharpened staves and glaring at them with menacing looks.

From that point on, the project became known as Operation Speedo, and everywhere along the way the defeated men were falling in their tracks. They collapsed from thirst, malnutrition, starvation, jungle diseases, and wholesale exhaustion. And if they weren't dead when they fell, their guards methodically hastened their deliverance from the evil of their creation by spiking them in the gut with their sharpened bamboo staves or stoning or kicking them to death. They used bayonets, wire, stones and bamboo clubs, but rarely did they use their rifles: it was considered a waste of a valuable resource to use a bullet to shoot a prisoner.

In Pierre Boulle's famous novel, *The Bridge Over the River Kwai*, the artful construction of a bridge is depicted as a combined effort between two contending colonels, Nicholson on the British side and Saito on the side of the Divine Empire. At the real site, there was never any conflict of opinion and none would have been allowed expression. The bridge, in fact, was but a minor event in Operation Speedo. The major episode was the building of the railway. A few hundred yards in length and five stories above the river, the bridge that is presumed to figure in the novel was completed in two short months. It took exactly one year more to build the railway to the Burmese border.

During that time, each of the camps along the Kwai and her sister rivers and tributaries (there were actually thirty-two camps between Ban Pong, Thailand and the Dawna Mountains in Burma) became a stinking, rotting bamboo village overflowing with crowded huts containing between five to eight thousand utterly defeated men, none of whom could find any meaning or purpose to his life. Not since the surprise invasion of the Japanese on the Kra Isthmus had any of them known a single moment of peace, and for not a few of them the importance of being alive had lost all meaning.

Their futile battles down the length of the Malayan Peninsula and their mad flight across the Causeway into the pit of Singapore's hell had been termed The Great Run, and

in the end, having finally reached the supposed sanctuary of The Gibraltar of the East, General Percival had ordered them to line up in neat rows on their parade fields, to stiffen their backs, push out their chins, stick out their chests, to maintain a soldier's dignity—and to stand by mutely as they were ceremoniously handed over to Japanese officers who barked at them like mad dogs, and eventually to be force-marched to the banks of the River Kwai to be turned into odious, nameless, numberless slaves.

At their many camps along the jungle rivers, the prisoners of war were continuously hungry and almost always sick, lonely and depressed. Most of them suffered from vitamin deficiency blackouts, and many of them had malaria and jungle fever. On occasion, a typhus epidemic would sweep through one or more of the camps wiping out hundreds of them at a stroke. Without medicines to combat their sicknesses, and brutalized by their captors day in and day out in their jungle prisons thousands of miles from freedom, all vestiges of morality swiftly disappeared from their lives, and it took no time at all before they gave in to a dog-eat-dog world without law in the humid jungle that had become their lair.

Those who could rise up at dawn from their hard bamboo beds to work knew that their days were numbered, and they didn't care. Their bodies were rotted with ulcers, bloated with beriberi, shrunken with dysentery and consumed with fever. Maggots fed on their ulcers, and the stench of rotting flesh permeated the atmosphere. Bedbugs and lice lived on their bodies, and many of them became temporarily blind or near-blind from their bland diets, a diet that often caused their skin to harden and split until it peeled like a ruptured onion.

If the Japanese had cared to dispense it, just a spoonful a day of the husk polishing taken from the raw rice would have provided the necessary vitamins to save the lives of thousands of them, but the Japanese didn't. According to their soldier's code, there was no reason to think of saving a prisoner's life.

The regimen quickly took its toll, and prisoners who were too sick to work were deposited in a place the prisoners called the Death House, a shack removed from their barracks where the terminally ill were taken to die. Once there, their flesh shrank from their bones until they seemed to evaporate from this earth. It was a house of no return, and within the heat and the humidity and the rotten stink of the jungle, those who were carried there either did not or could not protest. For them, their minds had left their wasted bodies long before their failing pulse beats.

In such an environment there was no such thing as morale: there was only a morbid philosophy of resignation and despair. In the winter of 1942, the opinion among the prisoners was that if they somehow managed to survive the hell of Operation Speedo, they should mentally prepare themselves to spend many more years in Japanese jails, prisons and work camps.

They felt empty, totally deserted, and they had no friends. They were even beyond thinking of foes. They lived one minute at a time, and they were grateful to have survived it. What allegiance they once had to normal military hierarchy and to law and order had vanished. What feelings they once had for their fellow man disintegrated into a shambles of anarchy, and within weeks of arriving at the camps along the Kwai they robbed, pilfered, cheated, filched, lied and reacted to one another like terrorized rats at a garbage pit. Worse still, the more depraved they became the more the Japanese reveled in their debasement: those pampered and indulged foreign villains were performing precisely in the way their Soldier's Manual said they would.

While their charges were fighting each other for the last grain of rice in an empty cooking pot, their Japanese masters spread out tables to dine on chicken and meat, duck and pig, the scent wafting from their cookhouse. Their meal finished, they took delight in tossing scraps and bones in a heap and watching the prisoners, arms and legs thin as matchsticks, scramble and grovel on all fours, fighting each other for a lick of sauce or the gristle on a chewed chicken bone. That provoked the guards into performing even greater acts of cruelty, until they ultimately went on to violate every civilized rule of behavior in the treatment of human beings and, in particular, to prisoners of war whose commanders had surrendered them to an enemy in good faith.

In the end, during the whole of World War II, four percent of all prisoners of war in German and Italian hands died in captivity. Those nations were signatories to the 1929 Geneva Conventions that established international standards for the humanitarian treatment and protection of military and civilian prisoners during a time of war. Fifty-three nations signed the Convention, but Japan would not. In their hands, close to twenty-eight percent of the prisoners of war died, many due to starvation, inhumane treatment and outright murder.

This cruel and inhuman aspect of the Japanese was known far from Asia and the banks of the River Kwai when, in the autumn of 1942, British codebreakers intercepted a confidential German War Office report on the Japanese Imperial Army, terming it "the most inhuman, bestial war machine on the face of the earth."

It has been estimated that for every mile of rail put down by the prisoners of war, three hundred of them paid for it with their lives—and this figure does not include the estimated 180,000-200,000 civilians who died in astonishing filthy work camps along the path of the railway. The numbers of dead Asians are harder to determine because they were non-combatants—often entire families—forced into hard labor, and they, men, women and children, were considered so inconsequential that virtually no records about them were kept, least of all by those who acted as their masters, those who had come to Southeast Asia proclaiming a new philosophy of Asia for the Asians.

As the months in the camps along the railway moved tortuously on, and lacking a fictional hero like Colonel Nicholson in their midst to command and inspire them; with no staunch and firm supporter of virtue and justice acting on their behalf and thinking of their well-being; without even a semblance of the stiff-lipped, die-hard officer found in the book and the film about the River Kwai, the prisoners went about fulfilling the will of the Japanese in Operation Speedo, each fending for himself, caring little or nothing about anyone else. They were on their own, cynical, depressed, lonely, with no connection to anything or anyone, becoming, as their captors described them, lifeless *maruta*.

Their makeshift hospitals were overflowing with the sick and dying, and there was no relief from the attacks of flies, white ants, lice, gnats and bedbugs. Maggots filled every wound and ulcer, and one could sense that his mind was going. Twenty young men died each and every day, and fires burned on the banks of the river where the bodies of those who had succumbed to cholera were burned. There was no escape, no hope, life had lost all meaning, and the cries of the dying meant nothing. Their pitiful sounds had become annoying, terrible to listen to. Didn't they understand that everyone was suffering? That everyone was in the same boat, and nothing was going to change? Another day, another week, another month — it was something that was going to go on until every last prisoner was dead.

That's how it was until it happened, something intangible, a slow-growing feeling, rising like the shoot of a bamboo, gradually opening, expanding. It was impossible to pinpoint, and much later when the survivors talked about it they were at a loss to explain it. It may not have been everywhere, it may not have been the case in every camp, and it may not have included everyone, but as POW Captain Ernest Gordon of the Argyll and Sutherland Highlanders was to tell it, there was a new feeling among them, a slow turning, a feeling of resilience. The war was in its second year, and in twelve months they had fought the jungle from Ban Pong to Burma. The railway and its death bridges had been built, their captors were less driven. But on the surface there were few changes. Trains were passing on the railway with troops and supplies heading west to conquer India, allowing the prisoners to work under less pressure. Even so, there was no improvement in their diet or their living conditions.

And yet they felt alone, trusting no one, talking to no one, simmering with hatred for those who had stripped them of their humanity and turned them into beasts. Captain Gordon was not alone wondering if there ever going to be something else, another way. Broken as they were, were they ever going to experience any kind of healing?

One afternoon he was pondering that very question when a sergeant approached to ask if he would lead a discussion group. "I think it would help," the sergeant said. "We're fed up with all we see around here. Men kicking their mates in the teeth when they're down, stealing from each other and from the dead ones, crawling to the Japs like rats for scraps from their swill pails. No, it ain't good, sir. No matter how you look at it, it's rotten, rotten, rotten."

Though not sure what could be achieved by men getting together and simply talking, Captain Gordon agreed to give it a try. He had no idea what the sergeant said to encourage anyone to attend, but from their very first meeting in a late afternoon in a shaded place under the trees he felt the sergeant was on to something. One man would talk, then another, and it was like opening a spigot. For the first time in months, men were voicing their views, speaking of the present, contemplating the future, talking of life and death and the possibility of a hereafter.

There were more meetings, and more groups were formed, and as the days passed there seemed to be small, almost imperceptible changes in their thinking. It had been eighteen months since their incarceration and in that time they had been systematically reduced to little more than groveling skeletons dressed in G-strings and loincloths. Months of debasement and humiliation had robbed them of self-respect, and having reached the absolute bottom where nothing and no one mattered, they were appalled to find they had nearly become as vile and inhuman as their subjugators.

There were some who said the new feeling was like a religious experience, and there were others who declared that it was actually a matter of self-adjustment. Others thought their new feelings were brought about by shame. Someone described it as being like a long-distance racer, running until he thinks he can run no more. But on the point of collapse, he gets his second wind and carries on to finish the race. What everyone was going through was like that, a race, and having run so far and having gone through so much, they were taking a deep breath and digging down to find the determination to finish it.

Perhaps, too, they had become weary of living like animals, of living in a poisoned atmosphere of hate and selfishness. They had experienced torture, known so much pain and seen so much death that it had to be justified. Why, they started to ask, would they consider giving up their lives while their unmerciful captors went on living? There was much anger and indignation in that, but underneath there was a new sense of determination: yes, they would fight to live, and yes, they would live to see that their torturers were punished.

Those were some of the reasons put forth for the change in their thinking, but no one really had a ready answer. All they knew was that individually, and then collectively, they began to trust in someone, to seek out a friend or two with whom to share, first their thoughts and then their few possessions. It wasn't anything dramatic, just a slow evolving back to an old way, a way of caring and sharing with others. In a way, it was a return to what they knew as the buddy system, having a mate, a cobber, a companion, the kind of thing every schoolboy, Boy Scout and military man knew.

In the mind of Captain Gordon, he felt it was a desire to get outside oneself, to have someone with whom to share thoughts and ideas and to exchange personal experiences. Later they might say it was nothing dramatic, just something basic. But it was important because it was a rekindling of life, and they were determined that they would not be defeated in spirit.

From the beginning of their enslavement anyone too sick to work was refused the normal handful of grey, dirty cooked rice doled out by the Japanese and Korean guards. But as the perspectives of the prisoners changed, teams were formed to collect and share their meager amounts of food with those who were ill, and in particular with those who were waiting for life to end in the Death House.

Soon, people were contributing a small ration of food to feed the sick, and the constant habit of stealing from each other slowed, then stopped as they regained the ability to think of themselves as a unit. It became part of a new creed which seemed to assert that to steal from one was to steal from all.

Men who had been too weak to walk found comfort and solace in new friends who volunteered to wash and shave them. And more importantly, they were inspired by friends who insisted that they refuse to give in to death.

Work groups were organized to begin cleaning up their living quarters and the space they occupied under the trees. As their will to live spread, it became epidemic, and the camps in which they were confined were no longer such appalling scenes of filth and waste.

In effect, what the fictional Colonel Nicholson had imparted to his men to inspire them in Boulle's book *The Bridge Over the River Kwai*, the real men in the real camps were doing for themselves. And from that time on there was no turning back to the figurative death house which had been their lives. Their minds were set; they were going to persevere—and to survive. Most of all, they had one very, very important objective: come hell or high water, they were determined to outlive their jailers.

At one point early in this period of transformation, a few of the men produced long-unused Bibles from concealment, and though it had been difficult for many of them to cling to anything spiritual in the face of so much violence and suffering, they began to gather in the evenings to read from them aloud to a congregation of fellow prisoners in the silence of the evening beneath the bows of the trees.

At about the same time, and for reasons never clearly understood by anyone, the Japanese began to pay the men a small wage in Thai baht for their labors. With the few coins they received they were able to barter and buy small amounts of food from the natives living in villages near their camps. Each day, more began coming to the edge of the camps carrying pineapples and mangoes, sweet potatoes or rice. Sometimes they had duck's eggs, and on occasion there would be a fish on offer.

The prisoners received the equivalent of about three US dollars per month, and from that sum many decided they would contribute twenty-five cents a month to a general fund to buy food for the sick, for those who would otherwise die because they were not working and consequently were not receiving a wage.

This volunteer larder became humorously known as the River Kwai Health Insurance Fund, and the money collected was used to buy eggs, fruit and fish from the villagers. Before long they were cooking more wholesome meals for themselves.

The self-appointed cooks in the various camps started experimenting with native herbs to make their cooked dishes more palatable. They discovered that hibiscus leaves gave flavor to boiled rice, and that many jungle plants were not only edible but could be eaten for their nutritional value. There were two biologists in their midst who helped them find edible leaves and plants in the jungle. From the villagers who came to sell, they purchased a root which they quickly dubbed "the wooden potato". It proved a healthy food that was cheap and readily available. When it was cooked with dried fish and a concoction of insects mixed up with coconut oil and bananas, it proved savory and filling. Many of them had learned the technique of trapping rats, and when mixed in a stew they said the meat was as tender and tasty as any they had known. It added valuable protein to their diets, and heaven help the ugly vultures which swooped too near the ground. It didn't matter to them how a vulture was cooked: roasted, fried or boiled, vulture seemed as delicious as any tender turkey, Snakes, too, found their way into the pot, and even the hideous cockroach was said to taste like a delicious crispy nut when fried for several minutes in a hot pan.

An important stage had been reached, a mountain had been scaled, and many things seemed to ease within their minds. One thing they learned was to stop complaining about the present. The haunting numbness of the past, the constant feeling of impending doom — those feelings slowly vanished from their minds as the future began to have new meaning. Men would continue to die, and yes, they continued to live at the whim of the Japanese and Korean guards, but their ingrained instincts had returned and they began to believe that it was truly possible to survive. Their lives at the Kwai were becoming a triumph of improvisation and there was a communal effort afoot to make life not just tolerable but actually workable. In the interest of pride and for the common good, they had forged and reconstructed their unusual society to resist the animal-like activities to which their captors had so thoroughly reduced them. In a word, they had discovered that to survive meant having a meaningful social structure, and to attain that demanded order and something called teamwork. They had begun by forging the teams; the next step was to mark out the path of survival.

Small but important attempts were made to decorate their bare living quarters, and amazingly, very old and very dog-eared magazines appeared, reading material that some of them had stashed away in their knapsacks when they left Singapore. It seemed important that they add color and substance to their lives, so they began to cut out and post photographs of things they missed and things they dreamed about. From the women's pages of the pre-war magazines they clipped recipes and photos of anything that looked as though it could be eaten, resulting in their palm frond walls being papered with images of sausages and steaming stews, platters of baked meat, crusty loafs of homemade bread, opened bottles of iced cola, and rich and fattening desserts galore.

From other magazines they cut out advertisements of whatever things people in the world beyond the Kwai and before the war had utilized to make life convenient, such as pictures of smiling ladies using washing machines; of another beaming woman measuring out soap powder to clean a sink of dirty dishes; of someone pushing a Hoover vacuum cleaner across the floor with a broad smile on her face; and of a pretty bride expressing delight as she pulled perfect slices of golden toast out of her new pop-up electric toaster. There were no pin-up pictures of shapely girls in swimming suits on those walls: in their frail and debilitated condition things like that didn't interest them.

As they gazed dolefully at their handiwork, they understood

they were looking ahead.

Once they became determined that they were going to outlive their jailers, they began to hunger for some kind of fulfillment. Sparked by that wish, in their heterogeneous midst they were to discover that there were surgeons and doctors, scholars and writers, lawyers, actors, poets, musicians, architects, designers, electricians, plumbers, botanists, engineers and inventors, all living together under the ever-scrutinizing stare of their jailers.[25]

Spurred on by the new sense of vitality that had entered their lives, the doctors began working with scraps of steel, fashioning and shaping them to make crude operating tools. A Dutch graduate engineer began working with odd bits of scrap iron and bamboo until he had succeeded in making an ingenious artificial leg. But what good was one strange-looking leg, he asked himself, when so many hundreds were needed?

The answer wasn't long in coming. He and a fellow inventor began devoting their spare moments teaching amputees how to make their own artificial legs, and throughout the camp men who had hobbled around on flimsy crutches or who had lain helplessly on their bamboo beds being waited on, were soon clunking and thumping about on new limbs.

Within weeks, these men joined together to form what was to become the camp's first industry of craftsmen, building artificial arms and legs out of bits and pieces of iron, steel, barrel hoops, bamboo, and wood with strips of animal hide for leather.

The railroad had been built, but they remained. There was work to be done maintaining the railway. Their efforts to sabotage the project occasionally paid off: loose spikes came out, a portion of

---

25 See Page 251, THEY SURVIVED

the rail bed would collapse, a bridge or trestle would become feeble. In the hope that white ants would perform like termites, they were often placed in the logs of a number of bridges. They didn't know if the ants obeyed their wishes, but thinking they did make them feel a whole lot better.

At all the camps, the atmosphere had become less tense, and at the end of the day the scholars and teachers in their midst began forming loose-knit study groups that met at twilight beneath the bows of the trees. In time there were so many willing students that they began to schedule regular classes, and it was then that Kwai University was born. Whenever time permitted, the teachers and their students would meet, and soon there were study courses in mathematics, history, architecture, carpentry, philosophy, economics, geology, biology, theology, archaeology, and more than a dozen languages. The list included Latin, Greek, Italian, Chinese, Russian, Sanskrit, French, German, Dutch, Spanish, and Esperanto — almost every language except Japanese and Korean.

Undeterred by the lack of textbooks, the students would work with their professors to compile their own. The professors wrote books from memory, jotting them down on scraps of paper that were passed from student to student, each in turn making copies of their own. And as if by magic, just as it had been with the concealed magazines, books of all sorts appeared from the bottoms of haversacks and bedding and wherever else they had been stuffed and hidden for so many months. Many of the books came from the POW library established at Changi Prison, brought along for rolling an occasional cigarette of dried leaves, and especially useful as toilet paper. But food for thought had become more important than a cigarette or latrine tissue, and so many books suddenly surfaced that the camp at Kanchanaburi found itself with a sizable lending library, though it was actually a library without books: notes of who had what book and where were posted near the latrines and near various huts. Albeit, many of their pages were missing: they had gone up in smoke or helped to fill one of the slit-trench toilets.

There was astonishing depth, and so much was being offered at Kwai University that some of the men found it difficult to decide which course to study. Some of the advanced students elected to study law along with Greek philosophy, and amazing as it seems, there were some who were able to read Plato's *Republic* and Aristotle's *Nicomachean Ethics* under the tutelage of an Oxford Classicist.

Oddly, as the lending library was being formed, one prisoner reached into his knapsack and pulled out *Mein Kampf*: he had kept Adolf Hitler with him as a constant companion during all his months of confinement. He had tucked the book and several others into his bag when he was preparing to leave Singapore with H-Group. There were other books in his stash, but when he was searched at Ban Pong the one by Hitler was the only one he was allowed him to keep. He despised his fascist companion, but when he tried bartering it for fruit or cigarettes, no one wanted it. So he read it and re-read it until he had it nearly memorized. Many were the times that he wished Europe's leading politicians had done the same before the war.

Art classes were formed with the artists making their own pigments from charcoal, crushed rock, boiled leaves, flowers, mud and roots. Their brushes were made using animal hair found in the cookhouse and with bristles of hair from their own heads. There were classes in woodcarving too, and one day after their first year of captivity the artists of Kwai University held an exhibition in one of the huts. The show displayed such a high degree of talent that even the most jaded among them were impressed. The Japanese guards who strolled through the exhibition cocked their heads, scratched, scowled, but made no comments.

In the blueprint and architecture classes, someone pointed out that the favorite project on everyone's mind seemed to be designing and constructing elaborate kitchens and bathrooms. That, said one of the professors, surely signified something.

But it was probably the Kwai university orchestra that was to prove to be the most ingenious and one of the most edifying experience for all those who lived on the banks of the river. It began when an assortment of food parcels and gifts received at one of the camps from the International Y.M.C.A. The usual procedure was for the guards to tear open the parcels and help themselves to whatever food, vitamin pills and delicacies they found. On one particular day the newly arrived parcels included six small children's violins. Having no use for the things, the guards appropriated what they wanted and passed on what remained.

It happened that on that day one of the men with a burning passion for music was standing close by. His name was Norman Whittaker, a Londoner, and before the war, music had been his entire life. He immediately seized one of the small violins, held it up and turned it over and over in his palms studying it. Then, taking up a bow, he tested it. Surprisingly, the sound was clear and resonant, and without giving it further thought he knew Kwai University was going to have an orchestra.

Not only did the man possess musical genius, he was imaginative and he had ambition. From whatever scraps he could find, he worked with other musicians to build and rebuild a number of instruments until he had perfected a few that pleased him. In the camp trash pit, from the villagers who came to trade, and from whatever source he could find, he collected tubes and metal that he was able to fashion in such a way that he soon reproduced some trumpets, a couple of trombones and a saxophone.

When word got around that Norman was building an orchestra, as if from nowhere real instruments began to appear. Almost certainly, they belonged — or had belonged — to the band members in A Group that had gone by ship to Burma.

From some source Norman learned that the Japanese officers had a piano at one of the camps. They had taken it from a bordello in Kuala Lumpur and had transported all the way to the middle of the Kwai jungle, only to neglect it. The genius with a passion for music appealed to the Japanese through Nagase Takashi, an English-speaking Japanese warrant officer, to let the camp have use of it. In an uncharacteristic gesture, the Japanese agreed.

With this highly unusual — even mad — assortment of instruments, the man they called the Maestro quickly found men who shared his passion and talent for music. He patiently taught them how to construct violins, violas and wind instruments using reeds and bamboo. From old oil barrels and tin food cans he fashioned together a timpani section, and for his stringed instruments he salvaged animal gut from the kitchens. Bamboo was everywhere and could be shaped to form the cases and necks of his stringed instruments. A large discarded wood box marked *Tea from Ceylon* was transformed into a bass viol, "as beautiful as any instrument in the renaissance," declared the Maestro.

Fortunately, the conductor was blessed with a photographic memory, and he set to work copying down complete musical scores on the tissue-like "paper" that clings to the inside of bamboo. He distributed the thin pages to his fellow musicians who conscientiously made copies of the work before passing the pages on to others. Finally, the individuals who would make up the orchestra got together and began to practice, and after a fortnight or so, in a carefully selected natural amphitheater against a hill, the maestro picked up his baton one evening and the Kwai University Orchestra played Beethoven's Fifth Symphony and Schubert's Unfinished, and concluded with selections from The Mikado.

The program had been purposely chosen to please all, including the startled Japanese guards who had commandeered positions close to the orchestra. They listened in disbelief as the eerie trills of Gilbert and Sullivan's story of Yum-Yum, Nanki-Poo, and Ko-Ko spilled out into the jungle and rose over the trees into the air high above the River Kwai and the Railway of Death. In the weeks that followed, the orchestra was to give repeat performances, each one better than the last.

Eventually, Kwai University had its own glee club, a debating team, a little theater, an acrobatic team, a modern dance group, and even a ballet troupe, each putting on regular performances. Artists among them built a small stage, painted backdrops using scraps and mosquito netting to create scenery. Some of the illustrated programs made for the performances still survive.

Loet Velmans, a Dutch prisoner who fled the Netherlands to escape the Nazis *blitzkrieg* only to be made a prisoner of war when the Japanese invaded Java, tells of a Japanese officer with a wry sense of humor ordering several musicians to appear outside his quarters every morning to play "Heigh-Ho, Heigh-Ho, It's off to work we go," the dwarves' marching song from Walt Disney's Snow White.

Three years and eight months after the fateful bombing of Singapore and the painful retreat down the Malay Peninsula, the men who built and survived the Railway of Death and the many bridges along the River Kwai were liberated. They had barely escaped Japanese reprisals after the atomic bombings of Hiroshima and Nagasaki, but in the end they had fortune on their side, and they were free. The doors of Kwai University were closed and the music from its orchestra faded into the eternity of the murky shadows of the valley. Their instruments were left behind, but the musicians went home.

In the end, the diplomas the prisoners took away with them from Kwai University were not certificates written on paper or parchment: they came in the form of knowledge that they had fought back the curtains of death and were at long last walking forward as proud, honorable and dignified men. In spite of the war, and in spite of the Japanese, the men at the River Kwai had regained self-respect.

Before the war ended, many thousands of the survivors of the River Kwai experience were transported back to Singapore where they were packed into the holds of prison ships and barges — known as Hell Ships — and taken to Japan where, upon arrival, they were lined up in groups on the docks and auctioned off to rich industrialists from Nippon Steel, Mitsubishi Corporation, Mitsui Company, Showa Denko, Kawasaki Industries, and nearly fifty other major and minor *zaibatsu* (Japanese conglomerates) that put them to work as slaves in their factories and mines. Many others like them, given no food and very little water, had sailed from Singapore in vessels displaying no red crosses to mark them as hospital or prisoner of war ships. Tragically, they did not reach the auction blocks of Japan: they had been sent to the bottom of the sea by torpedoes from American submarines.

The loss of so many of them in this way helps to explain why only half of the approximately 16,000 British and Commonwealth prisoners of war who died building the Death Railroad have been officially accounted for. Like the un-numbered Asians who slaved and died for the Japanese as forced laborers, they vanished from the world without a trace.

Of the British service personnel in Japanese prisoner of war camps along the River Kwai, only 37,583 were repatriated after Japan's surrender. The rest, more than 25% of them, had died building the infamous Railway of Death.

Ironically, after all the suffering and death associated with the project, few trains traveled the length of the railway from Bangkok to Rangoon. Due to the terrain and the heavy monsoon rains, bridges failed and embankments collapsed. Also, shortly after its completion, RAF planes began bombing it, making it a dangerous business to move vital supplies and troops along it. There was another factor as well: the prisoners had added their contribution to the railway's failure by making sure the tracks were insecure and dangerously positioned. Portions of the line were continually falling down the steep embankments and dumping supply trains into the river. The Japanese brought in work elephants and were compelled to spend a great deal of time recovering supplies and salvaging engines and rail cars from the bottoms of valleys and flooded rivers.

At the end of the war, the British government sold the railroad to the government of Thailand for six million dollars. The Thais ripped up much of the track for the steel and the wood ties were floated down-river for other uses. In recent years, the site has become an important destination for Japanese tourists who know of the Kwai story largely by way of rumor and word-of-mouth because the film *The Bridge Over The River Kwai* was effectively banned in Japan for many years. Someone at the top figured that people did not wish to see a Japanese officer outwitted by an officer from the West. Furthermore, many Japanese middle school textbooks devote but a single paragraph to the war in the Pacific, and for the past seventy years or more Japan has adamantly refused to make a full acknowledgement of the River Kwai or many other atrocities.

Years after the war, ex-Kwai POW Loet Velmans would spend a considerable amount of time in Japan in his capacity as an executive with a major American public relations firm. In his book *Long Way Back To The Kwai*, he writes "World War II was a topic not to be discussed with foreigners. For the Japanese, the war was treated as an intimate family album; its pictures were to be shown to family members, and as presented in the bland history books used in Japanese schools. When it came to wartime behavior, the Japanese appeared to be suffering from a case of collective amnesia. Under no circumstances was blame to be ascribed to any Japanese, dead or alive."

Further to that, the historian Stephen E. Ambrose says, "The Japanese presentation of the war to its children runs something like this: "One day, for no reason we ever understood, the Americans started dropping atomic bombs on us."

The bridge that tourists venture so far to see today is not the legendary structure shown in the film featuring Jack Hawkins, Alec Guinness and William Holden. That bridge, the one of logs and timber five stories high, was completely destroyed by RAF bombs early in 1943. The men who built it watched with glee and let out quiet cheers as the bombs struck and the huge timbers dropped into the murky river to float away. Two or three months later they were disappointed when a new bridge, a more permanent one of iron and steel, was brought up from Bangkok to replace it. It had been transported from Java, and section by section it was placed over the river on cement and stone pillars. Shortly after it was completed, however, the prisoners were able to give another cheer when a squadron of US B-25 bombers swept in at treetop level and severely damaged it. What remains over the Kwai today is that second bridge, much repaired.

A true reminder of what happened at the River Kwai can be found nearby, and in the early evening when the sky turns a rich red and violet color, and when the call of a thousand unseen birds interrupts the silence, a short walk takes you to it. Entering a gate, you step onto a beautifully manicured lawn. This is Don Rak, the space once occupied by Chunkai base camp, a sprawling area of thatched huts that the prisoners had hacked from the jungle. The headquarters of the Japanese in charge of building the railway had been there, as was the torture unit of the *Kempeitai* military police. There had been a makeshift hospital there too, little more than a leaky attap shack staffed by two, three and sometimes four POW doctors who attempted to perform miracles with no medicines. They forged their own tools from metal scraps to do hundreds of amputations and to perform an astonishing number of surgical operations. The fortunate ones survived.

The huts they lived in, the various shops that had been there to service the trains, the hospital with little on hand to treat dying men except brown bottles of iodine, the *Kempeitai* and their water boarding equipment… all that is gone now. In its place is a cemetery, its vast lawn containing six thousand seven hundred and ninety-two Christian and Star of David crosses. Casting a long shadow over it is the bridge, and at a certain time of day when the shadows lengthen and darkness is about to descend over the River Kwai, the bridge and the crosses appear to blend together. And in a sense they are joined: a memorial to those who died there, and a reminder of a time when military imperialism and decaying colonialism breathed its last gasp and millions upon millions of people who had never experienced self rule lifted their heads and found new life.

PART III

HIROSHIMA AND NAGASAKI

"Having found the bomb we have used it. We have used it against those who attacked us without warning at Pearl Harbor, against those who have starved and beaten and executed American prisoners of war, against those who have abandoned all pretense of obeying international laws of warfare. We have used it in order to shorten the agony of war, in order to save the lives of thousands and thousands of young Americans. We shall continue to use it until we completely destroy Japan's power to make war. Only a Japanese surrender will stop us."
President Harry S. Truman, August 9, 1945

"I didn't hate the Americans that dropped the bomb. It was such a horrible time. I hated air raids. I hated war. To my child's mind, the bomb ended it all."
Nine-year-old Hiroshima survivor Kimura Yasuko

JAPANESE INTELLIGENCE CHIEF Lieutenant General Arisue Seizo sat at his desk examining a top secret report that one of his aides had just handed him. It was July 1945, and the war was going badly. The once mighty Imperial Japanese Empire that had so recently included the Alaskan islands of Attu and Kiska in the north and swept south to the Solomon Islands near Australia had been eroded like the sands of a shore washed by relentless tides.

General Arisue was exhausted. He closed his eyes momentarily to rub them, and when he did an array of names flashed through his mind: Malaya, Singapore, Hong Kong, Guadalcanal, The Celebes, Guam, Leyte, Tarawa, Kwajalein, Eniwetok, Saipan...

The endeavors of so many years of planning, and the lives of so many valiant Japanese warriors, now all lost. In the far reaches of the Pacific, the fragmented fruits of Japan's swift victories had been encircled and were slowly being isolated. And since spring the American enemy had occupied the Japanese islands of Iwo Jima and Okinawa.

An air raid warning sounded and General Arisue went to the windows to pull the black curtains closed. Unconsciously, he first looked up for signs of approaching planes, and then he thought to himself that he had never before seen so many stars in the night skies over Tokyo. But that would be understandable, his logical mind told him: sixty percent of the sprawling metropolis no longer existed. The American bombers had become increasingly meticulous in their destruction of the cities of Japan, and Tokyo still remained their number one target.

A smoldering stench penetrated his office and stung his nostrils. General Arisue pulled the curtains together wrathfully and returned to his desk. Sitting down, he picked up the report and heaved a sigh. What hope remained for victory was in that handful of papers that had just been handed him.

The report was titled *Operation Ketsugo* — Operation Decision — and it was in two parts. Complex and detailed, it was the operational defense plan designed to repulse the enemy from the beaches of the Home Islands. In sum, it was a coordinated plan to destroy the enemy in the event of an attempt to invade Japan.

As he studied it, General Arisue pursed his lips and nodded. Even on paper, the plan was extraordinarily imposing. Since early in the year, his intelligence units had worked overtime trying to outguess the Americans. By carefully analyzing past battles and reviewing the radio messages that had preceded each of the previous amphibious landings the Americans had made against Japanese positions, he and his staff had put together a detailed summary of every move taken by the Allies since the beginning of the war. It was so impressive that after looking at it, the Imperial General Staff had come to a unified conclusion: the Americans would strike in force at two probable Japanese beaches: Miyazaki and Ariake Bay on the southern island of Kyushu.

Even as he was reading the report, Arisue knew that under cover of night those beaches were being continuously fortified with strong defenses. Furthermore, to meet the impending invasion, a formidable fighting force was being shaped with units already being deployed to those two areas consisting of fifty-three infantry divisions and twenty-five brigades, plus three tank brigades, together totaling nearly two and a half million well-trained troops.

To add depth, a back-up garrison of over four million trained Army and Navy civilians and the Patriot Citizens Fighting Corps, a reserve militia of twenty-eight million citizens, was being positioned in strategic locations to bolster the front lines the moment the command was given and they were called upon to fight for the survival of the nation. The Corps was composed of all healthy males aged 15 to 60, and all women 17 to 40, many of them armed with nothing more than longbows, muzzle-loading muskets and bamboo spears. Ammunition was becoming a serious problem, but forty percent of all the ammunition in the Home Islands had been allocated for the expected battle for

Kyushu.

The Navy, though no longer an effective fighting force, was preparing to move six aircraft carriers, four cruisers, one battleship and a large number of minor warships into the seas near the Kyushu beaches. Despite being short of fuel, the Navy had given assurances that it would have enough on hand for an additional twenty operational destroyers and forty submarines. Their Number One mission: to sink the enemy troop ships before they reached their destination.

Turning a page, Arisue paused to review *Operation Cherry Blossoms At Night*, the Navy's intriguing new plan to bomb California with deadly pathogens. Developed by Surgeon General Shiro Ishii's biological warfare Unit 731, five long-range I-400 submarines would be crossing the Pacific Ocean on a one-way *kamikaze* mission to bring about peace. Surfacing near Los Angeles, the submarines would launch a dozen planes carrying hundreds of balloon bombs filled with fleas carrying bubonic plague, cholera, smallpox, botulism and anthrax. Since the early days of the Sino-Japanese war, Ishii's bombs had been used on population centers and in two biological and chemical warfare camps in northeast China where it was figured they had killed an estimated 300,000 - 400,000 Chinese. Noting how effective his weapons had been in China, Ishii added a personal note saying he believed that the use of the pathogen bombs on a modern California city like San Diego would not only kill many thousands, it would immediately bring the Americans to the negotiating table.

Arisue put the report down. Good, he thought. Very good. The *Cherry Blossoms* plan seemed promising, in spite of the failure of *Operation Fu-go,* General Kasaba Tatsumi's grand scheme to terrorize the American public with high explosive and thermite fire bombs. It had been an expensive, time-consuming operation, with young schoolgirls all over Japan spending hours and hours on their hands and knees on the floors of their school gymnasiums pasting together the large sheets of *washi,* a tough, waterproof paper made from the leaves of mulberry bushes. Nearly ten thousand of the helium-filled balloons were released, rising up to catch the jet stream and be carried across the Pacific to North America. Each balloon had been fixed with an intricate timing device that, after reaching the continent in an estimated three days, would bring the balloons to the ground where it was hoped they would set off forest fires and cause panic. On the 5th of May, a woman and her five children enjoying a picnic in southern Oregon were killed when they came upon one of the balloons and sought to investigate it. And though the balloons were being found from Mexico to Canada, and even as far from the coast as Iowa and Michigan, there were no other casualties and there was no panic. *Fu-go* had not been a success. On the other hand *Yozakura,* the *Cherry Blossoms at Night* operation, was a thorough plan to be carried out by the navy, not something left to the winds of chance. It looked hopeful.

Turning his attention again to the preparations being made for the battle on the beaches, an additional surprise would be awaiting the foreign invaders: the new all-volunteer battle unit of 25,000 dedicated young warriors that had been designated the *Tokubetsu kōgeki tai,* or Special Attack Group. More units and more young men were being added to it daily. Tears of pride came to General Arisue's eyes as he read the list of units comprising the burgeoning *tokkōtai* unit, for it was an expansion of the suicidal Volunteer Defense Corps which had already tested the enemy's mettle the previous autumn in the seas off the Philippines during the Battle of Leyte. Initially composed of flying *kamikaze* suicide bombers which contained just enough fuel for a one-way mission to encounter enemy warships, this new group of young pilots would use a stockpile of planes of all types as living bombs to dive boldly into the American ships.

The word *kamikaze* means Divine Wind, and in previous acts by the unit the Americans had been struck with terror as planes flown by volunteer pilots twisted down from the heavens to explode on their ships during the naval battle in the Leyte Gulf. They had been horrified, for they were unable to comprehend how men could turn themselves into human bombs. It was inconceivable that young men would choose to die for their country in what seemed to be such an appallingly violent way. They did not comprehend because they did not understand Shintoism, the national religion of Japan. Yet every man, woman and child in Japan clearly understood the objective of those young pilots because Shintoism taught them that their Emperor was a living God, and that they owed their unquestioned fidelity to the state he represented. If those acting in the Emperor's name called upon a loyal subject to die, the call was considered a blessing for it not only allowed them to accomplish the noble aim of dying for the Emperor, it instantly transformed them into spirits - *kami* - and reunited them with their ancestors. Therefore, for the *kamikaze* dying while destroying the life of an enemy was upheld to be as easy as breathing.

Returning to the report, General Arisue read on. Now that the Americans were advancing on Japan, the Special Attack Group was being transformed into a frightening new fighting force with several important weapons developed by the military for suicide missions. One of these was the one-man underwater rocket that zipped undetected beneath the seas at more than fifty knots, each one loaded with more than one ton of trinitroanisole. Named the *Kaiten* or Flying Torpedo — frequently called the Heaven Shaker — it was calculated that one torpedo was sufficient to sink a navy destroyer and badly damage a loaded troopship. More than one

ASIA BETRAYED

thousand of them had been moved to the beaches and were now ready. Additionally, the suicide group had just added a new unit of more than 5,000 trained frogmen. Called the *Fukuryu,* or Crouching Dragons, the divers wore heavy packs of explosives lashed to their bodies. They had spent many hours learning to swim beneath the water for long distances while aiming at the hull of an enemy ship. Having reached it, they were to detonate their lethal charge, blowing themselves to bits and hopefully blasting a gaping hole in the vessel. If the job was performed correctly, the ship would be destroyed. At that very moment, the underwater "Dragons" were going through an intensive training program to ensure that their bombs would prove as successful as the military architects planned.

But there was more to come.

On the shores of Kyushu were skillfully concealed a huge number of lightning-fast speedboats, each one containing a devastating explosive charge in its bow. Called *Shinyo* — Sea Quake — the army had 3,000 of them at the ready, the navy had 6,200. These were to be launched and directed toward the enemy's landing craft and troop carriers. As the navy had more volunteers than speedboats, it was hurriedly preparing more of them.

The navy was also making ready hundreds of small motorboats belonging to local fishermen. Charges of powerful explosives were being placed in the bows of the boats as more and more fishermen volunteered to become part of the Divine Wind attack group.

Further to that, in the harbors of Kyushu the two-man crews of three hundred and fifty midget submarines loaded with torpedoes and explosives were awaiting attack orders, and at flying fields and airstrips across the south of Japan 10,000 airplanes of all types — fighters, bombers, old ones, new ones, damaged ones barely able to fly — were being loaded with bombs and high explosives in preparation for a mass *kamikaze* attack against the enemy's landing force.

Far from the beaches, a secret operation was underway to produce an enormous array of one-man rockets which would be flown on one-way missions against the slow and, until now, untouchable B-29 bombers that were roaming the skies at will, and at altitudes higher than any Japanese fighter plane was capable of flying. Soon, hundreds of those rockets with their super warheads would be able to strike the underbellies of the lumbering giants and deliver the United States Air Force such a stunning and horrifying surprise that it might possibly change the direction of the war.

Not just on the beaches but away from them, in cities, in villages, in the open countryside, on every sacred centimeter up and down the entire length of the island nation, the people were resolved, and they were determined. From their early years, school textbooks had taught them that their "bright and strong souls" made them the superior race, and their proper place was in the leadership of the Greater Asia Co-Prosperity Sphere. The Emperor's roots reached back 2,600 years to Jinmu, the first emperor, who was said to have lived 125 years. In uniting the various tribes of the land and instilling in them a privileged spirit (*Yamato-damashi*) his maxim, "All the world under one roof" (*Hakkō ichiu*) had, at the start of the war with China, become a political catchphrase meaning that Japanese imperial rule had been divinely ordained to expand until it united the entire world. However, anyone not Japanese — and in particular the Chinese and the people from the West — was said to be "devilish, animalistic", and therefore enemies. Now, awaiting the assault from these devils, the people remained unshakable in their conviction that Japan was on a sacred mission and that the gods would once again save them. As "the world's foremost people", everyone was preparing to do their part. Women, children, old men, people in shops, the wounded, the lame, fishermen and those working in factories and in the fields, they forged clubs into weapons and sharpened bamboo staves. School children and their parents gathered daily to practice using the staves against the larger and taller Western devil, school teachers taking the lead: "Not in the stomach, not in the body. Always aim for the throat. Thrust, kill, thrust, kill. Ten die for one, ten die for one, thrust, thrust, thrust..."

General Arisue allowed himself a smile. A page in the report referred to one of his personal remarks. He had stressed that a desperate situation called for desperate tactics, and therefore the primary mission of the Special Attack Group — unlike those in the past which were concentrated essentially against warships — should be to strike primarily at troop-carrying vessels and landing craft headed for the beaches. The new objective, he suggested, would create such hell and inflict so many deaths that the enemy's morale would be weakened to the point where he would soon agree to settle the war as swiftly as possible through a negotiated peace.

The huge American bombers, the *B-san* as everyone called them, would fall like leaves from the skies of Japan, and the seas off the Kagoshima beaches would be a dense scarlet with the blood of a million American dead. In days rather than weeks, the enemy would be counting his losses and would find them so agonizing that he would lose his will to continue the war.

Part two of the report was something General Arisue was familiar with, for he had helped to draft it. It was a detailed outline of the entire known strength of the United States fighting forces, naming precisely and accurately every Army, Navy, Marine and Navy unit in the Pacific Theatre of Operations. The might of the enemy was categorically listed, down to every air group, and even down to each individual unit. It represented the massive power then poised off Japan's shores, but one small thing puzzled General Arisue. On a page listing all B-29 bomber squadrons in the Pacific, someone in Arisue's own intelligence unit had made a notation dated May 8th: "One other bomber unit is available but its identity has not been ascertained yet."

General Arisue sat back and looked at the date on which the Imperial Staff had concluded the Americans would begin their attack: "In all probability it will be on the 1st of November 1945."

Arisue wondered why someone on his staff should concern himself about the location of a single B-29 bomber unit.

In the closing days of May 1945, a top-secret document was being circulated among a select group of high-ranking officers of the American forces in the Pacific region of operations. Code-named *Olympic*, it was the assault plan for the upcoming invasion of the Japanese Home Islands. The island that had been chosen for the attack was Kyushu. The two beaches selected for the American landings were Miyazaki and Ariake Bay. The date for the operation was set for the morning of November 1, 1945.

Three months earlier, in the waning sunset hours of March 9, three hundred and thirty-three B-29 bombers engaged in *Operation Meetinghouse* lumbered heavily off runways on Guam and Saipan in the Marianna Islands. They thundered northward like a concentration of silver-bodied bees. En route to Tokyo 1,500 miles (2,500 kilometers) away, they passed over the explosive eruptions coming from Iwo Jima where the remnants of the Japanese defenders were fighting their final battle in a fierce *banzai* charge against the United States Marines. Some of the Japanese defenders were half-naked, some armed only with spears, swords and broken bottles. Until now Iwo Jima, 750 miles from Yokohama, was the closest that the Americans had brought the war to the Home Islands of Japan, and the Japanese had been fighting with a ferocity unmatched in any of their earlier battles. The view from the Plexiglas windows of the B-29s was of a small wrinkled flower petal adrift in tranquil seas. Yet the fierce month-long battle for the five-mile-long island had cost the Americans nearly 20,000 casualties, including the lives of 6,817 U.S. Marines. In the end, of the 21,000 Japanese defenders of the island, there were only 216 prisoners of war, and most of them were badly wounded. Commanded to fight to the last man, Iwo Jima was a prelude to what the American forces could expect in November when they turned their sights on the beaches of Kyushu.

In his headquarters on Guam, Air Force General Curtis LeMay paced the floor nervously. Many times since January he had sent his B-29 bombers over the major cities of Japan, first from bases in China, now from bases in the recently-captured Marianna Islands.

"This damned outfit of mine has been getting a lot of publicity without really accomplishing a hell of a lot of results," he had complained to his fellow officers two weeks earlier.

Unlike Europe where factories had made large and obvious targets for Allied bombers, two-thirds of Japanese industry was dispersed in homes and in small workshops that were little more than scattered wooden sheds manned by thirty people or less. Easily identifiable factory structures with smokestacks and railway spur lines like those in industrialized Germany, Belgium and France were few, and the Bees—as they were popularly called—had become an irritant, constantly disrupting life patterns but no longer causing much in the way of damage. The major Japanese installations had been destroyed early in the bombing campaign, and apart from modest homes there was little left for the Bees to bomb.

General Curtis LeMay was about to change that. Two days earlier, and without consulting his superiors in Washington, General LeMay had devised a scheme that he had hoped would alter the picture and bring the Japanese nation to its knees. He briefed his crews and told them that he was removing all defensive weapons—guns and ammunition—from their planes in order for them to take on board more bombs. The weapons, he said, were a waste of weight for, after all, for the Japanese didn't have a plane capable of flying anywhere near them. All the fighter planes that had tried soon dropped back toward earth as their engines ran short of oxygen and stopped functioning.

Furthermore, General LeMay had concluded that it was a pointless exercise to continue using conventional bombs that were simply "digging huge holes in the Japanese earth." He decided to load his planes with something new, the M-47 devices which were napalm-filled incendiary bombs that split open one hundred feet above the ground and spewed out two-foot long napalm sticks that burst into searing flames upon impact. Lastly, to confuse the Japanese air defense, LeMay told his pilots to cancel their normal flights at 30,000 feet. That night he would have his planes fly across Japan at the surprisingly low level of 5,000 to 9,000 feet.

"That's close enough for those bastards on the ground to throw rocks at us!" one crew member frowned.

At midnight the sirens in the path of the B-29s shrieked and cried out their usual alarm. During the recent raids, the Bees had caused little damage, and few people paid any attention. When the first planes passed over the heart of Tokyo at 12:15 a.m. most of those who had been awakened by the sirens remained in their beds. A number of puffs of anti-aircraft fire blossomed in the dark skies, but their range was high, at 30,000 feet where the gunners had expected the bombers to be. Not a single fighter plane bothered taking off to seek the bombers. High octane aircraft fuel was in short supply, and experience had told them it would have been a futile gesture.

But General Curtis LeMay's attack was designed to put an end to gestures of all kinds, and when the bomb doors beneath his 333 planes opened and the bombs spilled out and then split open and the sticks of jellied gasoline fell to the ground, the darkened city of Tokyo was transformed into an absolute inferno. During the next hour, huge balls of flame leaped thousands of feet into the air whipping up winds of hurricane force. Thermal tornados sucked frail homes, large vehicles and huge trees into the perimeter of the flames which, like a gigantic vacuum, reached out for oxygen. The final bombers approaching the conflagration were shaken and tossed several thousand feet upward from the 2,000-degree heat, and their crews gripped their seats and clung to whatever they could as they wretched and vomited from the terrible stench of burned flesh.

By dawn, the center of the capital was a wasteland, laced here and there with the remains of a few concrete walls and a scattering of shattered telephone poles which continued to smoke like smothered candle wicks. The Sumida River flowing through the city had evaporated. Sixteen square miles of Tokyo were gone, and 130,000 civilians were dead.

When word of LeMay's bombings was flashed around the world, the people in the United States cheered. TIME magazine described the raid as "a dream come true". Surely, it reported, Japan's surrender would not be long in coming, and overnight General Curtis LeMay became a national hero whose cunning and daring convinced them that he had probably saved the lives of 500,000 to 1,000,000 American servicemen by bringing about a quick end to the war.

One month after LeMay's firebomb attack on Tokyo, on the third of May 1945, a Japanese Naval attaché stationed in Switzerland realized the significance of Berlin's impending defeat for Japan and he privately made contact with Allen W. Dulles. Dulles, as representative of the Office of Secret Service, was well-known for having helped arrange a separate peace treaty for Italy when it decided to opt out of the war against the Allies. With three civilian associates, Naval Commander Yoshiro Fujimura met with Dulles clandestinely on several occasions. Dulles told Commander Fujimura that the United States would be interested in opening formal discussions with any fully authorized representatives whom the Japanese government might select. His country, and that of its allies, Dulles said, was prepared to guarantee the safe air passage of any such representative to Bern, Switzerland for talks that would lead to the end of hostilities between Japan and the Allied nations.

Five days later, on the night of May 8, Germany surrendered. Observing the event, and with full knowledge of the violent destruction that had been wracked on Germany in the final weeks of the war by Allied bombers and Russian ground troops, Fujimura acted boldly. Along with several fellow conspirators, he sent a coded message to Tokyo informing them of their secret meetings with Dulles.

Six messages and eight days later, Tokyo finally responded: "There are certain points which indicate that you may be involved in an enemy plot. We advise you to be very cautious."

Despite repeated attempts by Fujimura and his confederates to expand their channels of communication to Japan, nothing more was heard from Tokyo. When Fujimura failed to contact him again, Dulles concluded that a Japanese Naval officer was acting on his own. Yoshiro Fujimura's peace efforts passed unnoticed into the pages of history where they were quickly forgotten. [26]

With the war in Europe at an end, General Curtis LeMay's operations to destroy Japan by fire continued without respite. On the afternoon of May 23rd, he sent 562 bombers on a mission to revisit Tokyo. They flew in low, dropped 3,262 tons of napalm incendiary bombs and returned without a loss. In the evening, he sent another 502 Super Fortresses to sear the Japanese capital. Although the airmen had been directed to avoid hitting the Imperial Palace, several huge fireballs leapt over the moat and jumped the walls. Twenty-eight members of the Emperor's three thousand member staff were killed in the ensuing fires, and that same night tens of thousands more people were incinerated in their homes, including sixty-two Allied prisoners of war who had recently been transported to Japan from Changi Jail in Singapore. They were some of the survivors who had spent the early years of the war working as slaves for the Japanese to build the Death Railway in Thailand.

In the week that followed, LeMay's planes paid visits to Yokohama, Osaka, and Kobe. After a little less than two weeks of fire bombing, more than thirteen million homeless survivors wandered about the countryside. Their dwellings had been

---

26 There's a fascinating account of Fujimura's involvement in the transfer of many tons of Japanese gold to the Nazis via submarine at http://www.i-52.com/index_files/Page4752.htm

obliterated, and the principal cities of Japan had been turned into cinders.

Poking through the layers of ashes that was all that remained of her library of ancient books which had included a superb collection of Chinese volumes from the Sung and Ming dynasty, an elderly scholar collected the fine white powder and placed it into scorched jars as a remembrance. Long after the war, she recounted the episode to a fellow scholar: "It made the smoothest tooth powder imaginable."

Deep in the Earth, beneath the smoldering capital, a special investigative staff composed of military and civilian experts from the Cabinet Planning Board came together in the bunker of the Imperial General Headquarters to add last-minute changes to *Operation Decision*, a confidential report they were about to present to Prime Minister Suzuki Kantaro. Suzuki knew what the Planning Board had in mind, and he was not comfortable with it. He was in the unenviable position of trying to create some semblance of order in a nation that he knew would soon be fighting its last-ditch battle on the beaches of the Home Islands. His was a tenuous position as well: the warlord Tojo who had ruled the cabinet during the glorious days of Japan's victories had been abruptly ousted after the loss of Saipan in July the year before; and the interim cabinet headed by Prime Minister Koiso was toppled by the military leaders in the government when the strategic island of Okinawa fell the previous month. There was no doubt in Suzuki's mind that further encroachments on Japanese territory were going to send him the way of Tojo and Koiso. Okinawa had been a shattering loss, for it provided the U.S. with an air base a scant 300 miles from all the major cities of Japan. And it left Japan temporarily without a Prime Minister.

It was at that point that the Emperor arranged with a number of his court "doves" to press the seventy-eight-year-old Suzuki back into service and ask him to form a new cabinet.

Suzuki was a former naval admiral, a scholar and a devout Taoist who was never happier than when he was sequestered from the world of politics and the cares of the world in his library of 20,000 books. Broadly speaking, Taoism, represented by the Yin-Yang (or *Taiji*) symbol, emphasizes freedom, nature, cosmology, self-cultivation, retirement from social life, and the search for immortality. Learning of Suzuki's possible return to office, the military members of the cabinet voiced no objections, for they thought the old admiral could be depended upon to fulfill their intentions of fighting the war to its last battle on Japanese home soil. On the other hand, Emperor Hirohito, who spoke of Suzuki as "a grand old uncle", knew him to be a master in the art of diplomacy and felt he could be trusted to support the embryonic peace efforts that he thought might soon have to be tested.

When the much-revised report was presented to Suzuki, it revealed a situation far more critical than anyone had imagined. Every single area of life within Japan was affected by an appalling lack of raw materials. Steel production was down by two-thirds, munitions production was half its expected total, and every area of transportation was crippled by enormous shortages, losses and a lack of manpower. Fuel reserves were so critical that aviation gasoline was now being extracted from pine-root oil distilled from trees in the forests, and in some areas the hillsides had been stripped bare of trees. The official food ration was two-thirds the minimum wartime standard, and facing the smallest rice harvest in over forty years, school children had been assigned the task of going into the forests to collect acorns for food. Holes and slit-trenches were being dug in backyards, in parks and along the streets to be used as bomb shelters, and women everywhere were sewing together 'bomb helmets', pieces of cloth stuffed with cotton to protect their children during an air raid. Carried over the shoulder, to go outside without one was to earn a severe reprimand. Neighborhoods were organizing groups of fire fighters — mostly woman and the very old — and instructing them in how to douse incendiary fires using a fire extinguisher and a damp mop.

So staggering was the report that Suzuki took immediate action and called for the formation of a special group to be placed in charge of the direction of the war. The group, comprised of the Prime Minister, the Foreign Minister and Japan's top four military chiefs, was titled the Supreme Council for the Conduct of the War, but almost immediately it became known as The Big Six.

On the 12th of May when the full *Operation Decision* report was formally read to The Big Six, a somber atmosphere gripped the room. Naval Minister Yonai was the first to speak, suggesting that perhaps some sort of immediate mediation be sought through diplomatic channels in Switzerland, China, Sweden or the Vatican.[27]

Equally stunned by the contents of the report, Army Chief of Staff Umezo stared gloomily at the table, and in what sounded like an afterthought he added that perhaps the Soviet Union should be selected as a go-between to mediate the end of the war. It was possible, he suggested, that with the surrender of

---

27 Edward Wiley, *The Uncertain Summer of 1945*, page 96. DOCID: 3928846, UNCLASSI-FIED, approved for release by NSA on 12-01-2011 Transparency Case#63853
https://www.nsa.gov/news-features/declassified-documents/cryptologic-quarterly/assets/files/The_Uncertain_Summer_of_1945.pdf
This was not a new thought. During a pre-war liaison conference (November 29, 1941) in which the Army and the Navy chiefs were brought together to explore how and when the war could be brought to an end, it was proposed that Prime Minister Tojo turn to the Pope to negotiate an end to hostilities. JohnToland, *The Rising Sun*, page 226

Germany the people of the United States would be interested in pressing for a quick end to the war for an early return of its servicemen.

Suzuki said nothing and showed no emotion, but in his heart he was pleased. He had achieved what he and the Emperor had thought impossible, but his insistence that the situation report be read aloud to an open meeting of The Big Six had forced the army and the navy to bring the forbidden subject of negotiated peace into the open at long last.

Two days later, The Big Six held another meeting during which they drew up a memorandum suggesting that their ambassador in Moscow initiate peace overtures through Russia. Because Japan was not at war with Russia, their representatives to the Kremlin had been treated as diplomats of a neutral nation.

"It should be clearly stated in the memorandum that Russia owes her victory over Germany to Japan, since we remained neutral with them during the European war," they advised Suzuki. "And furthermore, Russia should be reminded that she may soon need friends for she may have the United States as an enemy in the very near future."[28]

To Suzuki and the doves within the inner circle of government, the statement was considered a positive move in the right direction. Yet the statement, like the members of The Big Six themselves, was indirect. It was fraught with *haragei*, the traditional method of "stomach talk" which has always plagued Japanese discussions, whether amongst themselves, with friends, neighbors or adversaries, and whether in business or in war.

Haragei was their centuries-old method of saying one thing while intimating something else. It was a way of saying

---

28 http://nsarchive.gwu.edu/NSAEBB/NSAEBB162/42.pdf

everything—and a way of saying nothing. It was an ingrained trait, a method of dealing with topics both complex and subtle. To the Westerner, the Japanese mind was a maze of complex contradictions; to the Japanese, a man who could not speak *haragei* — and speak it well—was a fool. With *haragei*, the object is to speak in riddles and contradictions. The listener is meant to arrive at the truth of the remarks by a convoluted process of guesswork and elimination. The greater a man's ability to contradict and mislead, the more thoughtful and wise he is considered to be. It was *haragei* that helped push Japan to go to war, and it was "stomach talk" that was bound to plague the nation and prolong that war.

That is what Prime Minister Suzuki knew, and that is what frightened him.[29]

One week after the meeting in which a letter to the Japanese Ambassador in Moscow was proposed, the four military members of The Big Six had an opportunity to reflect upon their hasty reactions to Suzuki's reading of the *Operation Decision* report. They called for a special meeting in which they formally presented their own document to the Council. It was titled *The Fundamental Policy to be Followed Henceforth in the Conduct of the War*.

As presented, the Policy was a skillfully designed message meant to encourage the nation forward down the path of war,

---

[29] After the war Suzuki and others claimed that though they were secretly working towards peace, they employed 'the art of hidden and invisible technique' because they could not openly advocate it. This has been disputed by a number of historians, however Japanese historian Robert J. C. Butow writes, "Because of it's very ambiguity, the plea of *haragei* invites the suspicion that in questions of politics and diplomacy a conscious reliance upon this 'art of bluff' may have constituted a purposeful deception predicated upon a desire to play both ends against the middle. While this judgment does not accord with the much-lauded character of Admiral Suzuki, the fact remains that from the moment he became Premier until the day he resigned no one could ever be quite sure what Suzuki would do or say next." Butow, *Japan's Decision To Surrender*, pp. 70-71.

and it concluded with these words: "We shall prosecute the war to the bitter end in order to uphold our *kokutai* (our national essence), protect the Imperial Land, and achieve our National goals of conquest."[30]

In dismay and disbelief, Foreign Minister Togo rose from his chair and shouted across the table at the stern faces of the military members confronting him. "Going through the items in the *Operation Decision* report, and reviewing yours in favor of fighting, I can see no reason for continuing the war. To imply as you do here that the closer the battlefield comes to us the more advantageous it would be for Japan is ridiculous!"

One of the most powerful men in wartime Japan, the Minister of War General Anami, leapt to his feet as though he had been slapped with a glove across the face. "If we cannot fulfill our individual or collective responsibilities as advisors to the throne, we should offer our sincere apologies now by committing *harakiri!*"

As he sat down, a melancholy pall descended on the room. The two civilian members of the council knew they had been out-maneuvered, and the decision of the military officers to continue the war until the death of every citizen in Japan was passed into motion.

A few days later, on the 8th of June, the resolution was presented to the Throne. As custom dictated, the mere reading of an agreement before the Emperor was sufficient for Imperial approval. This was baffling to people outside Japan, but to the Japanese the Emperor was the ultimate father figure, a descendent of the Sun Goddess *Amaterasu*, human in form but in reality a deity. As such, he was responsible only to his ancestors,

---

30 John Toland, *The Rising Sun*, Vol 2, page 925

never to his living subjects. They were the Emperor's children and as their god and father those serving in his cabinets or as his ministers or as his military leaders automatically inherited a portion of his deity. According to the Imperial Constitution, "The Emperor is the head of the Empire; The Emperor gives sanction to laws and orders them to be promulgated and executed; The Emperor has the supreme command of the Army and Navy." Moreover, first and foremost, Emperor Hirohito was a firmly committed nationalist determined to preserve the monarchy and protect Japan's interests abroad.

It would be many years after the end of the war before it became clear that Hirohito had such a strong hand and was adept in asserting his influence behind the scenes in the lead-up to it, including his sanctioning the army's seizure of Manchuria in 1931 and giving subsequent approval to the Biological and Chemical Warfare Research Division, Unit 731, to conduct biological and germ warfare and to carry out deadly poison gas experiments on Chinese civilians.[31] The facility was responsible for chemical weapon attacks, torture, surgical experimentation on POWs, forced labor, and sexual slavery. Chinese citizens, as well as prisoners of war and even children, were operated on without anesthetic because "vivisection should be done under normal circumstances." Rivers, wells and springs were poisoned, and during a four month period in 1938, in what is known to the Chinese as the Defense of Wuhan, the record shows that Hirohito personally transmitted orders to use poison gas on 375 occasions,

---

31   http://pricegraphicarts.tripod.com/WorldWideTerrorism/id43.htm

contributing to the deaths of 400,000 Chinese.[32]

On the throne for only five years in 1931, the Manchurian acquisition not only expanded Hirohito's empire, it gave Japan new agricultural land while helping to redress the problem of Japan's weakness in natural resources such as coal and iron ore. From that point forward, "national emergency" became the rhetoric of the military, allowing Hirohito to sanction a large expansion of the military budget and to authorize a threefold increase in the size of the army in north China. In addition, just after the Marco Polo Bridge "incident" in 1937 leading to Japan's all-out war with China, Hirohito signed a directive confirming that Japan was not bound by the Hague Conventions regarding the humane treatment of prisoners of war—even though Japan had not signed the Conventions. Though it was repeated again and again after the war that the Emperor was nothing more than a figurehead, he possessed, in fact, all the power necessary to rein in his military. But he chose not to do so.

On this day in June 1945, not quite forty-three years of age, he had spent almost a quarter of his life as Emperor of a nation at war, first with China, then with the world. And now, he would again sit in silence listening to his nation's leaders as they discussed the course of the war. They, meanwhile, would be carefully studying his face to fathom whether he approved or disapproved of the direction of the meeting. At any sign of displeasure they were prepared to change the discussion to arrive at a different conclusion.

---

32 The Chinese estimate that 2,000,000 Japanese produced chemical weapons were buried in China at the end of the war. For nearly fifty years, -- until 1993 when Japan and 165 nations signed the Chemical Weapons Convention, Japan refused to acknowledge that it had left the weapons or dumped any into the Nen (or Nenjiang) River in northeast China. After signing the Convention, Japan built a factory to recover and dispose of them. Yuki Tanaka, Poison Gas, the Story Japan Would Like to Forget, Bulletin of the Atomic Scientists, October 1988, page 17; https://en.wikipedia.org/wiki/Japanese_war_crimes, Use Of Chemical Weapons; https://en.wikipedia.org/wiki/Unit_516; https://en.wikipedia.org/wiki/Japanese_war_crimes, Use Of Chemical Weapons

And so it was that when the principles for *The Conduct of the War* were read to him, Emperor Hirohito, a master who had early on learned the game of displaying an inscrutable countenance, sat listening in silence with his hands folded. It has been stated that in the fourteen years he had been on the throne he had spoken but twice to his various cabinets or councils. In 1931 he had issued a mild rebuke to the army for the murder of a Chinese warlord when the army sought a contrived way of expanding its war in Manchuria. On the October 10, 1941 he sat on his dais and listened to the arguments of the military and heard their proposals that would lead to the decision to bomb Pearl Harbor and launch attacks on targets throughout Southeast Asia. When they had finished their discussions before the throne, the Emperor surprised his audience—some of whom had never before heard his squeaky, high-pitched voice—by unfolding a piece of paper and reading a poem written by his grandfather, Emperor Meiji:

> "All the seas, everywhere
> are brothers one to another.
> Why then do the winds and waves of strife
> rage so violently through the world?"

In awe at hearing him speak, but uncertain whether they had just been censured by their living god, the military officers adroitly made a minor change in their policy of war to skirt around any objections he might have had: they agreed to continue going through the motions of negotiating with the Americans for peace while stepping up their preparations for war. Then they bowed to their Emperor, left the meeting—and proceeded to force Prime Minister Fumimaro Konoe from office because he dared to show his displeasure over their wish to force a full-scale military confrontation against the powers of Great Britain, the Netherlands, and the United States.

On the day following the reading of the council's plan to pursue the war to its suicidal end, Hirohito summoned Foreign Minister Shigenori Togo to his bunker at the palace. He had retreated to it soon after General LeMay's bombers destroyed parts of the palace killing several of the household staff. The retreat was a deep underground chamber his staff euphemistically called His Majesty's Library.

Togo had only recently assumed the Foreign Minister's position again, having held it in the years leading up to the start of the war. At that time he, like Konoe before him, had been adamantly opposed to going to war with the United States and Great Britain, declaring it would be a war Japan could not win. He was ignored by everyone associated with the planning of it, and when, after the bombing of Pearl Harbor, he said Japan must agree to the terms of the Geneva Convention with respect to the treatment of civilians and prisoners, he was shunned. That was the tipping point, and he submitted his resignation to the Emperor. He had spent the war years in retirement, but returned earlier in the year when the Emperor called him back into service. During their first private meeting in February, he advised the Emperor to begin negotiations to end the war. Hirohito firmly rejected the recommendation saying he was still looking for *tennozan*, a great victory.[33]

Now, six months later and at this supremely crucial moment, the two met away from all ears behind closed doors. Hirohito opened the conversation by talking about the secret Imperial Underground Headquarters being constructed northwest of

---

33 Fujita Hisanori, Jijûchô no kaisô, Chûô Kôronsha, 1987, pp. 66-67, Bix, page. 489
    https://en.wikipedia.org/wiki/Hirohito#cite_ref-33

Tokyo under Mount Maizuru.[34] In addition to ten thousand Korean conscripts, thousands of others were working twelve-hour shifts preparing a huge complex for what the Army was calling its Final Battle, and copies of the 1941 Soldier's Code were being distributed throughout the land underscoring the lethal demand being made on all Japanese citizens: When attacking, be determined and positive, always taking the initiative, fighting vigorously and stubbornly, vowing not to cease until the enemy is crushed, and in defense, always retain the spirit of attack and always maintain freedom of action. *Never give up a position but rather die.*[35]

Twice, the Emperor said to Togo, the Army had asked him and the Empress to leave Tokyo to join them in their underground complex. An armored train was prepared to take them to it and their safety was assured. He had declined the offer. More recently, he had learned the Army was secretly building an underground palace at the site, something he wouldn't have known about if it hadn't been that the person who was to build it had no idea what an Imperial Palace looked like and had approached the Emperor's staff seeking design information. Five times larger than a baseball stadium and covering 77,000 square feet, work had been continuing day and night on the project, shoeless laborers struggling to bore endless chambers and eight miles of tunnels out of solid rock. The death toll was so great that an Auschwitz-type crematorium had been constructed at the site, and nearby villagers said for the past ten months smoke never stopped coming from its chimney.

While the two men were talking, the earth began to shake as

---

34   Drea, Edward J. (2003). In the Service of the Emperor: Essays on the Imperial Japanese Army, P.206; https://en.wikipedia.org/wiki/Matsushiro_Underground_Imperial_Headquarters#cite_note-Drea206-5
35   http://www.duhaime.org/LawMuseum/LawArticle-1625/1941-The-Japanese-Military-Field-Code.aspx

bombs exploded nearby. Then, in a muted voice, the Emperor revealed his fear that the militarists were conspiring to take him to the Matsushsiro underground shelter to isolate him so they could rule in his name and carry out their suicidal ambitions in a sacred war. The time had come, he said, to seek out a nation willing to mediate the end of the war.

Togo left the Emperor's underground 'Library' and proceeded to carry out the Emperor's order. Unfortunately, he once again made the unwise decision of trying to make contact with someone at the Soviet Embassy.[36]

It was mid-July when a new president of the United States sat down in a wooded German village near Potsdam under the flags of the United States, Great Britain and Russia and spoke once more of *"unconditional surrender."*

Former President Roosevelt had first used those words during an informal chat with newsmen during the Casablanca Conference with Churchill in 1943. The two Allied leaders had gone to North Africa with their staffs to work out the initial details of the forthcoming invasion plans of Europe. Alone with newsmen from the U.S. and Britain, Roosevelt had declared: "The elimination of German, Japanese and Italian war power means the *unconditional surrender* of Germany, Italy and Japan." The startled newsmen asked him to repeat his remark. He did, and from that moment on the idea of offering the enemy nothing except surrender without any terms or preconditions had become Allied policy.

When Roosevelt died in office in April of 1944 and the Vice-President, Harry S. Truman, inherited the office of the presidency, he inherited the previous president's strategies. Now Truman

---

36 http://nsarchive.gwu.edu/NSAEBB/NSAEBB162/42.pdf

was at Potsdam speaking of unconditional surrender in the same way that Roosevelt had. When the conference was concluded, a proclamation which had been agreed to by the three powers was beamed openly to the war's final belligerent:

"Continuation of the war would lead to the utter devastation to the Japanese homeland unless Japan surrendered unconditionally. Japan would be confined to her four main islands and would be under American occupation until such time as a new order was established and there was convincing proof that her capabilities of making war were destroyed forever. The criminals responsible for the war would be tried in a military court by the Allies."[37]

A number of Truman's aides had wanted him to amend the proclamation to state that the Allies were agreeable to the idea of preserving the ancient Emperor system. But President Truman had been advised by his new Secretary of State, James Byrnes, that a recent Gallup Poll in the United States showed that one-third of the American people had favored executing Emperor Hirohito, and 37% had come out in favor of putting Hirohito on trial as a war criminal. Most Americans believed that the Emperor shared a large role in starting the war, and only 7% of the people polled said they thought the Imperial Emperor of Japan should be allowed to continue on the throne.

With the Gallup figures in mind, President Truman signed the Potsdam Proclamation and gave no more thought to the Emperor or his status. He knew nothing at all of *kokutai* - the Japanese national essence - and it wouldn't have mattered if he did.

The morning following Truman's declaration, Japanese newspapers carried the full text of the Potsdam Proclamation signed by Truman and Churchill. The *Yomiuri Shimbun* editorialized it as "a laughable matter, a thing of no great importance. It will only serve to re-enhance the nation's resolve to carry the war forward unfalteringly to a successful conclusion," they said.

Many thousands of miles away, the *New York Times* of July 30, 1945 displayed its reaction to the Japanese response with a banner headline reading: JAPAN OFFICIALLY TURNS DOWN ALLIED SURRENDER ULTIMATUM.

Three days later, all schools in Japan were closed, all school children were mobilized, the civilian population was being armed, caves were fortified, and there was a fast start in building more underground defenses.

At precisely eight-fifteen and seventeen seconds on the morning of August 6, 1945, in the Japanese year Showa 20, meaning the 20th year of the reign of Enlightened Peace, the 12-man crew of a B-29 Superfortress named the *Enola Gay* felt their plane lunge abruptly upward. Nine thousand pounds lighter, it rose swiftly, banked violently, and then nosed down rapidly to gain as much speed as possible to depart from the serene skies over Hiroshima. A blue-pink flash of lightning enveloped the men in the plane as Little Boy, the code name of their bomb, exploded 2,000 feet (660 meters) above the ground.

That sudden flash was the culmination of over six years of scientific labor that had begun in 1938 at the Kaiser Wilhelm Institute in Germany when it was thought that it might be possible to smash the atom and release its energy, energy which many believed would be as powerful as the sun.

Aboard the *Enola Gay*, no one had any certainty that their mission would be a success, or even that their bomb was even going to work. Only three weeks earlier, an experimental prototype had been exploded at night and in secret in the New Mexican desert of the southwestern United States. The scientists in charge of the operation had been instructed to give an instant report of the results, and word of the success of their one small bomb was immediately wired via code to Babelburg, Germany where Truman, Stalin and Britain's new Prime Minister, Clement Attlee, (Churchill had just been ignominiously voted out of office and had left the conference) were concluding their talks at Potsdam.

At that precise moment Truman was particularly irritated that Stalin was talking about including Russia in the war against Japan. Until that time, Stalin had resisted all Allied efforts to declare war on Japan and place that country in the position of fighting a war on two fronts. The new President of the United States was not fond of Stalin, and he did not trust him. He especially resented Stalin's claims that his army "had broken the back of Japanese resistance." By doing what? Truman had been tempted to ask.[38]

Truman had been strained in his dealings with Stalin, but looking at the message about the success of the new bomb he suddenly became relaxed. With the conviction that the United States had a new and powerful weapon capable of ending the war in one blow, he began searching in earnest for a way to negate Stalin's earlier commitments in which he, Stalin, had promised Russian intervention in the war against Japan "at the right moment".

Additionally, all secret Japanese codes had been broken in the months—in some cases, years—before the outbreak of the Pacific War, and President Truman was very familiar with the deteriorating situation within Japan and of her recent feeble

---

38 William Craig, *The Fall of Japan*, Open Road Media, September 29, 2015, page.50

efforts to seek peace through the Soviet Union—efforts which Stalin had conveniently neglected to report to him. He knew, too, that the Japanese leaders were engaged in a deadly battle among themselves as they played for time in the hope that the Allies would grow weary of the war and consent to a compromise peace settlement. What Japan had quietly proposed through neutral diplomatic channels was an arrangement whereby they would quit all the areas they presently occupied while retaining those areas they had possessed at the outbreak of hostilities with the United States, the Netherlands and Great Britain on December 7, 1941. They added that as their war with China was an older one between two longstanding Asian enemies—a war that the Chinese (they claimed) had instigated—they insisted that they had a natural right to continue their war against China.

Truman scoffed at that, and he was concerned and annoyed about the territorial ambitions of Joseph Stalin. If that wasn't enough, he now had new and serious considerations on his mind. The secret reports of Dr. J. Robert Oppenheimer—the man responsible for the design of the new bomb—had stated that in his estimate a single explosion of such a bomb over a Japanese city would probably kill twenty thousand people.

Truman reflected on that as he sat next to Stalin and Attlee, pondering the bomb and what his Assistant Secretary of War, John McCloy, had suggested: he thought the President should send a message to Emperor Hirohito informing him of the new bomb and its devastating possibilities, and he suggested, too, that Truman should threaten the Emperor by announcing that the United States would use it if Japan did not surrender immediately.

A number of other suggestions had been put forward by the Joint Chiefs of Staff, notably one by Secretary of War Henry L. Stimson who thought that a bomb should be dropped off the coast of Japan to "rattle their windows and give them pause for thought."

But on everyone's mind, and especially on Truman's, was the important question: Would the bomb work? The scientists on Oppenheimer's team had labored through the war to build it, yet when it came down to it and the men on the small Pacific island of Tinian assembled the components and put the bomb into a B-29 and sent the plane on its way, not even Dr. Oppenheimer could give Truman any assurances.

Now, advised of the success of a small atomic device exploded in the New Mexico desert, there seemed a distinct possibility that the U.S. had a weapon that could bring a quick end to the war. But Truman decided to say nothing to Atlee or Stalin about it.

At ground zero in Hiroshima, the 10,830 degree heat (6,000 C) melted granite from the walls of the buildings. House tiles, bricks, glass windows, asphalt, steel, bone and flesh evaporated into a billowing cloud that rose to an altitude of 50,000 feet. A huge firestorm erupted as oxygen was pulled into the center of the blast from all directions to feed the flames, and for nearly a mile from ground zero, the exact point where the bomb had exploded, oxygen was sucked from the lungs of the living and the walls of their chests collapsed. When the fire subsided and the dust cleared, the ground was flat as far as the eye could see. What clocks and watches remained were stopped at 8:15 a.m. That day, four square miles of a large industrial city were leveled and 66,000 human beings died, including 20,000 Imperial Japanese soldiers and twenty-two American prisoners of war who were there as slave laborers. In the months to come, nearly as many people were to die of burns, injuries and radiation poisoning.

The B-29 unit that had been of such concern to someone in Lieutenant-General Arisue's intelligence bureau had finally been located. It was the 509th Composite Group which, at the time that Arisue had been reading the report listing the strength of United States fighting units, had disappeared from the rolls of the various Air Force installations in the Far East. The 509th Composite Group had been in Cuba learning how to drop atomic bombs on the cities of Japan.

The Suzuki council appointed to discuss the conduct of the war held an emergency meeting in its underground bunker. To various observers in Japan, the bombing of Hiroshima was a golden opportunity to end the war while allowing the nation to save face. No longer would it appear necessary to blame the military or their shortcomings for losing the war.

At the meeting, Foreign Minister Togo rose first and made a motion that the Potsdam Proclamation be agreed to and accepted immediately.

"Hiroshima drastically alters the whole military situation and offers the military ample grounds for ending the war as quickly as possible," he said.

But as he had done in the past, whenever the word surrender was intimated, the hawkish samurai warrior, General Anami, jumped to his feet. His face turned red as he glared at the members of the Council.

"Such a move is uncalled for," he bellowed. "Furthermore, we do not yet know if the bomb was atomic. What do we know? We have only Truman's word for it. It might be a trick!"[39]

After the bomb had been dropped and Truman had been notified of the results, he issued an immediate statement to the generals of Japan: "If Japan does not accept our terms, she may

---

39 John Toland, *The Rising Sun*, Vol 2, page 982

expect a rain of ruin from the air, the like of which has never been seen on this earth."[40]

However, after almost 14 years of war the military officers were accustomed to hearing threats, as well as making them, and for the most part they treated Truman's words with ambivalence. But Foreign Minister Togo had no desire to let them push the issue aside. Taking a cautious and neutral step backwards, he argued that he was of the opinion that no nation on earth had enough radioactive material to mount the kind of attacks Truman had threatened. "But even if the United States and its Allies did," he added, "world opinion would not allow the use of such inhuman weapons."

General Anami jumped to his feet again in irritation. "Talk of surrender is unthinkable!" he shouted. "It is absolutely un-Japanese! The *Soldier's Manual* has not taught the Japanese soldier how to surrender. All soldiers, millions upon millions of them, understand what it means when they read *'always save the last round for yourself'*." He pounded his fists together. "No, the soldiers of Japan will never surrender!"[41]

Togo waited until Anami sat down. The August air inside the shelter was humid and heavy, and perspiration rolled down his face as he stood again and chose his words carefully. "Even if we offered the sacrifice of twenty million Japanese lives, what would we have to gain in return?"

General Anami didn't bother getting to his feet. "If we are resolute," he countered, "and if we are prepared to sacrifice the lives of twenty million Japanese lives in a final effort, victory shall be ours," he said.

This was becoming a debate between the Foreign Minister

---

40   Ibid, page 979
41   Richard B. Frank (1999). *Downfall: the End of the Imperial Japanese Empire*. New York: Penguin

and the Minister of War, and the other members of the council were, for the present, prepared to remain silent. Togo spoke again.

"If only we had any real hope of victory, no one would for a moment think of accepting the Potsdam Proclamation. But winning one battle or two battles will not win the war for us," he said quietly.

General Anami bristled. He leapt to his feet a second time.

"What are we doing here? What we should be talking about is not peace but war! If we are to have peace, it must be peace with honor. Without it, the army will continue to fight on without quarter, showing no mercy to the enemy."

He paused and looked about the room for someone to accuse. The members of the council stared down at their hands resting on the table before them. General Anami was piqued by their submissiveness.

"Some of you may now seem to forget it," he said, "but the army has not. And I have not! This is a Holy War, and it was designed as one for the protection of the Land of the Gods. And I remind you again that we are here to talk about our destiny, and about war with honor. The Japanese army will not talk about peace!"

They went on talking and shadow-boxing for nearly two hours in the stuffy basement bomb shelter, totally exhausted from the heat, the tension—and the *haragei*. When the Army Chief of Staff Umezo finally displayed his hand by siding with General Anami, Anami changed tactics for a moment. He wondered aloud if the bomb that had destroyed Hiroshima was anything more than a new type of incendiary weapon. He returned to his original remarks about the possibility of the whole business being nothing more than an enemy trick.

On that evening, the day of the destruction of Hiroshima, the only thing that was agreed at the meeting of The Big Six was a proposal that Japan's Intelligence Chief Arisue and Japan's leading nuclear scientist, Doctor Nishina, visit the scene of devastation and return with a report on the situation.

Dr. Nishina wasted no time. He went to Hiroshima immediately, and returned to tell Intelligence Chief Arisue that the bomb that destroyed the city had indeed been nuclear. In fact, he said, it was a uranium-type bomb similar to the one he and other Japanese scientists and physicists had been working on in secret for the past several years. When he asked Arisue if he should continue work on their own bomb, General Arisue was silent.

Foreign Minister Togo left the Council meeting a disturbed man. He walked hurriedly to his office where he drafted a cable. Immediately after receiving a memorandum from Arisue's intelligence office confirming that the U.S. President had spoken the truth and that Hiroshima had indeed been destroyed by a new type of weapon called a nuclear bomb, Togo gave the cable to an aide with instructions to have it urgently transmitted to his Ambassador in Moscow. The aide went down the corridor and dictated the message to a code operator:

THE SITUATION IS BECOMING SO ACUTE THAT
WE MUST HAVE CLARIFICATION OF THE
SOVIET ATTITUDE AS QUICKLY AS POSSIBLE.
PLEASE MAKE FURTHER EFFORT TO OBTAIN A
REPLY IMMEDIATELY.[42]

In Moscow, Ambassador Naotake Sato had been waiting. After

---

42   John Toland, *The Rising Sun*, Vol 2, page 984

making several requests for an official appointment, he finally received a message. He was mystified, for it did not appear to be a response to his application for a meeting: instead, it appeared to be a summons directing him to appear at the Kremlin.

The *Enola Gay* had paid its visit to Hiroshima two days earlier, and when Ambassador Sato was ushered into the study of the Russian Foreign Minister Vyacheslav Mikhaylovich Molotov, the atmosphere within the room was oppressive. Sato was not even invited to sit down. Molotov picked up a single piece of paper from his cleared desk and began to read: "I have here, in the name of the Soviet Union, a notification to the Japanese Government," he read in a dull and unemotional voice. "True to its obligation as an Ally, the Soviet government declares from tomorrow — that is, from the 9th of August 1945 — the Soviet Union will consider herself in a state of war against Japan."

Molotov stared coldly into Ambassador Sato's eyes and the Ambassador returned his gaze for a second, then bowed, turned, and walked from the room. Stalin had finally decided that this was "the right moment", and even as Ambassador Sato walked from Molotov's study, one million six-hundred thousand troops under the command of Marshal Vasilievsky began crossing the Russian frontier into Manchuria.

At that same moment, across from Molotov's study in the rambling Kremlin complex, Joseph Stalin had summoned five of Russia's leading scientists to his office where he ordered them to develop an atomic bomb. "Regardless," he said, "of the costs."

The Big Six gathered again. It was their third meeting since Hiroshima, and more and more it appeared to Prime Minister Suzuki and Foreign Minister Togo that these council meetings were becoming nothing but endless rounds of fruitless debates between two civilian ministers in a search of understanding, and four military strategists dedicated to destroying the Japanese nation. It occurred to Suzuki that this Council was not going to come to any agreement, and that worried him for a very good reason; namely, that the real power in Japan rested not in his hands but in the hands of the military. Modeled after similar cabinets in England or the United States, Suzuki's cabinet differed in that it had no authority unless there was the complete agreement of all parties. That meant that each member of The Big Six had to vote yes or no together, and in this cabinet there would be no such thing as a majority decision. Nor would there be any abstentions.

In the matter of accepting the Potsdam Proclamation and ending the war or, conversely, rejecting the Proclamation and continuing the war on the beaches of Kyushu, the Supreme Council for the Conduct of the War was split down the middle. The civilians Suzuki and Togo stood on one side of the issue in favor of accepting an immediate end to all hostilities. At times the Navy Minister Yonai, a military officer but a liberal famous for opposing Japan's alliance with Germany in 1940, appeared to be with them on the side of the doves. Then again, sometimes he seemed on the side of the hawks. He spoke *haragei* so effectively that no one really understood his ambiguities or where in the world he stood on any given issue at any given moment. Nonetheless, when counting votes to size up his position, in Suzuki's mind he was 80% convinced that he could include Admiral Yonai on the side of ending the war.

Opposing him was the sixty-year old Navy Chief of Staff, Admiral Toyoda; the sixty-three-year old Army Chief, General Umezo; and the ferocious fifty-eight year old model of an ancient samurai, the Minister of War, General Anami.

As they met for another bout of *haragei*, a new fear began preying on Suzuki's mind. The more time that passed, and the more the members of the Council argued their positions, the more the danger arose of another strictly indigenous Japanese concept, that of *gekokuju*. Roughly translated, *gekokuju* means insubordination. Applied by the military, it was something to fear. History and tradition had legitimized such action on the part of the military as a way of seeking redress for grievances or as a means to settle injustices, real or imagined. The weapons of *gekokuju* were force and assassination, and no one on the Council understood its terrors better than Suzuki. In February of 1936 there had been a military uprising by a number of young hotspurs demanding that Japan free herself from what they believed to be medieval politics and grab her fair share of the rich regions available in China. The faults of Japan, they felt, were caused by the decrepit politicians who governed the nation, and in their zeal to make war they set an ambush. Because he was an old politician of the old school, they attempted to kill Suzuki. His body still showed the marks made by the four bullet wounds, one of them still lodged near his heart.

Now, poised on the threshold of total destruction from the forces of the United States and Great Britain—whether by invasion or by atomic bombs—Suzuki was growing alarmed about being destroyed by *gekokuju* and the military fanatics within his own country.

His logical mind that had permitted him to survive so long in the world of political intrigue grasped the paradox: even if he were to succeed in his efforts to bring about peace, the Allies would undoubtedly put him on trial and hang him as a war criminal. On the other hand, if he failed to mediate peace and if the military was permitted to continue down their avenue of total annihilation, they would surely single him out and kill him as a traitor.

That was the situation in which Prime Minister Suzuki

found himself late on the night of August 8 when he entered the meeting room at Imperial Headquarters for another round of discussions with his fellow members of The Supreme Council for the Conduct of the War.

It was just before dawn on the 9th of August when a B-29 named *Bockscar* groaned down a runway on Tinian Island 1,500 miles south of Tokyo with "Fat Boy" — thought to be code-named after Winston Churchill but in fact named after British actor Sidney Greenstreet — tucked securely inside its bomb doors. Slowly, interminably slowly, the B-29 strained forward toward the end of the long runway and finally lifted up into free space to turn toward Japan and seek out the ancient castle city of Kokura.

Off the south coast of the island of Kyushu where secret plans were being acted upon and thousands upon thousands of *kamikaze* warriors were assembling at newly-constructed bases, the powerful engines of a single bomber could be faintly heard. It flew so high it required no fighter protection. The officers in charge of operations on the ground looked up into the dawning sky and smiled. They had just begun to receive the new one-man flying rockets that would soon be able to blast those deadly nuisances from the sky. But today was not that day: their instruments of destruction were to be kept in reserve as a diabolical surprise for the day the American ships appeared off the coast and attempted an invasion.

Far overhead, *Bockscar* began flying in wide circles as it waited to rendezvous with two escort planes that were to fly with it to the target. Within several minutes, one plane appeared and the two of them circled in an ever-widening arch waiting for the third one, a camera plane that was to record the entire operation for posterity.

After forty-five valuable minutes, the camera plane still hadn't appeared and by then *Bockscar's* crew discovered that they had a problem. One of their fuel selectors hadn't been functioning properly, and after making calculations the plane's engineer told the pilot that they had 600 gallons less fuel than they thought they had on board.

"To hell with it then, I'm not going to hang around here waiting for a damn camera plane to come," the pilot said to his crew on the plane's intercom. And then he banked to the right and flew north toward his target.

At a pre-flight briefing session, the weather advisory office on Tinian Island had told the pilot and his navigator that the skies over Kokura would be clear. But by the time *Bockscar* arrived over the city it was virtually hidden from view by a cover of smoke caused by General LeMay's recent firebombing of nearby cities. Nonetheless, once over the city the bombardier, Kermit Beahan, took control of the plane from his Plexiglas observation position in the very nose of the bomber. Sitting alone and squinting into his bombsight attempting to see through the haze covering Kokura, Captain Beahan became a troubled man for he was under explicit verbal instructions from Air Force Headquarters in Washington, D.C. to turn off his radar and use his eyes. "This is to be a visual drop only, and no mistakes will be tolerated!"

The radar was off and he was using his eyes, but as *Bockscar* lumbered slowly over Kokura he could see no visible landmark and he could find no clear target marker. Taking a deep breath, he directed the pilot to pass again over the city and he felt the plane bank, turn, and come back for a second run.

Moments passed, then: "We waited too long to get here," Captain Beahan exclaimed to the pilot on the intercom as he pressed his eyes ever tighter against the bombsight. "All I can see down there is smoke."

And then the plane had passed beyond Kokura again.

Realizing it, the pilot turned sharply and the huge plane came in over the city from another angle. Minutes and seconds ticked by and the crew sat in taut nervousness feeling the throbbing of the engines as they waited for the upward surge their plane would make once the big bomb had been dropped.

A voice over the intercom system suddenly broke the tension. "The fuel situation is getting critical, Captain," the flight engineer said.

There was a long pause in which time seemed to stop, and then the crew heard the voice of the pilot talking quietly, first to Beahan, and then to the navigator. "Okay, mission aborted. Let's proceed to our secondary target. Let's get going to Nagasaki."

Shigeykoshi Morimoto was a superstitious man. Three days earlier he had been working in a factory in Hiroshima when a sudden blinding flash lit up the skies like an exploding sun, and a terrible tremor had shaken the earth. A wind like none he had ever known blew and whistled past him, and he fell to the earth in sudden darkness. When he regained his sight, the city of Hiroshima had become a desolate plane. In terror, he ran, not knowing exactly where to go except to flee from the horrible demons that had come out of nowhere to destroy the earth. He ran as fast as he could, and somewhere, somehow, he found a railway, and there was a freight train on the tracks and it was still running. It was moving slowly, and he hurried to it and climbed on and clung to it as though it was the last living thing in the world. Through the entire day and night and the following day the train rolled on, and when it finally stopped he realized that the train had taken him back to the city of his birth, the city that was the home of his family. As though awakening from a terrible dream, Morimoto was filled with joy. He leapt from the train and rushed through the streets to return to his house where he knew his wife would be waiting. As he ran, he could think of no words to express his happiness at having escaped the demons and being safely transported back home. Back home to Nagasaki.

For many years, people spoke of Nagasaki as the San Francisco of Japan. It was, they said, a beautiful city of 200,000 people, with lovely streets and narrow lanes that wound lazily up and down its many rolling hills just as they did in San Francisco. Those who had visited it claimed that it was the most Europeanized and the most Christian city in all Japan. It had a musical history as well, for looking out as it did over the beautiful blue harbor and the East China Sea; it was the legendary home of Madame Butterfly. Standing on one of its hills and looking out at the sea, one could almost hear her haunting song and feel her sorrow as she sang of her love for a naval officer who would never return again.

Running through the streets, Morimoto drew near to his house, and hearing his cries his wife rushed into the street to meet him. Embracing, they clung to each other tearfully, and then Morimoto began to shake with fright. He wanted to tell his wife of the terrifying things that he had witnessed, of the demons that had just visited Hiroshima. But what he had seen and heard was so incomprehensible that he couldn't find the words to speak. Instead, he grasped her fretfully and stared into her eyes — and at that very moment, a flash of light brighter than a hundred suns enveloped them. Reflected in her tearful eyes he saw again the same pink flash he had seen at Hiroshima. In anguish, he pulled his wife to the ground and buried her beneath the weight of his thin body. Holding her, he began to cry. The demons had followed him home.

A survivor from the *HMAS Perth*, an Australian destroyer that had been sunk off Java by the Japanese in the opening days of the war, was taking a brief rest before going back underground to work. Almost three and a half years earlier he had been pulled from the warm waters of the Java Sea and transported to Japan aboard a Hell Ship where he and 1,859 other prisoners of war from other countries—Dutch, British, Javanese, Australians, Americans—were put together in groups of twenty, thirty or fifty on the wharfs and auctioned off in bulk lots to financiers and businessmen who owned factories and mills and munitions plants. He, along with seventy-three other survivors from the *Perth*, was sold to the operators of the Omuta Coal Mines across the bay from Nagasaki on Hashima Island, and he spent most of the past twelve months underground in the darkness of the coal shafts. It was one of his small pleasures to stand above ground every now and then breathing the clean air, feeling the sun on his face and daydreaming of home and his family while staring out at the horizon. On this day he tilted his head back and watched something that was truly free and unrestrained. He gazed up at a solitary B-29 that moved in a straight and even line to bisect the cloudless blue sky. He had an understandable tinge of envy as he thought of the American fliers aboard that plane, and as he looked he saw a large object fall from its opened underbelly. He was puzzled why such a huge bomber had flown so far to drop but a single bomb.

When he regained consciousness he was lying at the bottom of a mine shaft. His body hurt, but he didn't think he'd been badly injured. He moved carefully, and after crawling painfully back up to the surface he looked about. He was alone, his guards were gone. And so, too, were 35,800 others.

Admiral Yonai, the naval minister Suzuki counted amongst those on the side of the doves, finally stopped speaking *haragei*.

"We might win the first battle for Japan, but we won't win the second. The war is lost to us. Therefore we must forget about 'face'. We must surrender as quickly as we can, and we must begin to consider at once how to preserve our country."

The Big Six had been meeting to discuss the damage that had been done to Hiroshima when an officer rushed into the room and reported the atomic destruction of Nagasaki. That, coming on the heels of news that Russia had just declared war on Japan, caused the Admiral to drop his mask. Looking Suzuki directly in the eyes, he came out from behind his veil of 'stomach talk...'

"We must approach the Americans directly," he said.[43]

General Anami again became furious, standing to blare his words at the members of the Council. He denied that Japan was defeated.

"Japan must at least have its final chance," he shouted. "Japan must be allowed to repulse the enemy on our beaches and attain life out of death."

His little Mount Fuji-shaped moustache which was always perfectly trimmed bristled as he began reciting once again the means by which the Army and the Special Attack Forces would destroy the enemy on the beaches, and of the many thousands of them who would perish even before they reached the beaches.

Looking at him out of the corner of his eye, Suzuki watched a man bellowing with rage, his thick neck like that of a bull's, his chest as large as that of a *sumo* wrestler. Suzuki closed his eyes and chewed on his cold cigar. He realized it would be impossible for him or anyone else to deal with such an infuriatingly obstinate man.

When Anami finished his recitation, he dropped back down into his chair like a boxer returning to his corner between rounds.

---

43   Kazutoshi Hando, The Pacific War Research Society, *Japan's Longest Day* (Tokyo: Kodansha International, Ltd., 1968), pp.11-53

With a frown, Foreign Minister Togo got up and turned cautiously to General Umezo and leveled a question: "In your opinion," he asked, "can the military offer any hope of victory?"[44]

Along with Anami, General Umezo was one of the two most powerful men in Japan. But with his long arms, his short frame, his deadpan face and his large nose, Umezo looked almost too pedestrian to be controlling the nearly seven million men in the army's fighting machine. He looked more like a village grocer. "With luck," he said slowly, "and with the help of the Special Attack Forces, we will be able to repulse the invaders before they land. I can say with absolute confidence that we will be able to destroy the major part of an invading force before it reaches the beaches."[45]

Foreign Minister Togo appeared impatient. Thousands of young Japanese boys were dying while they quarreled and debated and made claims and formulated policies on the basis of hope. He pressed General Umezo further. "But what difference would that make?" he asked. "You will destroy one force and the enemy will simply launch a second. And then a third. Where will it end? And *how* will it end?"[46]

Umezo was silent. He, like General Anami, appeared to be hypnotized. Both seemed to be locked in on a single subject: the final, decisive battle for the Home Islands. Like the others in the room, they could not fully grasp the significance of Hiroshima and Nagasaki. To the generals, one United States plane with one bomb destroying an entire city was not all that different from three hundred and thirty-three planes dropping 2,000 tons of incendiary bombs on Tokyo and burning it to the ground in one evening. It was terrible, it was disgraceful, but that was war. In

---

[44] John Toland, *The Rising Sun*, Vol 2, page 807
[45] Ibid
[46] Ibid

the end, it was something the nation would have to live with. In the minds of Umezo and Anami, the most authentic peril facing them now was how to deal with the nearly two million Russians that were sweeping across Manchuria and into Korea even as they sat there quarrelling about the lamentable bombing of two of their cities.

Still, the talking continued for nearly three more hours, and yet they were no nearer to a resolution than when they began. It seemed to Suzuki that the unnerving news of the destruction of Nagasaki had been almost forgotten as the military waged its war of words and demanded a final opportunity to display its might on the battlefield. In despair, he adjourned the meeting. While the others left the room he remained in his chair, and when the last one had shuffled out he stood up, picked up his cane, and hurriedly went out to search for Marquis Kido, the Lord Keeper of the Privy Seal. Marquis Kido was a close confidant and an advisor to the Emperor. Suzuki knew that he was overstepping his bounds by turning to someone in the court for help, but time was running out and he would have to have an ally. Apart from Kido, there seemed to be no one else to whom he could turn.

"The Council is at an impasse," Suzuki said to Kido. "There is only one solution and I need your help. We must ask the Emperor to make the decision."[47]

Suzuki and Marquis Kido knew full well that the Emperor's role did not include the initiation of policy, but they were also both aware of the importance of the next few days for Japan. And they both understood that only the unprecedented intervention of the Throne would save the nation.

Apart from Korea, most of the Chinese mainland, Formosa

---

[47] Ibid

(Taiwan) and the Home Islands, the last remaining area of any great significance left to the collapsing Japanese Empire was the Southern Region Army, commanded by Field Marshal Count Hisaichi Terauchi. An aristocratic veteran of the old school, extremely independent and a fanatical imperialist, he categorically rejected any thoughts of peace or defeat. Far from Tokyo in his Saigon headquarters, he was surrounded by maps with their telltale pins and arrows which clearly showed the shrinking territories of his army. For many weeks he had been out of touch with the Philippines and General Yamashita, the Tiger of Malaya, who had conquered Singapore with — compared to the British forces — what appeared be a token army. When he learned from external radio sources that the American General Douglas MacArthur had conquered Luzon and its capital Manila, he assumed that General Yamashita had died a hero's death. Of that, Japan could be proud.

His information from other areas of the Southern Region was equally unfavorable. Reports from Burma told of the British entering Mandalay, and they were beginning to march south toward Rangoon. He had just heard about the bombing of Nagasaki from monitored radio broadcasts picked up from stations in Australia and San Francisco, but he sensed that the enemy was not telling the truth. Although his army was technically surrounded, he still commanded a formidable army and was in full control of a huge zone of operations that consisted of Siam (Thailand), the Dutch East Indies (Indonesia), Malaya, Singapore, Hainan Island, Hong Kong, and Indochina, which included Vietnam, Cambodia and Laos. It was evident from a quick look at the maps on his wall that he was in command of an empire, and Count Terauchi was resolutely determined that he and his army would atone for the massive assault that was being unleashed on his homeland. He and his army would do it, he vowed, if it meant fighting to the very end. Even if he lost Siam and Burma, or Hong Kong and some of his territory in the north, his forces in Java, Sumatra, Borneo, Malaya and Indochina would, if necessary, fight the Allies alone. It would be a war that would continue for many, many years. Of that he had no doubt whatsoever.

To fight such a war would require the determination and essence of samurai discipline. It would also require unyielding self-sufficiency. His army would survive and it would win, and to make that possible it would be necessary to affect a number of changes in policy. He had not forgotten that when Japan set down the details for this campaign it was designated as a Holy War for the eternal protection of the Land of the Gods, and the Yamato Spirit would see them through, allowing them to overcome whatever disproportion there was in fighting material—even though he knew there was such a shortage of iron and steel that people were asked to collect the fragments of American bombs so they could be melted down and reused in Japan's factories.

Nodding his head as though in approval of what he had to do next, the Field Marshal went to his file cabinets and withdrew a folder that contained a list of all the military and civilian prisoner of war camps within his area of command. He put the file on his desk, reviewed its contents quickly, and then he called in a secretary and ordered him to draft an immediate communiqué. "This," he began, "is to be addressed to all Prisoner of War camp commanders in the Southern Region," and Count Terauchi began to dictate the message:

"On the day the Allies begin an invasion on any area in this command, every last prisoner of war, whether military or civilian, will be executed, and all visible signs of their internment camps will be destroyed and evidence of the existence of the camps will be eradicated from the earth. After the duty is performed, every officer and man responsible for this

JOHN BELL SMITHBACK

action will join an active fighting unit or, if that is not possible, will go into the jungles and continue the war by conducting guerrilla activities against the enemy."[48]

If the secretary had any reaction to the order he didn't show it. He copied the message in shorthand, and when General Terauchi indicated that he was through dictating, the secretary stood up, bowed low to his commanding officer, and then strode from the room. Back at his desk he transcribed the message from shorthand before handing it over to the radio operator with instructions to transmit it to all POW camp commanders from Hong Kong to Borneo, from Siam to Sumatra.

At that moment, nearly one million virtual skeletons of men were living in captivity behind barbed wire in the areas that remained under Field Marshal Count Terauchi's command, including forty-two thousand civilian woman and forty thousand children.

Also at that same moment, in the headquarters of Lord Louis Mountbatten who was in command of the British forces in the Burma sector of operations, the final details of an invasion schedule had just been ironed out. His officers had made their final notes and reviewed the maps and it was decided that, on the morning of August 18, an amphibious armada would land on the southern beaches of Siam and strike out toward Bangkok. Following that, on the 9th of September, Mountbatten's forces would begin an all-out assault on Malaya. The Siam operation

---

[48] In March 1945 a general order to kill all POWs was issued in Tokyo by Lieutenant General Kaneshiro Shibayama, the Imperial Japanese Vice-Minister: http:/ibiblio.org/hyperwar/PTO/IMTFE/IMTFE- 8.html (Section 1043) An earlier order, dated February 26, 1945, was found in the office of the Governor General of Formosa (Taiwan) http://histclo.com/essay/war/ww2/pow/jap/powj-mo.html Additionally, ex-POW Lauren's Van Der Post writes that Major General W.R.C. Penney, Director of Intelligence, South East Asia Command uncovered a copy of the order at Terauchi's Saigon office. Laurens Van Der Post, *The Night of the New Moon*.

was exactly nine days away.

After his conversation with Suzuki, Marquis Kido met in secret with the Emperor, and the Prime Minister's exceptional request for an Imperial Conference was granted. Marquis Kido had acknowledged the truth just as Suzuki had: if the total destruction of Hiroshima and Nagasaki and the anticipated tidal wave of Soviet troops descending on Korea and the islands of Japan could not convince the generals and admirals of the hopelessness of victory and the logic of surrendering, what could? In addition to that, it had just been learned from General Anami that an American pilot held by the *Kempeitai* had confessed that the United States had at least one hundred atomic bombs at its disposal, and his understanding was that the next target would be either Kyoto or Tokyo.[49]

Under the stark light of an August moon, the members of the Big Six were led down a steep stairway to the Emperor's underground bunker sixty feet below the Imperial Library. It was just before midnight, and they were puzzled by this call to a sudden and unexpected meeting. In the sweltering heat of the narrow corridors in the subterranean conference chamber their swords clanged ominously as they took seats at two parallel tables. They placed their hands on the table and sat facing each other in the oppressive heat. At the head of the table there was a smaller one, and behind it was a gold-paneled folding screen.

At that same moment at the Imperial General Headquarters, the supreme military commanders were still in session rolling

---

49 In reality, the pilot, Marcus McDilda, knew nothing of the Manhattan Project, and simply told his interrogators what he thought they wanted to hear. The lie, which caused him to be classified as a high-priority prisoner, probably saved him from beheading. See:Imperial Intervention and Allied Response: http://nations.wikia.com/wiki/Surrender_of_Japan

out maps and plotting strategy for the final defense of the Home Islands.

The Minister of War, General Anami; the Army Chief, General Umezo; and The Navy Chief, Admiral Toyoda, looked around the room with suspicion. They were visibly upset by this sudden call to a midnight conference. They suspected that their old Taoist Prime Minister was up to something. Then the room became silent as an aide came in and began passing out printed copies of the Potsdam Proclamation. The officers at the table fingered through the pages without bothering to read them.

Another aide appeared and placed before each of them a single page of paper. They read it with disbelief as it listed Japan's solitary condition for the acceptance of the Potsdam Proclamation. The condition had been written by Foreign Minister Togo, and it stated that the Potsdam Proclamation would be accepted if the Allies agreed to preserve *Kodo*, the Imperial Way. This would assure that the Emperor system would continue to prevail in Japan.

They had barely scanned the page when, to their consummate surprise, doors opened, and in what seemed like an intrusion, the small conference room began to be filled with others. The military chiefs looked about and saw the directors of the army and navy Military Affairs Bureaus. Then two generals from the Tokyo area entered the room, followed by the Chief of the Combined Planning Board, the President of the Privy Council, and the Cabinet Secretary.

Suzuki had pulled out all the stops in his attempt to outmaneuver the military and resolve the stalled proceedings. It was a bold, unprecedented move, and as he carefully studied the faces of Anami and Umezo, his mind flashed back to that cold day in February 1936 when the dissenting hot-bloods had appeared from behind bushes at his home and began pumping bullets into his body. He gave a slight shudder and looked about. The room was full, it was hot, and a hoard of savage mosquitoes swarmed around their heads. But this was an Imperial Conference, so the members of the council placed their hands on their knees and sat in impassive silence awaiting the arrival of the Emperor.

When Hirohito finally entered the room from behind the gold-framed folding screen at midnight, those at the tables scrambled to their feet. They bowed respectfully low, and when the Emperor had taken his seat on a small dais before them, Prime Minister Suzuki cleared his throat and began the meeting by reciting the details of the debates from the previous meetings of the Supreme Council for the Conduct of the War. Having set the stage, he tactfully called upon each of the members of The Big Six to make a statement.

It fell upon Foreign Minister Togo to speak first.

"It is both humiliating and terribly difficult for Japan to accept the Potsdam terms," he began in a self-possessed voice. "However, circumstances compel us to accept. The atomic bomb and Russia's participation in the war have suddenly changed the situation. Especially now that the Soviet Union has resorted to arms, negotiations for peace have been made impossible."

He paused and his eyes looked directly into those of the War Minister.

"I think it is better to present the Allies with one condition only, that of *kokutai*. We must ask that the national essence be maintained and that the maintenance and security of the Imperial family be guaranteed. That would make the terms of the Potsdam Proclamation acceptable."[50]

He sat down slowly and it was the turn of the Naval Minister

---

50 Lester Brooks, *Behind Japan's Surrender: The Secret Struggle that Ended an Empire*, McGraw-Hill, 1967 -World War,1939-1945, page77

to speak. Admiral Yonai had only a short statement to make:

"I agree with the Foreign Minister," he said quickly.

War Minister Anami was the next in line. He moved his chair back swiftly and stood up straight as a rod.

"I oppose the opinions I have heard," he said in a strained voice as he tried to maintain his temper. And then he suddenly lost it and launched into a tirade attacking the peacemakers and the doves whose minds, he said, were filled with fear and treachery. He went over his previous arguments in the meetings of The Big Six, and he pleaded again for an opportunity to stage one last decisive battle to save the Home Island and to preserve Japan and the destiny of her people. With tears coming to his eyes, and with his voice rising almost to a roar, he looked into the face of the Emperor and pleaded.

"I am quite sure we could inflict great casualties on the enemy, and even if we fail in our attempt, our one hundred million people are ready to die for the honor of glorifying the deeds of the Japanese race in recorded history. Indeed, our slogan 'One Hundred Million Die Together' is not just a phrase. It is taken literally by everyone. This is total war, involving every citizen. If we can give a great blow to the enemy, we can then settle for better terms."

Anami sat down and there was a long period of silence before Army Chief General Umezo got to his feet.

"I am of the same opinion as the War Minister," he said in a quiet, passive voice. "Although the Russian attack has made the situation unfavorable, we have made our preparations for the final battle and I do not think we need to abandon the opportunity to deliver one last blow to America and England. If we surrender now, it would be inexcusable to our thousands of dead heroes."[51]

His speech delivered, he sat down, but before Admiral Toyoda could rise to speak, a new voice was heard. The Privy Council President, Baron Hiranuma, stood and began to question General Umezo.

"Personally, I am very uneasy about these matters," he said. "I would like an explanation of the extent of air raid damage done on the homeland."

General Umezo stood again, his shaved head glistening with sweat. "Although it might be difficult to avert disaster from these special bombs totally, it might be checked to a certain degree if proper measures are taken. These bombs alone will not bring about the conclusion of the war. We will never surrender to the enemy because of air raids alone."[52]

Baron Hiranuma was a civilian and a constitutional lawyer. He had been summoned to attend the meeting by Suzuki, and his very presence in the room during an Imperial Conference was considered extraordinary. Convinced of their infallibility, the military listening to his words grew intensely resentful of Hiranuma's role as devil's advocate. Their belligerence only served to inspire Baron Hiranuma to ask more questions and demand less ambiguous replies concerning their plans and the extent of their defensive measures.

"It is of concern to me to know the precise number of planes in the air force, and in addition to that, the means you intend to employ them against the enemy's air attacks," Hiranuma told the general.

Umezo continued to sweat, and Hiranuma, a man with a reputation as an ultra-nationalistic patriot, was provoking him.

"Heretofore," Umezo replied wrathfully, "our air force has

---
51 Ibid, page 79
52 Ibid, page 82

been concentrated in readiness for the decisive battle of the homeland. When the enemy attempts to land, we expect to counter-attack using considerable strength," he fumed.[53]

The zealous Hiranuma pressed him again and again demanding facts, data, details, statistics. Finally, the Navy Chief Admiral Toyoda could take it no more. He had remained silent, but these attacks on a Japanese military officer by a civilian lawyer caused him to rise from his chair.

"The fighting spirit of Japan still prevails among the people," he said in a muted but caustic voice. "We are speaking of *seisen*, a holy war, and they wish a decisive battle. They are prepared for that."[54]

The old man, Suzuki, bent his head forward so that his weak ears could hear the Admiral's remark. Disheartened, he shook his head from side to side and was overcome with sadness. It had happened again: Toyoda, The Navy Chief of Staff, had reverted to speaking *haragei*. Did he mean to side with the generals, or was he simply making a statement to absolve himself of any role in a decision to stop fighting? Was he speaking for the people of Japan, or was he speaking for himself? It was difficult to know, and it was 2:00 in the morning and the room was stifling. There were no more trees in Tokyo to absorb the heat and generate fresh air.

Suzuki was exhausted, and what's more, he had no wish to listen again to the same old restated arguments. The time had come, he said to himself. Without waiting for Admiral Toyoda to elaborate his position, Prime Minister Suzuki got up from his chair and stepped forward to face the Emperor on the Imperial Throne.

The move was so unexpected, and it was such an

---
53 Ibid
54 Ibid, page 85

unprecedented breach of court etiquette, that everyone in the room gasped at Suzuki's effrontery.

"Mr. Prime Minister!" General Anami cried out.

If Suzuki heard the call, he gave no sign of it. He advanced to the foot of the Emperor's small podium as though completely beset by deafness. He bowed low, and when he straightened up he looked directly into Hirohito's face. When he spoke his thin body wavered and his voice sounded weary.

"Your Imperial decision is requested," he said.

Emperor Hirohito nodded slightly and lifted a gloved hand to motion Suzuki back to his chair. Then, very slowly, he got to his feet. Spellbound, those in the room watched the scene as though everything was happening in slow motion and then, almost as one, they remembered that their Emperor was standing before them and they quickly lowered their heads and bowed. Never in the recorded history of the Imperial throne had the Emperor been called upon to make an expression of his own will. Never before had he taken any part at these ritualistic meetings. And, apart from Suzuki, every man in the room felt a sense of impending disaster.

Emperor Hirohito was dressed in the uniform of the Marshal Commander of the Armed Forces, ill-fitting because no tailor was allowed to touch him to get a proper measurement. He wore white gloves and stood straight to the point of being stiff. At that moment he looked every bit the military chief as he gazed for several moments at the lowered heads of his officers and ministers. Then he began speaking, and his voice sounded strained and weak.[55]

"I will state my opinion," he began. "I agree with Foreign

---

55 Thomas B. Allen and Norman Polmar, *The Radio Broadcast That Ended World War II*, The Atlantic, Aug 7, 2015

Minister Togo. After serious consideration of the conditions facing Japan at home and abroad, I have concluded that to continue this war can mean only destruction for the homeland and more bloodshed and cruelty in the world."

Suddenly every man in the room was aware that their Emperor was weeping. Contagiously, the crying spread and the room was instantly filled with the sobbing sound of the weeping civilians and military officers. Slow, agonizingly slow, Hirohito went on speaking.

"I cannot bear to have my innocent people suffer further," he said through his tears. "Ending the war is the only way to restore world peace and relieve the nation from the terrible suffering it is undergoing."

His voice broke, but he went on. "Some advocate a decisive battle in the homeland as the way to survival. In past experience, however, there has always been a discrepancy between the fighting services' plans and the results achieved. If, in conditions such as these, Japan should be rushed into a decisive battle in the homeland, how could an enemy be repulsed? What would become of Japan? I do not want to see our people continue to suffer any longer. Moreover, I do not desire any further destruction of our culture, nor any additional misfortune for the people of the world."

Once again he paused and the sobs of the shaken leaders of the Empire were clearly audible. With a gloved hand, Hirohito reached up to brush tears from his cheeks.

"I am afraid that faced with a situation such as this, the Japanese people are doomed, one and all. But in order to hand the country of Japan to posterity, I want as many people as possible to survive this war and rise again in the future. I feel great pain when I think of all those who have served me so faithfully, and indeed, the disarmament of my brave and loyal military is excruciating to me. It is equally unbearable that those who have rendered me their devoted service during these years should be considered war criminals. However, for the sake of the country it cannot be helped. To relieve the people and to maintain the nation, we must bear the unbearable. When I recall the fortitude of my Imperial Grandfather, the Emperor Meiji, I swallow my own tears."[56]

Again he faltered and sobbed.

"If we continue the war, Japan will be totally annihilated. If even a small number of Japan's people's seed is allowed to remain, there is a glimmer of hope of an eventual Japanese recovery. For that, I am willing to go before the microphone. All of you, I think, will worry about me in this situation. But it does not matter what will become of me. Determined, as I have stated, I have decided to bring the war to an end immediately. For this reason, I agree with the Foreign Minister's proposal."[57]

That was it, the god-sent ruler of the Great Japanese Empire had made his decision. Twenty-six hundred years of tradition had been put aside in the longest official speech of his life, and when Hirohito sat down the seventy-eight-year old Suzuki rose slowly from his chair and looked across the table at the members of the Supreme Council for the Conduct of the War. To a man, they were bent over the table, their heads on their arms, unashamedly weeping.

An abrupt pain suddenly filled his chest and Suzuki cleared his throat. "The Imperial decision has been expressed," he said. "This conference is adjourned."

It was two-thirty in the morning of August 10th. Hirohito

---

[56] Lester Brooks, *Behind Japan's Surrender: The Secret Struggle that Ended an Empire*, McGraw-Hill, 1967 – World War,1939-1945, page 107-108
[57] Mutsuo Fukushima, *Generals Foiled Aug. 15 Palace Coup - Pair's Actions Credited with Ensuring Hirohito Surrender Decre*, Japan Times, History Article Aug 12, 2005

moved from sight behind the gold folding screen and the sobbing men at the tables wiped their eyes. They pushed back their chairs slowly, and with lowered heads they filed up the stairs. All too abruptly they were back in the real world under a black sky in their scorched and blackened capital.

At dawn, the people of Japan would awake to find that War Minister Anami had placed the nation under martial law, and the first newspapers of the day contained a statement from the general addressed to the army: "The only thing for us to do is to fight doggedly to the end, though it may mean chewing grass, eating dirt, and sleeping in the field."[58] His brother-in-law, Lieutenant Colonel Masahiko Takeshita, spent the morning urging Anami to lead a coup. Anami refused.

Far from Japan, on their final mission at sea, the crew of a lone Japanese submarine heard the sound of an approaching ship. Apart from the submarines in reserve for the *kamikaze* journey to drop plague bacterium on the coastal cities of southern California, the I-58 was one of the last in the once-impressive Japanese undersea fleet, and it was the only one still on duty at sea. As the captain listened to the throbbing engines of the approaching vessel he took his submarine up to periscope depth to have a brief look. He had no doubt it was an Allied vessel as there were no longer any Japanese ships in those waters. Recently outfitted with six of the *Kaiten* suicide torpedoes, the captain had received orders to return to the waters of Japan to participate in the final battle for the Home Islands. But Lieutenant Commander Mochitsura Hashimoto, a thirty-five-year-old son of a Shinto priest, had been taking his time, lingering at sea hoping for one

---

58 Thomas B. Allen and Norman Polmar, *The Radio Broadcast That Ended World War II*, Aug 7, 2015, The Atlantic

last opportunity to sink an enemy ship.

Now, hearing the pulsating sound of an approaching vessel stirred old feelings in the captain and he dimmed the interior lights to begin a slow and even ascent. The U.S. Navy had ruled the waters off Japan for two years, and to a man everyone in the submarine knew that they were involved in a risky action. But the thought of destroying one more enemy ship outweighed all thoughts of danger.

When the captain's periscope broke above the surface he found himself looking at a large naval ship moving toward him in a straight course taking none of the evasive maneuvers ships normally take while on the open seas. It was pitching in the waves, and in the light of a rising moon Hashimoto thought he was looking at a battleship. It was indeed on a leisurely voyage, and as far as the captain could tell it was sailing alone. Spinning his periscope around, he scoured the horizon to confirm that there were no other ships in the immediate vicinity. He felt his pulse rate increasing as he began calling out navigational instructions and gave notice to the *Kaiten* volunteers to prepare themselves for the transfer to their loaded torpedoes once he surfaced. Quickly donning their dress uniforms and slipping on ritualistic *hibachi* — headbands with words of encouragement inscribed, sometimes written in blood by family members and friends — they moved close to the hatch to await the surfacing of the submarine, each young man alone with his thoughts, each one gliding his fingers a final time over the thousand-stitch sash presented to him on his final visit home. Worn as a belt or wrapped around under his uniform, it was a strip of cloth three feet long and perhaps three inches wide covered with tiny needlework stitches in red thread, each one sewn there by a different person — his sisters, his mother, or by women in the marketplace, in the rail stations, on the bus, by passersby in the streets. They were Shinto tokens said to protect the wearer from harm. To soldiers in battle they were said to deflect enemy bullets. To *kamikaze* and *Kaiten* pilots, the *senninbari* imparted strength and gave them the luck to inflict the greatest possible damage upon the enemy.

As they waited, Commander Hashimoto stalked the course of the ship through the eye of his periscope, slowly making mental calculations concerning its speed and distance. Under the sea, every second seemed an hour, and every breath they took seemed strained and shallow. Then the voice of Hashimoto interrupted the silence. It had become clear that the *Kaiten* would not be necessary and he ordered the pilots to stand down. Still following the ship he waited for the most advantageous moment, and then gave the order: "Fire One... Fire three... Fire two..."

The I-58 shuddered as six projectiles rushed from the submarine and sped through the water at close to sixty miles per hour. Hashimoto held his breath. Moments later, three of the torpedoes slammed into the side of the speeding ship. A horrendous blast split the warship into two parts, followed by another blast so great it shook the submarine. The sky overhead burst alight with sparks and flame, and after a third explosion there was silence, and then total darkness. In a little less than twelve minutes the ship had vanished, and nine hundred sailors without lifejackets or lifeboats were thrashing for life in the shark-infested waters. It would be five days before the ship's survivors would be rescued. Of the 1,106 men aboard the ship, only 317 survived, and the incident would become known as the worst shark attack in U.S. naval history.[59]

If Commander Hashimoto was witness to any part of the frenzied scene on the surface, it would not have changed his course of action. Downing periscope, he took the I-58 far beneath

---

59 Alex Last, *USS Indianapolis sinking: 'You could see sharks circling'*, BBC World Service, 29 July 2013

the choppy surface of the sea and cut his engines. In silence, he listened for the sound of destroyers that might be approaching with depth charges. Time passed, and there was no sound to be heard apart from the ticking of his watch. Finally, he allowed a smile and ordered a restart of the engines. Immediately, there was a shout as his crew experienced a pitch of excitement and a sense of relief. Then, in silence, they faced Tokyo and bowed deeply. Later, having set course for the long journey home, Hashimoto went to his quarters to record the time, the date, and the sinking in his log book, noting that he believed the vessel to have been a battleship.

What the captain and his crew did not know was that the ship they sent to the bottom of the Pacific was the *U.S.S. Indianapolis*, a cruiser, not a battleship, and it was the last ship to be sunk by a Japanese submarine. The *Indianapolis* had just performed one of the most secret missions of the entire war: it had been to Tinian Island delivering uranium and the components for the atomic bombs that were dropped on Hiroshima and Nagasaki. When the I-58 found it, it was under orders to go to the Leyte Gulf in the Philippines to prepare for the invasion of Japan.

And what only a few people in the military and in Washington knew, and least of all what no one in Tokyo knew, was that the elements that the *U.S.S. Indianapolis* had delivered to the U.S. Air Force on Tinian represented the only atomic bomb material immediately available. Apart from two bombs code-named Little Boy and Fat Man, the United States had no other bombs in its nuclear arsenal.

In Tokyo, however, the imperial decision had been made, and presumably the long war would be over. Yet it would be another five days before the people of Japan would even learn of their

Emperor's decision to surrender.

In the meanwhile, Suzuki's worst fears were realized. Immediately after the conclusion of the Imperial Conference in the early hours of August 10th, the military was plunged into a state of semi-organized rebellion. *Gekokuju*, the act of legitimized military insubordination, was planned by men from every branch of the military services and Prime Minister Suzuki, Foreign Minister Togo, and anyone else who had openly expressed doubts about continuing the war, went into hiding.

Naval ships moved into Tokyo Bay, took up positions, and waited for orders to begin shelling Tokyo. The general of the Imperial Guards was murdered when he refused to join the revolt and allow the rebels access to the Imperial Palace. Airmen and pilots of the Special Attack Squadrons, the *kamikaze*, put what gasoline they could find into the tanks of their planes and waited in a state of readiness at nearby airfields. They were under orders from their squadron commanders to attack anyone who attempted to hinder the efforts of the tigers who were about to take over Japan. Firmly convinced that the Emperor had been ill-advised by the doves and had been betrayed, they spread the word that the Emperor had suffered a mental relapse brought about by the pressures of the war, and that the traitors Suzuki and Togo and a number of civilians had taken advantage of his weakened condition to force their will upon him.

Then, on the 14th of August, and in one of the most daring acts of *gekokujo* ever committed by disenchanted or impetuous military rebels, using forged documents they had forced their officers to sign at gunpoint, the hotheads, believing themselves to be the new samurai, betrayed the Imperial Guard, murdered its officers and moved one thousand troops into the Imperial Palace. They heard a rumor that the Emperor had made a recording in which he would proclaim Japan's surrender. It was said to be on a resin disk about to be played over the radio to the people of Japan, and in a frenzy fifty soldiers entered the Imperial Household Ministry and went from room to room kicking in doors and overturning desks and furniture searching for it. Failing to locate it, they sent a squad of soldiers to the offices of NHK, the Japanese broadcasting studios where the offices were nearly wrecked in the search that followed.

The previous evening, NHK was told to report that an important announcement would be made at noon the following day, and radio technicians were called to the palace with their recording equipment. When they arrived they were taken to the audience hall of the Household Ministry building to await Hirohito. He arrived at 11:00 p.m., and looking somewhat dazed he was directed to a microphone. "How loudly should I speak?" he asked, and a nervous engineer suggested he speak in his normal voice. After reading his prepared statement, the engineer stepped forward. "There were no technical errors, but a few words were not entirely clear," he stammered.

Stepping up to the microphone again, the Emperor read the rescript a second time, and before he was done his eyes were filled with tears. Soon everyone in the room was crying. Though only four-and-a-half minutes long, the speech had to be 'cut' on two separate records. The first set was thought to be the best, but the engineers put both sets in two metal cases and then in khaki bags, and, having heard rumors of army mutineers staging a coup, they spent a fearful night in the palace. The bags with the records were put in a safe in one of the offices, then hidden beneath a pile of papers.

In the early hours of the 15th, a group of renegade soldiers with bayonets fixed to their rifles located the engineers and imprisoned them in a barracks. They forced one of the engineers to lead them on a search for the recording. Unfamiliar with the palace, he led them on a journey up and down corridors and into and out of offices, all of which were left in a shambles by the soldiers. Unbeknown to them, the Emperor was watching the proceedings through a peek hole in the metal shutters over his windows.

Empty-handed after hours of searching, the mutineers left the palace grounds. Figuring it was safe to come out, the NHK engineers divided the two sets of recordings and, in two cars travelling by two different routes, they delivered the surrender message to the broadcasting studio.

It wasn't until five days after the seizing of the palace that a group of generals loyal to the throne could mobilize their forces in sufficient strength to secure it. In the interim, the Emperor had been in hiding, waiting it out in his underground 'Library'. When a semblance of order was finally restored in Tokyo, the zealots, for whom the word 'surrender' did not exist, had fought their final battle. The disks they had been searching for, the *Gyokuonhoso* – the Jewel Voice Broadcast – were played on airwaves across the nation, though because the Emperor was speaking in classical Japanese, not everyone hearing it understood what he was saying. Furthermore, he didn't speak of surrender; he spoke of accepting the terms of the Potsdam Declaration. Most, however, were able to gather the meaning of the speech from the title given to the special broadcast: The Imperial Rescript On The Termination Of The War. In a weak and trembling voice, the Showa Emperor had praised his subjects for their bravery, spoken of his personal distress and told everyone to remain calm. He concluded by saying it was painful to think of their past and present sacrifices and called upon everyone to cooperate with the American occupation forces. Everywhere, people began weeping, realizing that Japan had been defeated. It was as though the heart of the nation had stopped beating.

Until that moment, Japan's China Expeditionary Army had won every battle it had fought. With a strength of 1.05 million men, during eight years of war, an estimated 15-20 million Chinese had died (3-4% of China's entire population) including 3.2 million Chinese soldiers. More than half of China was under Japanese occupation, and the Japanese Army seemed unstoppable. To General Yasuji Okamura, the Army's commander, the order to surrender "came like a bolt of lightning from out of the blue."

"So when it came to the order of surrender, we still had the fighting strength to defeat our enemy and we were put in a very awkward position indeed. Our country had surrendered, so we had no choice but to surrender. The frontline troops weren't able to listen to the Emperor's entire August 15 broadcast, and I heard that many of them thought the Imperial Edict was just an exhortation to fight even harder."[60]

Fortunately, the entire army obeyed the Emperor and laid down its arms.

Suzuki, who had changed hiding places seven times in five days, now wondered if it was safe for him to come out of hiding and resume his official duties, duties which would now include making preparations for the surrender. As it turned out, it didn't matter for he was told his services to the nation had been rendered in full, and he immediately returned to his books and faded from public view.

Far to the south, codebreakers at Admiral Louis Mountbatten's

---

[60] Han Lianchao, *The U.S. Was the True Mainstay in the Fight Against Japan in World War II*, translated by China Change. Chinafile, September 3, 2015

headquarters in northern Burma had been picking up distressing information regarding Field Marshal Count Terauchi's determination to continue the war. He was sending instructions to his officers to create mass destruction before taking their troops into the jungles to fight a hundred-year guerrilla war. When the information was forwarded to General MacArthur, he sent a stinging message to Tokyo telling them to have Terauchi stopped.

Acting immediately, the Emperor arranged for his cousin, Prince Kan-in Kotohito, to fly in secret to Saigon to convince Count Terauchi to lay down his arms and accept the terms of surrender. Guaranteed safe passage by MacArthur, the Prince set out in an ancient bomber that was so tattered there were serious concerns about the plane being able to reach its destination. Terauchi might have wished it didn't, and though he raged because he was not to be permitted to continue the war so he and his soldiers could die honorable deaths, he finally ordered the 680,000 men in the Southern Region Army Command to lay down their arms. And then he suffered a heart attack. Mountbatten thought Terauchi's heart attack was feigned and sent an Allied team to Saigon to have Terauchi arrested and dragged to the surrender ceremony in Singapore. The team reported back that Terauchi's attack was genuine and that he was indeed hospitalized. In his stead, Singapore's commanding general, General Seishiro Itagaki, met the British to put his signature to a document of surrender.

Meanwhile, a war of another kind was burning inside Japan. On the 17th, 18th and 19th of August the mop-up of rebel stronghold units was continuing. A group of four hundred soldiers who had taken over Ueno Park in the center of Tokyo agreed to surrender, but they only acquiesced after their leaders had committed suicide. Nearby, on the summit of Atago Hill, a fanatical group of patriots armed with pistols, swords and hand grenades held off the police for another week before finally joining hands in solidarity and pulling the pins from their grenades to blow themselves to bits.

In virtually every part of the nation, similar acts of *gekokuju* continued, and in his headquarters General Anami, who had steadfastly refused to join the revolt, lay down a ritual *seppuku* mat in the corridor outside his office, opened an ornamental case with a ceremonial sword, and plunged it into his belly to rip open his stomach. Then, faithful to samurai tradition, he thrust the sword into his throat.[61]

Elsewhere in Tokyo, Admiral Takijiro Onishi, the naval officer who worked with the British traitor Lord Sempill in the development of the Imperial Japanese Naval Air Service, apologized for the deaths of 5,000 pilots before drawing his samurai sword across his belly and bleeding to death. Known as the father of the *kamikaze*, his plea to sacrifice 20 million more lives to achieve victory had fallen on deaf ears.

Throughout Japan, officers with trusted airplane mechanics were dispatched to air bases to remove the propellers from all the airplanes so that none of the dedicated *kamikaze* pilots could carry out their threats to dive their planes into the forthcoming surrender ceremonies. At the same time, throughout the countryside posters that had appeared on walls and telephone poles reading KILL SUZUKI, KILL KIDO, and KILL TOGO were being pulled down. And while they were being destroyed, hundreds of officers from every branch of the military services performed their final act of allegiance to their Emperor by following General Anami and Admiral Onishi's example and

---

61   There are at least two descriptions of Anami's suicide (1) Gideon Rose: *How Wars End: Why We Always Fight The Last Battle*, page 92; (2) *The Pacific War Online Encyclopedia*: "His self-inflicted wounds were not immediately fatal, and after three hours a staff officer ordered a military physician to give Anami a lethal injection to end his death struggle."

committing *harakiri*.[62]

On the morning of 2 September 1945, a new Foreign Minister, Mamoru Shigemitsu, and the old Army Chief of Staff, General Yoshijiro Umezu, walked onto the deck of the United States battleship Missouri in Tokyo Bay to put their names to a document of surrender. At the nearby Atsugi Airbase, *kamikaze* pilots hunted in frenzy for the missing propellers for their ancient warplanes. They failed to find them, and after eight years, one month and three days, the war that Japan started on July 7, 1937 at *Lugou qiao*, the Marco Polo Bridge near Peking, was over.

There is no doubt in the minds of Allied and Japanese intelligence sources that if the war had been carried to the Home Islands of Japan, the Japanese defense plan utilizing the *kamikaze* Special Attack Group would have increased the number of Allied dead and wounded by at least five to seven times and the war would have continued for another fifteen to eighteen months. Japan would have been a destroyed nation, and an estimated five to seven million Japanese would have died, either in the fighting or from starvation and illness. In General Terauchi's Southern Command, the order to kill all civilian internees and prisoners of war would have been implemented, and the native people in the areas occupied by his army would have suffered to an extent beyond measure. And the war in China would have continued.

While we know approximately how many people died at Hiroshima and Nagasaki, there is no way of knowing the number of lives that might have been lost had General Ishii's bacteria bombs been dropped on San Diego and Los Angeles. Nor is it known how close scientists in Japan were to having their own

---

62 The Sydney Morning Herald (NSW: 1842 - 1954), *Fanatics Commit Hara-kiri*, page 1, Aug 29, 1945

atomic bombs, bombs they could have dropped on Honolulu, Seattle, San Francisco and Los Angeles.

In 1939, the same year President Roosevelt gave American scientists the go-ahead to look into the building of an atomic weapon, Japan had initiated two similar projects, the N-Go Program by the army and the F-Go Program by the navy. The navy lost interest in its program in 1943 after a Committee on the Research in the Application of Nuclear Physics concluded that "it would probably be difficult even for the United States to realize the application of atomic power during the war." The army, however, continued its program, and after searching for uranium ore in Korea, China and Burma and finding none, it requested uranium from Germany. Germany obliged by sending 1,230 pounds (560 kilograms) of unprocessed uranium oxide to Japan aboard the submarine U-234. While at sea, Germany surrendered, and the U-234 surfaced off Newfoundland in the Atlantic Ocean to surrender to the US Navy. There were twelve notable passengers on board, including a high-ranking German *Luftwaffe* general, four German naval officers, a group of civilian scientists and engineers, the general manager of production of the world's first operational jet fighter, the Messerschmitt Me 262, who was to supervise the production of a new Japanese jet fighter, and a German Naval Fleet Judge Advocate who was journeying to Tokyo to open a probe into the German diplomatic corps following the exposure there of Stalin's spy, Richard Sorge. In addition, there were two Japanese naval officers aboard accompanying the uranium oxide. When told the submarine was going to surrender, they took an overdose of barbiturates and committed suicide.

At war's end, Japanese troops moving out of China left behind 700,000 unused germ bombs that had been destined for use on the cities and villages of China.[63] In defense of the Home Islands, the army could have used those bombs against the Americans. Possibly twenty million people had already died in China since the Japanese invasion in 1937, over a million people in the Philippines; one and a half million in Indochina; four-plus millions in the Dutch East Indies, one hundred thousand people in Malaya, Borneo and Sarawak; and somewhere between twenty-five to fifty thousand people in Hong Kong and Singapore. One life, one hundred thousand lives, even ten or twenty million lives—numbers had never mattered much to the Emperor or his generals. *Tennozan*, the great victory, was the only thing that weighed on their minds.

All projections aside, *Operation Downfall*, the code name for the planned invasion of Japan, was to commence on November 1. It was to consist of two landings, the first, *Olympic*, would target the beaches of Kyushu—precisely where the Japanese expected the invasion to take place, and where they had spent almost a year making preparations for it. The second, *Coronet*, was scheduled for March 1, 1946 on the Kantō Plain near Tokyo. The first operation would have put 14 US divisions—550,000 troops—ashore. Because the B-29s and other bombers had been meeting little or no opposition in the skies over Japan, US intelligence concluded that the Japanese had only 2,500 functional airplanes available in the Home Islands and Korea, but as they were critically short of fuel it was supposed only 300 planes would take to the air to oppose them. A careful analysis of aerial photographs of the *Olympic* site showed signs of troop concentrations and of new ground construction. But a lesson had been learned from the battle for Okinawa in April, an island 330

---

63   Nicholas D. Kristof, *Unmasking Horror -- A special report: Japan Confronting Gruesome War Atrocity*, The New York Times, March 17, 1995

miles (550 kilometers) from the main Japanese islands, where every civilian—old, young, men, women, boys, girls—rose up to oppose them, many with only bamboo staves and makeshift weapons.[64] There were cases of women and elderly citizens dying while attacking armed soldiers with nothing more than a broken bottle. The Okinawa battle had seen fighting of a ferocity never before experienced, and in 82 days it had cost the United States 82,000 causalities. The Army and Marine Corps counted 12,500 dead, 768 aircraft were lost, 225 tanks destroyed, and 368 Allied ships sunk—including between 36 to 42 from *kamikaze* attacks—killing 4,907 sailors and wounding 4,874 others. Two generals, the highest ranking officers to be killed in action since the American Civil War, were killed by artillery and machine gun fire. The Marine Corps Gazette made note that U.S. casualties included thousands of cases of mental breakdown.

On the Japanese side, the Okinawa battle they called *tetsu no bōfū* (Typhoon of Steel) had cost them approximately 110,071 soldiers, 16 ships—including the super battleship *Yamato* that had sailed to Okinawa on a one-way suicide mission—roughly 1,430 planes, and 27 tanks. Many of the civilian population, told that the US invaders were murderous barbarians, fought and died alongside the military. In the end, as many as one hundred thousand civilians, or roughly a third of the entire population of the island, died. A peace memorial on the island today contains 240,734 names.

Filing a report on the battle, *New York Times* reporter W. H. Lawrence wrote, "Stated in its simplest terms, we were able to announce the victory of Okinawa because the enemy had run out of caves and boulders from which to fight and we were nearly

---

64   Ben Hills, *The Emperor's Day of Reckoning: The Himeyuri girls. How Hirohito killed his children and why his son feared to visit Okinawa*. Sydney Morning, Herald, April, 17 1993, page 43

out of Japanese to kill."

With the fall of Okinawa, General Douglas MacArthur turned his attention to the invasion plans for Japan itself and his projections indicated it was going to cost the US more than one million casualties by the end of 1945. The US Sixth Army Command which was to carry out the major fighting on Kyushu estimated a figure of 394,859 casualties in the first 120 days. In Washington, the Secretary of War's planning staff submitted its projections for the defeat of Japan: it was going to cost five to ten million lives and 1.7 - 4 million American casualties, including 400,000 - 800,000 fatalities.

Accordingly, the War Department ordered the immediate manufacture of 500,000 Purple Heart medals, a medal routinely awarded to combat casualties.[65]

Using a combination of cunning guesswork and accurate military intelligence, in early 1945 the Japanese High Command had determined not only where the Americans would land, but when. Consequently they advanced plans to make preparations, and rather than facing an army of ill-trained conscripts the Americans would have found themselves pitted against an elite army composed of 790,000 fanatical defenders backed up by seven mixed brigades, three tank groups, and thousands of sailors in naval brigades, many of them living underground and in deep bunkers with hospitals and command posts connected by miles and miles of tunnels with dozens of entrances and exits. The air

---

65 During World War II, nearly 500,000 Purple Heart medals were manufactured in anticipation of the estimated casualties resulting from the planned Allied invasion of Japan. To the present date, total combined American military casualties of the seventy years following the end of World War II — including the Korean and Vietnam Wars — have not exceeded that number. In 2003, there remained 120,000 Purple Heart medals in stock. The existing surplus allowed combat units in Iraq and Afghanistan to keep Purple Hearts on-hand for immediate award to soldiers wounded in the field.

force, which had been conserving planes, fuel and pilots for this final battle, had secreted away 12,725 planes in 35 camouflaged air bases and nine seaplane bases. Disassembled planes were hidden in basements, in garages, and underground. There were an additional 58 concealed airfields in Korea and throughout the main Japanese island of Honshu, plus 20 suicide takeoff strips on Kyushu where the plan was to strike the invasion fleet while it was still 180 miles (290 kilometers) offshore. American intelligence expected 300 *kamikaze* planes in the assault. The Japanese were preparing to send 2,000 in one wave, followed by a second wave of 330 naval combat planes to attack naval warships, followed by a third wave of 825 suicide planes that would single out the troop transports. As the invasion fleet moved closer, 200 to 300 suicide planes were to be launched each hour the first, second, and third days. They hoped to continue such attacks non-stop for ten days. The chief weakness was that they lacked *kamikaze* pilots. There were 8,000 trained ones on standby and they were scrambling to fill the ranks with raw volunteers.

Once the fleet anchored and landing craft began transporting troops to shore, five aircraft carriers, 23 destroyers and 46 submarines would have been in the nearby waters waiting. From that point on, the invasion force would have been under attack from the Crouching Dragon frogmen, 2,142 Sea Quake speedboats, 393 *Kaiten* submarines, a literal swarm of Heaven Shaker rockets, hundreds of additional *kamikaze* airplanes flown over from Korea, a sea of two-man submarines, the Cherry Blossoms At Night germ bombs, the possible release of poison gas, and a fanatical Japanese civilian population armed with axes, clubs and bamboo spears. As part of an official program introduced in early 1943, those who were wounded or unable to attack were to commit suicide. The strategy was called *Gyokusai* – meaning "The Shattering of the Jewels". The tactic had been initiated during the battle of Tarawa in November 1943, after which only 17 soldiers of 4,600 were still alive. In the battle of Biak in May 1944, 520 of 10,000 survived. Closer to the Home Islands, in the battle of Saipan in June-July 1944, of a force of 28,000 only 921 remained alive. After Okinawa where virtually the entire male population was conscripted and boys as young as fourteen were forced into uniform, of the 120,971 defenders only 10,801 men and boys were captured or surrendered.

The United States planned to commit 40 percent of its uniformed service personnel to *Operation Downfall* – but at what cost? The year before in *Operation Overlord* – the Normandy invasion of German-occupied Europe – the 156,000 troops that went ashore on the beaches of France had far outnumbered the German defenders and it had cost the Allies 37,000 dead among the ground forces and a further 16,714 deaths in the Allied air forces. Kyushu would have been different: once ashore, the Americans would have been outnumbered 3 - 2, and the bloodshed could well have continued for at least fifteen to eighteen months. Or it could have failed altogether.

If the War Department had known what was awaiting them on the beaches of Japan, they might have considered revising their figures for Purple Hearts sharply upward.

In retrospect, the number of lives lost at Hiroshima and Nagasaki must be thought of as small in comparison to the number of lives that would have been lost if the war had been allowed to continue. And that's the tragedy. From the time of the military takeover in Japan there was one man who could have called out to stop it, but he didn't. Despite Japan's quick victories in the early months of the war, it had become increasingly apparent that it was a war Japan was not going to win.

ASIA BETRAYED

As far back as February 1942, Marquis Koichi Kido, Lord Keeper of the Privy Seal, had realized that American preponderance over Japan must in the end be the deciding factor, and he had secretly advised the Emperor "to grasp any opportunity to bring about the earliest possible termination of the war." Others, as the war wore on, came to the same dangerous conclusion—dangerous, because the Army did not share it.[66]

Had the Emperor called for an end to hostilities in late 1943, untold millions of lives on all sides would have been saved. The United States navy had grown overwhelmingly powerful, and Japan had lost most of its navy. With no ability to protect or supply its far-flung outposts, the millions of young men who had been transported there had no hope of return. And because surrender had never been an option, they had been sent there to die. Thousands upon thousands of them. His Majesty's *Shattered Jewels*.

In history, it has repeatedly been one man standing apart— Caesar, Napoleon, Stalin, Franco, Mussolini, Hitler, Mao, Chiang Kai-shek, Pol Pot—one man determining the destiny of a people. The man of the moment in Japan was Hirohito. It was he who decided who lived and who died while promoting a morbid, obsessive culture of death throughout the entire nation, promising *katsu* and *tennozan* (victory) as crowds waved flags and cheered young high school students marching off to war blissfully singing "Come home to death, we do not expect to return alive."

There was no one to cry STOP! No one. And nothing. Until Nagasaki.

---

66 Kazutoshi Hando, The Pacific War Research Society, Japan's Longest Day (Tokyo: Kodansha International, Ltd., 1968), pp.11-53

JOHN BELL SMITHBACK

EPILOGUE

"What don't you force mortal hearts to do, accursed hunger for gold!"
From Virgil, Aeneid 3,57, quoted by Seneca as
'quod non mortalia pectora coges, auri sacra fames'

It is January 30, 1965, and outside my home in Pacific Grove, California, I notice a small woman moving back and forth with uncertainty. She studies my house, bends forward to read the address, then moves on. I turn on my television and find there is wall-to-wall coverage of Winston Churchill's funeral in London. A barge with his coffin is moving slowly up the Thames past Tower Bridge and the event is being described as one of the most moving tributes in modern history.

My doorbell rings and I open the door to find a frail and bewildered woman standing there. She's the same one I'd seen earlier, and she says she's visiting from England. She's lost, she exclaims, and can't find the house of her family. I ask for the address and assure her the house that she is looking for is nearby, just around the corner and down the block. She is obviously exhausted so I invite her in, offering her a cup of tea and a chance to rest.

"Winston Churchill's funeral is on television, live and direct from London," I say. "Come in and watch, and then I'll drive you home."

She stiffens and makes a disagreeable face. "Young man," she scowls, "those of us who lived through the horrible days of the war owe everything to that great man. We stood alone, and his speech about fighting the Germans on the beaches strengthened us and led us through those terrible times. Even now, I can remember listening to his words on the wireless, and no thank you, I will not come in. I wouldn't think of watching Sir Winston Churchill's funeral on American television!"

Such determination... and so wrong. It was not Churchill's voice she remembered hearing on her radio. That particular speech about fighting the Germans on the beaches was delivered by a BBC newsreader giving an extract of a speech Churchill presented in the House of Commons, and the words themselves were borrowed in part from a speech given by Georges Clemenceau in Paris in 1918 that Churchill attended: "I will fight the Germans in front of Paris, I will fight the Germans in Paris, and I will fight the Germans behind Paris..."

In fact, few of Churchill's speeches were broadcast during World War II, although his "finest hour" speech on June 18, 1940 was. The speeches were delivered in the House of Commons to members of Parliament, and it wasn't until nine years after the war that Churchill, sensing the historical, political, and financial gain to be had, visited a studio to record them for posterity.

This wasn't the first time he had the public believing what Winston Churchill wanted it to believe, and he could very well have been characterizing himself when he described Russia as a riddle wrapped in a mystery inside an enigma.

Born to an aristocratic family in 1874, he was nearing thirty years of age and in Parliament when Queen Victoria died. On the first of January 1886, she was presented with the nation of

Burma as a New Year's gift by Winston's father, Lord Randolph Churchill, the Secretary of State for India. Lord Randolph has been described as a man totally driven by an imperial turn of mind. Though most ordinary citizens in Britain had no idea where Burma was, they rejoiced on hearing of the New Year's gift, taken in by what has been described as the "religion of Empire", an attitude Lord Randolph's son Winston absorbed as second nature. His dogged determination to reclaim by hook, crook or deceit every last centimeter of British colonial soil taken away by the Japanese during the war had its genesis in the era of his father, and in many respects he, too, remained a man of that time. That was often apparent as, for instance, during the development of radar, the single most indispensable technology in Britain's air defense. Churchill initially belittled its importance in favor of a bizarre scheme to scatter aerial mines across the sky over England, a fantasy straight out of the pages of H.G. Wells.

Yet it was Winston Churchill who, nearly alone in the early years of the Nazis, recognized Hitler as "a mainspring of evil" intent on taking Europe into another war, writing that the Third Reich represented an "unprecedented cult of malignancy". Surrounded on every side and on every level of British society and government by naysayers, fascist sympathizers and political compromisers, he kept resistance to Nazi malevolence alive, calling upon his government to obstruct the Third Reich.

"Stop it! Stop it! Stop it now!" he said. "Hitler constitutes the greatest danger for the British Empire!"

His warnings fell on deaf ears as his fellow conservatives, mocking him for his Victorian pomposity and criticizing his melodramatics, gave full support to Prime Minister Neville Chamberlain's efforts to appease Adolf Hitler.

Having previously created a close relationship with US

President Franklin D. Roosevelt, Churchill turned to him to secure vital aid through the Lend Lease Act which allowed Britain to order war goods from the United States on credit. Apart from that, however, the strong isolationist mood that prevailed in the United States tied Roosevelt's hands and prevented him from offering Churchill more than moral support and a number of obsolete destroyers. Americans wanted no part in another European war.

Later, when German bombs began falling on England, the Luftwaffe intentionally avoided London, leading Churchill to stand in the back garden at Number 10 Downing Street shouting up at the sky, "Why don't you come here? Bomb us, bomb us!" He understood that only a devastated London was going to gain America's sympathy and convince it to come to Britain's rescue. Without it, he knew that England would be lost.

The war that began on the first of September 1939 was by that point in its eighth month. In five weeks, the German *blitz* had overrun Poland and occupied Denmark, Norway and Belgium. Then the momentum abruptly stopped. It appeared that Hitler was waiting. But for what? As the days dragged on, people began calling it "the Phony War," but Churchill knew better. He had been in the Prime Minister's residence only eight days but he understood Hitler enough to know that this was just the beginning, that the man in Berlin was an apocalyptic dreamer set on total war. It wouldn't be long before he had the island nation in his sights. From his previous position as First Lord of the Admiralty, Churchill knew exactly what England would be up against and how inadequate her military defenses were. With the battle for Britain about to commence, it was his duty as First Minister to do everything possible to defend it and to save it. But how?

JOHN BELL SMITHBACK

As he lathered his face in the bathroom and began to shave, his son Randolph appeared at the half-open door. Churchill paused for a moment, then turned to his son.

"I think I see my way through," he said.

It was the morning of May 18, 1940 and the miraculous evacuation of the British Expeditionary Force from Dunkirk was seven days away.

"Do you mean that we can avoid defeat?" Randolph asked. Winston Churchill picked up his razor and studied his face in the mirror.

"Of course I mean we can beat them," he replied. "I shall drag the United States in."[67]

To accomplish that he would need an astonishing amount of luck, a Scottish Lord, a slow-moving steamship and the collaboration of the Japanese. In return, he would lose Asia and bring about the eventual fall of the British Empire. But in the end, Winston Churchill would prevail. He would defeat Hitler, free Europe and save England.

While the calculatedly slow release of official papers of the British government has helped historians and journalists write Winston Churchill down in many respects, little has been written about the two acts of calculated deception that facilitated Japanese imperial aggressions in the Far East, a stratagem designed to drag the United States into World War II and give Franklin Roosevelt the justification needed to overcome domestic resistance and join England's war. The first involved William Francis Forbes-Sempill, the 19th Baronet of Craigievar, AFC, AFRAeS, who became a spy for Japan. A hereditary member of the British House of Lords, he had been a decorated pilot in World War I and

---

[67] Martin Gilbert, *Churchill And America*, page183

also flew with the Royal Navy Air Service. In 1921 the Imperial Japanese Navy sought England's help in setting up its nascent naval air service. For some time the navy disregarded Japan's request, but in the hope of negotiating some lucrative arms deals the British Admiralty relented and appointed Sempill to lead the government's advisory delegation to Tokyo.

When he left for Japan, Sempill carried with him the plans for two new British aircraft carriers, the *HMS Argus* and the *HMS Hermes*, and he proceeded to convince the Japanese of the advantage of basing naval warplanes on ocean-going carriers instead of on airfields. His suggestions were immediately acted upon, and Sempill remained in Japan for 18 months training pilots in techniques of flight control and shallow-water torpedo bombing, skills that twenty years later the Japanese Empire were to employ to disastrous advantage in attacking the United States fleet at Pearl Harbor.

Acknowledging Sempill's "epoch-making service" to the Empire, Prime Minister Tomosaburo Kato awarded the Scottish lord Japan's highest honor, the Order of the Rising Sun, "for his especially meritorious military service". Sempill returned the favor, and for the next two decades he was handsomely paid to provide the Japanese with secret information on the latest British aviation technology, helping Japan become a world-class naval power. It was only when Franklin Roosevelt's administration raised concerns about Japan's growing naval strength that the British government questioned Sempill about leaking secrets to Tokyo. A resulting investigation revealed that Sempill was an active member of several far-right anti-Semitic organizations in England, including the fascistic Anglo-German Fellowship, a secretive group dedicated to ridding the Tory Party of Jews.

Sempill wasn't the only member of England's establishment elite at that time to embrace fascist ideology. The most famous, Sir Oswald Mosley, the 6th Baronet of Ascoats, founded the British Union of Fascists and its activities received positive press from London's *Daily Mirror* newspaper owned by the third richest man in England, Lord Rothermere, a Viscount. At the time of Hitler's rise to power in Germany, Mosley's organization was attracting dozens of viscounts and dukes, earls and barons, and a wide assortment of Lords and Ladies of the realm sympathetic to fascism and opposed to the rising Labour Party. Years later it would be revealed that Rothermere had been carrying on a correspondence with 'Adolf the Great,' and had congratulated him for the annexation of Czechoslovakia. Describing his work as 'great and superhuman', he encouraged him to invade Romania.[68]

Even the Royal House of Windsor — formerly the German House of Saxe-Coburg and Gotha — contained ardent supporters of Hitler's cause. Until being forced to renounce the throne "for the woman I love", Edward VIII, later Duke of Windsor, maintained such friendly relations with the Nazis that Albert Speer, Hitler's arms minister, lamented the abdication: "I am certain that through him, permanent friendly relations could have been achieved. If he had stayed, everything would have been different. His abdication was a severe loss for us."

One year after the outbreak of World War II, the disgraced Duke of Windsor and his American wife were living in neutral Portugal where they met with Hitler's representatives to negotiate a Nazi-sponsored return to the British throne upon Germany's defeat of England. The twice-divorced Duchess stated that she would become Queen of England "at any price".

---

[68] Neil Tweedie and Peter Day, *When Rothermere urged Hitler to invade Romania*, The Telegraph UK, Mar 1, 2005

In Britain, the appeasement policy of Prime Minister Neville Chamberlain had been quietly encouraged by members of the House of Windsor who feared that Britain's involvement in the war would spell the loss of its colonial empire. When the Duke of Windsor's brother became King George VI, The Queen was heard saying she would be happy enough if the Nazis invaded — "as long as they kept the royal family."

Recently discovered photographs of the time show the King and Queen in the palace garden teaching their two young daughters, Princess Margaret and the present Queen Elizabeth, how to perfect the Nazi salute.

For a time, neighboring Norway entertained hopes that an arrangement with Hitler to remain neutral would keep the Nazis at bay and the monarchy intact. But when Norwegian royalty and the entire Norwegian cabinet suddenly showed up on England's shores as refugees, barely escaping the Nazi occupation, Neville Chamberlain finally submitted his resignation to Buckingham Palace. The date was May 10, 1940, and at the pleasure of the King of England, the First Lord of the Admiralty Winston Spencer Churchill was instated as Prime Minister of Britain.

As Churchill prepared to move into No. 10 Downing Street he was handed a document from the war government's new Bletchley Park Code and Deciphering Unit. The report showed that Sempill was still receiving payments, funneled through the Mitsubishi Corporation, to spy for the government of Japan from his position in the Admiralty Office. For reasons of his own, the new Prime Minister chose to ignore the evidence and Sempill kept his post at Admiralty where he continued to have unlimited access to sensitive information about military maneuvers, military hardware and official secrets. Though nearly all of the intelligence files on Sempill's subsequent activities have mysteriously disappeared, surviving records show that he traveled with Churchill to meet with President Franklin Roosevelt at the Atlantic Conference held in Newfoundland in August of 1941. Four months earlier, a Gallop Poll indicated that three-quarters of Americans would support joining England's war — but only if they believed there was no other way to defeat Germany. Bolstered by the poll, Roosevelt sent his close friend and special advisor Harry Hopkins to deliver a private message to Winston Churchill in London declaring that the United States had every intention of *"carrying you through"*.

At the Atlantic Conference, however, Roosevelt reminded Churchill that the 1937 Neutrality Act enacted by the U.S. Congress prevented direct intervention, and that the strong isolationist element in Washington still tied his hands. The America First Committee, the conservative anti-war movement formed in 1919 soon after the end of World War I, persuaded many citizens that enough American blood had already been shed in Europe, and the sentiment was shared by isolation-minded progressives within the President's own party. Many of them were isolationists who expressed disappointment that Europe was "acting so tribal" and seemed unable to attend to its own affairs.

A Republican senator, Robert Taft, the son of a former president, spelled it out bluntly: "Even the collapse of England is to be preferred to the participation for the rest of our lives in European wars. If we enter the war today to save England, we will be involved in her wars the rest of our lives."

It's possible that he and a number of other senators had no knowledge of the extent of the covert deal struck between Roosevelt and Churchill whereby the United States, during that period of neutrality, was providing Britain with clandestine naval assistance. On assuming office, and with the Suez Canal under threat from the Italian army advancing through Libya, Churchill, former First Lord of the Admiralty, addressed a message to Roosevelt, former Assistant Secretary of the Navy, "from one naval person to another" appealing for ships and a naval escort to convoy troops to Egypt. In June, Roosevelt obliged by pressing into service six vessels, including two large cruise liners, the *S.S. America* and *S.S. Manhattan*, all manned by US crews and escorted by the US navy. Stripped of their luxurious interiors and liberally camouflaged, the liners were renamed the *USS West Point* and the *USS Wakefield*. Over time they would make twenty trips, carrying thousands of British and Commonwealth troops around the coast of Africa to Egypt and beyond. Termed Winston's Specials, at the time of the US entry in the war they were at sea transporting troops to Singapore.

Though a great many of the details of what transpired at the Atlantic Conference remain cloudy at best, we know that two weeks before the meeting Franklin Roosevelt had closed the Panama Canal to Japanese traffic, and in retaliation for the Japanese occupation of French Indochina he ordered the seizure of Japanese assets in the United States. The governments of Britain and the Dutch East Indies quickly followed suit, with the result that virtually overnight Japan was deprived of 88 percent of its imported oil supply.

We also know that at the Atlantic Conference Roosevelt again reminded Churchill that because of the Neutrality Act the U.S. could only offer a token contribution to the British war effort.

"At least for now," Roosevelt said.

"Unless," Churchill asserted, "you are attacked."

Roosevelt agreed: "Unless we are attacked first."

And if that attack on America came from Japan? At Guam or Wake Island? Or in the Philippines, or even Pearl Harbor? Would the United States concentrate its forces in the Pacific rather than in Europe? In other words, when could England count on America's attention?

Franklin Roosevelt, a New York patrician of Dutch-English descent, reassured Winston Churchill, the son of an American mother, that the United States was "with him all the way". In the event of such an attack, America would throw her full weight behind Britain to defeat Germany and liberate Europe. Until then, fighting a war in the Pacific would be put on hold.

Churchill had cause to press his point: he knew that in a matter of months — even weeks — the United States would, somewhere in the Pacific, be attacked by Japan. Even Roosevelt knew something ominous was transpiring for at that very moment all Japanese merchant vessels were being called home, presumably in preparation to transport troops and war material to points in the Far East targeted in Japan's invasion plans. But Churchill had other, more personal reasons for bringing Sempill to the meeting with Roosevelt. In the first instance, Sempill's paymasters in Tokyo would learn that Roosevelt was giving them a considerable period of grace — perhaps as long as two or even three years — in which to solidify their gains. And secondly, Sempill's boss, Winston Churchill, knew he would need a scapegoat for what was about to happen to Britain's colonies in the Far East. It was, after all, a matter of political preservation, for at that point only he knew the significance of the capture of a steamship named the *S.S. Automedon*.

Within five days of the Atlantic Conference, the codebreakers at Bletchley Park deciphered a series of messages to Tokyo from the Japanese embassy in London containing nearly word for word the conversations that had occurred between Franklin Roosevelt

ASIA BETRAYED

and Winston Churchill aboard the *USS Augusta* and the *HMS Prince of Wales* off the coast of Newfoundland. When Churchill read the transcript, he acknowledged it was "pretty accurate stuff", then signaled for Sempill's removal: "Clear him out while there is still time."

Called before the Chief of Naval Air Services, Sempill received an ultimatum: quit or get sacked. However, before Sempill could clear his desk, Churchill reversed his order to fire the spy. "I had not contemplated Lord Sempill being required to resign his commission," he said, "only that he be assigned elsewhere in the Admiralty."

The story of the *S.S. Automedon* had yet to be disclosed. Best to keep a first-class spy like Sempill close at hand for a future bailout.

On the 28th of September 1940 under a lead-colored sky in a somber part of the world, a merchant ship flying the British ensign left the port of Liverpool bound for Singapore. Hugging the African coastline to avoid detection by German submarines, the slow-moving vessel eventually steamed around the Cape of Good Hope into the relative safety of the Indian Ocean. Three days later, making its way east through calm seas, the *S.S. Automedon* was detected by a German military ship, the *Atlantis*, part of a fleet of surface raiders known as "ghost ships" that, flying false flags with their guns concealed, sought out and destroyed enemy merchant vessels carrying cargo to the Far East.

During a short encounter, the wireless operator aboard the *Automedon* had time to send a distress call that was picked up by two nearby merchant ships flying the British flag. They immediately sent coded messages detailing the incident to naval listening stations in Singapore and Durban, South Africa. In turn, both relayed word of the ship's imminent capture to

London. Overwhelming evidence indicates that British military authorities at the highest level were made fully aware of the *Automedon's* fate almost from the moment of its capture.

At the scene of the encounter a boarding party from the German ship found the *Automedon's* captain dead at the helm. A report filed by its leader, First Lieutenant Ulrich Mohr, stated that "the ship proved to be unarmed and the crew gave up without a struggle. Unobstructed, we got to work on the strong room where we found fifteen bags of secret mail, including one hundredweight of decoding tables, fleet orders, gunnery instructions, and various British Naval Intelligence reports, including all the top-secret post en route for the Far Eastern Command, Singapore." [69]

Included in the haul was a complete set of Royal Navy Fleet ciphers, new Merchant Navy ciphers scheduled to become valid in two months, a wealth of British Admiralty shipping and intelligence summaries, and several green bags containing 6,000,000 freshly minted New Straits Singapore dollars.

Lieutenant Mohr's report continued: "Our search of the Chart Room brought us far greater rewards. Our real prize was a long narrow envelope enclosed in a green bag marked HIGHLY CONFIDENTIAL - SAFE HANDS - TO BE DESTROYED. It was addressed to the Commander in Chief, Far East, with the words TO BE OPENED PERSONALLY. It was equipped with brass eyelets to let water in to facilitate its sinking should it prove necessary to dispose of it at sea."

The money, the reports, the codes, the intelligence reports, the green bags, the crew—the entire haul—was taken aboard the *Atlantis*. Then, stripped of its information and valuables, the *Automedon* was dispatched to the bottom of the Indian Ocean

---

[69] https://en.wikipedia.org/wiki/SS_Automedon

with German explosives. As the captain of the *Atlantis* sorted through the haul, he realized that he was looking at a mountain of intelligence information — a cache so vast, so significant, that he transferred six of his crew and Lieutenant Commander Paul Kamenz to a Norwegian tanker his raider had taken as a prize only hours before the sighting of the *Automedon*. The *Atlantis* took the crew of the *Automedon* to its port in the Desolation Islands, while Kamentz, aboard the *Ole Jacob* with its Norwegian crew and 10,000 tons of aviation gasoline, set course for Kobe, Japan.

As evening fell over Japan on December 5, 1940, the haul from the *Automedon* arrived at the German Embassy in Tokyo.

Over the next three days, Admiral Paul Wenneker, a German naval attaché, carefully photographed the codes and Chief of Staff reports taken from the *Automedon* before turning the haul over to a fellow officer, Captain Paul Karmenz, for delivery to Berlin. Karmenz went first to Vladivostok in Russia — for the present, a neutral nation — then crossed Russia by train, travelling day and night on his urgent mission. If there was trouble, Admiral Wenneker planned to send a four-part coded telegram to Naval Command Headquarters in Berlin summarizing each of the captured reports. But the plan wouldn't be needed. Safely delivered and deciphered, the messages were circulated among the Nazi top brass, and, on December 12, under orders from Hitler, the Japanese naval attaché in Berlin was summoned to German Naval Command Headquarters. When he arrived, Captain Yokai was shown a copy of Wenneker's summary which he immediately relayed in code to his superiors in Tokyo.

Yokai's message to Tokyo was intercepted by an American listening station in the Pacific, probably on Guam or Hawaii, where it was to sit in someone's in-basket. It wasn't to be deciphered until August 19, 1945, four days after Japan surrendered.

In Tokyo, things were moving considerably faster. On December 12, Admiral Wenneker presented copies of the report to the Japanese Naval Chief of General Staff, Vice Admiral Kondo. The Admiral read the contents and shrugged. "These codes and position documents," he said, "they have been allowed to fall into our hands to mislead both the Germans and the Japanese governments. This, of course, is a deception."

"I doubt that emphatically," replied Wenneker. "The *Automedon* was an unarmed merchant vessel whose captain was killed outright in our initial shelling. To a man, the crew surrendered without a fight, and upon boarding her First Lieutenant Mohr went directly to the captain's quarters where he found the sealed bags containing these documents. No, this is hardly a deception. The plain truth is that the ship's encounter with the *Atlantis* was too short and swift to afford anyone an opportunity to destroy them."

To make his point, Wenneker showed Kondo photographs of the green bag and a copy of the SAFE HANDS report that was meant to be handed over personally to the Far East Commander-in-Chief. "This information is marked to the personal attention of Air Marshal Robert Brooke-Popham," he added. "And what we have here is an intimate view inside the British War Cabinet. These, Admiral, are the full minutes of the Cabinet's meeting of August 8, 1940, a meeting in which a complete assessment of the Far East situation was presented. Included in it is a highly confidential Chief-of-Staff report on the defense of Hong Kong, Singapore and the Far East with respect to their defenses against any Japanese attack."

Kondo was silent, perhaps overwhelmed. "So," he said slowly, clicking his heels sharply and bowing generously to Wanneker. "So, these are the minutes of the British War Cabinet, with their diplomatic and naval codes." He whispered as if only half-believing his eyes and ears: "And, of course, full information on the defense of Hong Kong and Singapore."

"Perhaps I can remind you, Admiral," Wenneker said, giving weight to his words, "that it was Herr Hitler himself who directed that this information be shared with you."

"Certainly, Admiral. I assure you that this material shall be given careful scrutiny. And you must extend Japan's gratitude to your Führer," replied Kendo, clicking his heels and making his exit.

Three years earlier, Kondo had been part of the military coalition that swept aside the civilian cabinet in Tokyo and took control of the government, making Japan a military dictatorship much like Nazi Germany. Within five months the coalition had put together a war plan and, on July 7, 1937 — in the dead of night and without warning — Japanese troops launched an undeclared war against China.

As the coalition had surmised, the Chinese would be no match, and by 1940 Japan controlled every important city in China. There was only one exception, and that was the British Crown Colony of Hong Kong. Putting one boot across the border would, the invaders realized, incur the wrath and power of the British Empire. Instead, Japan turned its attention to nearby Siam (today's Thailand), where, by diplomacy and threat, it established a large naval base and built a number of military airstrips.

Then, quite unexpectedly, on June 22, 1940 France surrendered to Germany and Nazi troops occupied Paris. Seizing the opportunity, Japan presented an audacious request to the collaborationist Vichy government: "As Germany's ally, we demand that France relinquish immediate control of all its colonial possessions in French Indo-China." When a positive reply was forthcoming, Japan's military leaders made preparations to take over Vietnam, Laos, and Cambodia.

Back in England, Winston Churchill had just become Prime Minister, and as war raged across Europe, Japan's expansionist policies began to encroach on Great Britain's Far East possessions. Directing his War Cabinet to evaluate the situation with respect to Hong Kong, Malaya, and Singapore, Churchill wanted to know the size of the fleet that would be required to safeguard England's Far East outposts in the event of war with Japan. Referring to a study made a year earlier, it was determined that the minimum needed to meet Japanese aggression would be a flotilla of ten battleships and two battle cruisers, plus several cruisers and escort destroyers. It might even be necessary to send an aircraft carrier or two—an action requiring seventy days or more.

As if by chance, the German Luftwaffe chose that same moment to send 348 bombers and 617 fighter planes across the channel to bomb England. The first raid lasted two hours, followed by a second, then by a third wave of bombers. They came during daylight, they came at night, and the bombing of England continued for 57 days. Homes vanished, factories were destroyed, cathedrals burned. Entire cities were devastated.

In Berlin, Hitler issued Directive #16 setting in motion preparations for Operation Sea Lion, the Nazi plan for an event unprecedented since the Spanish Armada: a military invasion of the British Isles by sea. "As England still shows no signs of willingness to come to terms," Hitler declared, "I have decided to prepare, and if necessary, to carry out a landing operation against her. The aim of this operation is to eliminate the English

Motherland as a base from which the war against Germany can be continued."

Meanwhile, urgent pleas were arriving in London from the governors of Singapore and Hong Kong: "Where are the promised troops? Where are the promised ships? Where are the promised airplanes of the RAF?" The governments of Australia and New Zealand were asking the same questions. In response, Winston Churchill convened his top advisers, ordering the British Chiefs of Staff to update their earlier estimates about the size of the fleet needed to protect Hong Kong and Singapore. The report, 87 pages long, was gloomier than anyone could have imagined: Britain was in no position to resort to war if Japan attacked Hong Kong, Malaya, Singapore or the Dutch East Indies. The Far East was indefensible, and without the active involvement of the United States, Britain's remaining colonies were doomed. In the event of a Japanese attack, the Prime Minister was advised that Britain must make concessions and adapt a delaying strategy. In other words, to write off her Asian colonies.

Churchill's reaction was to gather all the information together and dispatch a copy of the report to his newly-appointed Commander-in-Chief of the British Far Eastern Command. It was a new command, making Air Marshal Robert Brooke-Popham responsible for all defense matters in Singapore, Malaya, Burma, and Hong Kong.

In the interest of secrecy, Churchill's decision was to hand the bag containing the full diplomatic report over to the captain of the *S.S. Automedon* for delivery.

Six thousand miles away in Tokyo, the Council for the Conduct of the War pored over the intelligence report drawn up after careful review of the documents captured by the Germans from the *Automedon*. Captain Yamaguchi Bujiro, Head of the Fifth Intelligence Section dealing with the USA, and Captain Horiuchi Shigetada, Head of the Eighth Intelligence Section dealing with Britain and India, offered this prediction to the Japanese General Staff: "Even if Japan sends forces into Indochina or beyond, Britain will not go to war." The Council then sent the following message to Naval Marshal Admiral Yamamoto: "In the event it is decided to go to war in Southeast Asia to neutralize the United States Pacific Fleet it is imperative that you begin drawing up plans to attack Pearl Harbor."

On November 26, 1941, The *Kido Butai*, the Japanese First Air Fleet consisting of six aircraft carriers, nine destroyers, two battleships, two heavy cruisers, one light cruiser, and three submarines, left Iturup in the Kuril Islands northeast of Japan, cut all ship-to-ship radio communications and began a 3,000-mile journey across the Pacific Ocean towards its American target.

Within a week of the Atlantic Conference meeting with Churchill, an Army-Navy board in Washington presented the results of an ongoing study to the White House: in the event of War Plan Orange (war with Japan), the Philippines could not be defended and would have to be yielded by default. The following day Roosevelt signed a bill permitting the Army to keep men currently in service for an additional 18 months. Then, perhaps on a hunch, he ordered four of the seven aircraft carriers out of Pearl Harbor and back to the west coast of the US, along with a number of cruisers and destroyer escort vessels, three battleships, and 21 tenders, fuel ships, and minesweepers. The carriers remaining at Pearl Harbor were to be assigned missions away from Hawaii. In the Philippine Islands, General Douglas MacArthur had only recently been recalled from retirement and made Commander in Chief of the US Army Far East.

Additionally, immediately after Churchill's meeting with Roosevelt, British ships loaded with Hurricane fighters en route to Singapore were abruptly ordered to change course. The planes promised to Singapore were instead dispatched to Libya. Experienced troops in Malaya and Singapore—the men best prepared to defend the Peninsula and save it from Japanese conquest—were put aboard ships and sent to India, the Crown Jewel of the dissolving British Empire.

Churchill's earlier authorization to send a fleet of fast torpedo boats to defend Singapore was similarly rescinded. In Hong Kong, Royal Air Force combat planes were ordered out and dispersed to Burma and India. Munitions and supplies from Canada meant for Hong Kong's defense were sidetracked to the Philippines. Additionally, every ranking government official in Hong Kong from the Governor down to the Director of Public Works, was abruptly recalled to England or transferred to a location removed from danger. Next on the agenda, nearly all merchant and naval ships received orders to leave the harbors of Singapore and Hong Kong—immediately!

Sometime between the hours of 2:30 and 3:00 on the morning of December 8 (Hong Kong time), as a fleet of merchant ships was hurrying out of Hong Kong harbor, important individuals including Madame Sun Yat-sen, widow of the Republic of China's first president, were also leaving. It would appear that the man behind the desk at No. 10 Downing Street knew not only what was about to happen in Hong Kong, Malaya and Singapore, but *when*. And he was making last-minute adjustments.

When the attack came, the defence of Hong Kong was left

to a volunteer militia comprised of two thousand civilian businessmen, lawyers, merchants, bankers and other professionals, some armed with only pistols and World War I rifles. Canada, which had been asked to provide support troops, had responded by sending two thousand men, a number of whom were fresh recruits who had not completed basic training. Through a bureaucratic blunder, the young soldiers arrived in Hong Kong while their baggage and gear was sidetracked to Manila in the Philippines. Three days later, the bombs fell. They had come prepared for garrison duty and found themselves in a war.

From London, Winston Churchill took to the airwaves to warn the military planners in Japan that, though under constant attack from the Germans, England had no intention of abandoning "one single inch of soil" in the Far East. As a consequence of its aggression, he said, Japan would have to reckon with the fearsome might of Great Britain. As proof, he said he'd already dispatched the *HMS Prince of Wales* and the *HMS Repulse* to the region. On the third day of the war, these two ships were almost effortlessly sent to the bottom of the South China Sea by a squadron of Japanese torpedo bombers.

On the east coast of the United States it was 1.55pm in the afternoon of Sunday, December 7, 1941, and Japan had gone on the attack. Across the Pacific, Pearl Harbor was burning and Asia was on fire. To a shocked world, Pearl Harbor would be universally described as a surprise attack, and for the next 44 months America would be at war.

In his book *The Second World War, Vol. 3*, Churchill would write: "No Americans will think it wrong of me if I proclaim that to have the United States on our side was to be the greatest joy...

England would live. Britain would live. The Commonwealth of Nations and the Empire would live... I went to bed and slept the sleep of the saved and the thankful."

Winston Churchill finally had his war and the island kingdom of Great Britain would be saved. In yielding Asia, however, these are the lands that would be given over to occupation by the Empire of the Rising Sun:

* Hong Kong
* British New Guinea
* The Philippines
* Guam
* Dutch East Indies
* Portuguese Timor
* Malaya
* Andaman and Nicobar Islands
* Straits Settlements (Singapore)
* Kingdom of Sarawak
* Brunei
* North Borneo
* Marshall Islands
* Nauru
* Imphal
* Solomon Islands
* Wake Island
* Gilbert and Ellice Islands
* Christmas Islands
* Attu and Kiska Islands

One year after the capture of the *S.S. Automedon*, the crew of the *Atlantis* were invited to the Emperor's Palace in Tokyo where Captain Rogge was presented with a samurai sword by Emperor

Hirohito. Only two other Germans had received such an honor: Field Marshal Hermann Goering, and Field Marshal Erwin Rommel, the war hero known as The Desert Fox.

Franklin Roosevelt, the 32nd president of the United States, died while still in office, at Warm Springs, Georgia on April 12, 1945, aged 63. He was in his fourth term as president, and his death was mourned by millions around the world. It has been said that Roosevelt's most powerful political asset was his ability to charm, and he enjoyed promoting uncertainty and confusion to "keep his options open". Even his closest associates often didn't know what he was going to do until he had done it. When the Japanese attacked Pearl Harbor on December 7, 1941, Roosevelt skillfully directed the organization of the nation's manpower and resources to prepare for global war, firstly to save Britain. His death came one month before the surrender of Germany, four months before the surrender of Japan.

Sir Winston Churchill, KG OM CH TD PC PCc DL FRS RA, lived 20 years longer, passing away peacefully in his own bed in London, aged 90, on January 24, 1965. His state funeral would be described as the largest in the world. In Britain, the Secrets Act protects official papers from public scrutiny for a period of thirty years. However, before leaving office, Churchill locked his official and personal papers out of public reach for a period of fifty years after his death. His secrets about Sempill and the *S.S. Automedon* would be carried to the grave, but during the terrible days that Singapore and Hong Kong were under attack, he issued these words to their doomed defenders: "There must be no thought of sparing the troops or population; commanders and senior officers should die with their troops. The honor of the British Empire and the British Army is at stake."

The man in Singapore to whom the order was addressed, Air Marshal Robert Brooke-Popham, a man who at the height of the battle for Malaya was thought to be at the point of a nervous collapse, was relieved of his command and boarded a ship that would take him to the safety of Australia. It was he, the Far East Commander-in-Chief, to whom Churchill had earlier sent the TOP SECRET, HIGHLY CONFIDENTIAL documents. Via the *S.S. Automedon*.

Just before Christmas, Churchill sent a follow-up message to the defenders of Hong Kong where a force of eight thousand British, Canadian, Indian, and Hong Kong Volunteers were trapped by a frenzied army of thirty thousand battle-hardened Japanese warriors. "Fight from door to door, the reputation of Britain is at stake," he demanded. A similar message was sent to General Wavell in Singapore with the instructions that "the battle should be fought out, if need be, in the ruins of Singapore."

To deter his detractors in Parliament who were calling for his censure over Singapore's perilous situation, he belatedly began sending reinforcements, and from early January 1942 until February 5 he sent a total of 45 troop ships. Having traveled halfway around the world, most of the men arrived on the docks of Singapore in time to be surrendered to General Yamashita, never having fired a shot.

Churchill's directives to Hong Kong and Singapore had been issued from the United States where he'd journeyed to address Congress and thank the American people for becoming partners in the war. "What kind of people do they (the Japanese) think we are?" he asked. "Is it possible that they do not realize that we will never cease to persevere against them until they have been taught a lesson that they and the world will never forget?"

Returning home, he reflected that his discussions in the White

House had not been entirely to his satisfaction. Roosevelt had declared that when the war was over Hong Kong should be returned to Chiang Kai-shek. He was, in fact, working out the details of a compromise deal with the Generalissimo whereby Britain would hand Hong Kong back to China and Chiang would immediately declare Hong Kong a free port. Barely controlling his rage, Churchill huffed, "I will not give away the British Empire."

Shortly afterwards, a visiting State Department advisor to London announced that "it was time that Britain did the right thing and give up her Asian colonies." Learning of this, Churchill had the man brought before him. "Hong Kong," he growled, "was a British creation which had benefited the whole world." Following up on that, in November 1942 he told the House of Commons, "I have not become the King's First Minister to preside over the liquidation of the British Empire" and he directed Whitehall to set up a deputation of governments-in-waiting to be "piggy-backed in" the moment the United States liberated Hong Kong, Malaya, and Singapore. Called the Far Eastern Reconstruction Committee, the Hong Kong Planning Unit consisted of nine Hong Kong veteran civil servants, headed by N.L. Smith, Hong Kong's former Colonial Secretary who had sailed out of Hong Kong harbor on a merchant ship just hours before the first Japanese bombs fell. Ironically, his vessel, the *S.S. Ulysses*, passed the arrival of his replacement, Franklin Gimson, who was entering Hong Kong on the *S.S. Soochow*, a cargo ship from Rangoon carrying a full cargo of rice.

"To appease the American liberals" — as they were to phrase it — the Hong Kong Planning Unit weighed making a change to the existing living restrictions in a reclaimed Hong Kong whereby the Chinese would no longer be barred from living on the Peak or from riding on the upper decks of the buses and ferries. The same would hold true for Chinese wishing to build or live on the previously exclusive hills on the offshore island of Cheung Chau. For good measure, the Unit recommended that a future government should no longer be involved in the trafficking of opium. "To comply with the wishes of the United States, it is laid down that government traffic in opium should at least be abolished, and the use of it stamped out." [70]

In their words, everything must change, so that nothing might change.[71]

What irony. One hundred years earlier, its Bengal warehouses jammed to the rafters with chests of opium, the British trading firm of Jardine Matheson decided to expand its market and began smuggling the drug into China through the port of Guangzhou (Canton). Ten years on, over half of all Chinese males over the age of forty were addicted to it, and after the overdose death of his own son, the Daoguang Emperor asked a scholar-diplomat, Lin Ze-su, to eradicate the drug from China. Lin immediately closed the Pearl River Channel, trapping the British traders in Guangzhou. Chinese troops boarded their ships, thirteen factories and numerous warehouses on shore were raided, and 20,000 chests of opium were seized and burned. Lin Ze-su then wrote a letter to Queen Victoria in which he questioned the moral reasoning of a government that sanctioned the trafficking of such a drug, saying in effect, "If you will allow the import and sale of opium into England, we will allow the import and sale of opium in China." Peeved, William Jardine journeyed to London where he persuaded Parliament to use the Royal Navy to protect his enterprise. That, in 1839-1842, was the First Opium War, and at its conclusion Jardine demanded nine million dollars

---

70   Pledge to the people of the colonies, given by the Colonial Office, July 1943. Endicott and Birch, *Hong Kong Eclipse*, page 279; 318-19
71   Philip Snow, *The Fall of Hong Kong*, page 200

in reparations for the chests of opium Lin destroyed and that Hong Kong Island be given over to Great Britain, declaring "You take my opium, I take your Islands in return." In time, Jardine's partner James Matheson would inadvertently define the character of the new Imperial Taipan. When told that one of his captains had refused to unload a cargo of opium because it was the Sabbath, Matheson ordered him sacked. "We have every respect for persons entertaining strict religious principles," he said, "but we fear that very godly people are not suited for the drug trade."

In the years, the months, the days leading up to the Japanese invasion, ninety-eight percent of the Hong Kong population was Asian. The remaining two percent was either British or other Westerners. Similar ratios of British administrators to the indigenous population prevailed in Singapore, Malaya and Burma, and though there were 8,000 men from several ethnic groups incorporated in the British army in Burma, there were no Chinese among the defenders of Hong Kong or Singapore. There were, however, as many as 130,000 fit and ready Chinese men in Hong Kong alone who were willing to pick up a gun to protect their homes, their freedom, and their families, but neither Churchill nor his minions wished to arm anyone who was Asian or part-Asian. Had Churchill done so, he might very well have had it both ways: there would have been no surrenders and the Japanese conquest of Asia would have stalled or could have failed altogether. Owing to his Victorian mindset, Churchill was incapable of seeing that he possessed the means of saving both England and Asia. In the end, his fear of losing even an inch of colonial soil was so great that he denied the Asian people the basic right to defend themselves. And yet it was he who, after abandoning them and the Commonwealth soldiers he'd sent to Asia, would write, "There is no worse mistake in public leadership than to hold out false hope soon to be swept away. What kind of leadership is that?"

As demonstrated, he was a man of contradictions. On a personal level, Winston Churchill could be brusque and exasperating, taking no notice of the private lives of people on his staff. He was a tough and exacting boss, intolerant, often spoke too quickly to his stenographers, and frequently growled at them in admonition. His wife Clementine wrote him a June 1940 warning, "There is a danger of your being generally disliked by your colleagues and subordinates because of your rough, sarcastic and overbearing manner." He responded that he would try to change. His staff said change didn't happen.

Eulogized as a defender of freedom, the man TIME magazine declared 'launched the lifeboats' to save England, in recent years historians have been taking a second look at Winston Churchill. In the words of *Atlantic's* literary editor Benjamin Schwarz, "Churchill's reputation as 'a great man' has evolved as scholars re-examine his doings in many directions and find them wanting. Throughout his long career, Churchill made colossal misjudgments and played a central role in a series of disasters, including the Dardanelles fiasco in World War I, the ruinous intervention in the Russian Revolution, the failed Norway campaign at the outset of World War II, the near-catastrophic 'second Dunkirk' in western France in 1940, the costly Dieppe raid, the rout experienced on Crete, the fall of Singapore..."

Time-Life Books in its *The Battle of Britain* added to that, citing "the reckless blowing up of the French fleet at Oran harbor which, in twelve minutes, claimed the lives of two thousand Allied sailors; his strategically unsound decision to send an expeditionary force to Greece only to see a huge number of them almost immediately captured; and, to serve his ends, his total disregard for the lives of just about anyone, whether they be British citizens or the Empire's Asian subjects in her far-off colonies."

The Dardanelles Invasion—better known as the Gallipoli Campaign—took place from April 25, 1915 to 9 January, 1916. It was proposed by Churchill—then the First Lord of the Admiralty—as a means of breaking the stalemate on the Western Front. He was locked in on the idea that it was disastrous to confront an enemy directly, that an oblique hit was the key to victory. Hence Gallipoli in the Ottoman Turkish Empire, a place far removed from the trenches of France. It was a disaster of the first order, resulting in the deaths of more than 60,000 Australian, British, French, Australian, New Zealand and Indian soldiers. The defeat never left him, and 27 years later he was virtually paralyzed when American and British military planners advanced plans for a cross-channel invasion. Fearing a war of attrition, he first convinced Roosevelt to take the Germans on in Africa, then to fight them in Italy. While the planners worked on *Operation Overlord*—the Allied landings in France—Churchill kept trying to convince them of his alternative plan: land at Lisbon, march across Portugal and Spain, then cross over the Pyrenees and hit the Nazis in their soft underbelly in southern France. Fortunately, his fatigued planners resisted, and on the 6th of June 1944 more than 160,000 troops successfully crossed the channel to Normandy and met the Nazis head on. But for his protests, it has been speculated that the United States could have carried out a successful invasion of the continent in 1943, shortening the war by nearly two years and saving millions of lives.

Yet for all his faults, it was Winston Spencer Churchill who conjured up the way to get the United States into the war against Hitler. The top secret documents captured at sea on an unarmed steamship may or may not have been part of his plan. But he was a masterful politician and a brilliant conniver who knew there were 96 seats in the United States Senate and 435 seats in the United States House of Representatives, each one occupied by an aging snail. And the old patrician knew it was going to take an event like Pearl Harbor to get them to morph into gazelles. Placing so much highly secret information on a vulnerable steamship—'a rusty old tub' was how the Germans described it—could have been an error. Or not.

But he did, and Japan took the bait and followed through. Keeping Sempill at his side as long as he did may have been a mistake. Courtesy of the *S.S. Automedon,* Japan's warlords had all the information they needed, so of what further use could a spy like Sempill be to Churchill? Perhaps, as Max Hastings says in *Winston's War: Churchill 1940-1945,* "He wanted war, like life, to be fun."

William Francis Forbes-Sempill, 19th Lord Sempill and Baronet of Craigevar, AFC, Third Class Commander in the Order of the Rising Sun (Japan), died eleven months after the death of the Prime Minister who protected him, at his Craigevar Castle in Aberdeenshire, Scotland at the age of 72. Ten days after the outbreak of war in the Pacific, at the moment Hong Kong was on the verge of surrendering, Sempill was discovered making calls to the Japanese Embassy in London. His office was raided and sensitive information was discovered. With the approval of Churchill, the Admiralty asked him to retire immediately. Sempill was said to be outraged. He threatened to sue for defamation, demanding that the evidence against him be revealed. That was not possible, for to do so would reveal that the codebreakers at Bletchley Park had cracked the Japanese ciphers. But giving consideration to his royal connections—his father had been *aide-de-camp* to King George V—it was decided it would be too embarrassing to the government to prosecute him and he was saved him from the hangman's noose.

Like a great many of Winston Churchill's papers, most of the documents relating to Sempill's treasonous activities and those relating to the capture of the *S.S. Automedon* have disappeared from government archives. Upon Germany's surrender in 1945, Admiral Wenneker's original detailed war diary report of the capture of the *Automedon* was found at German Naval Headquarters in bombed-out Berlin. It was turned over to British authorities in London, from where it promptly vanished. And yet the treachery of this forgotten man of history and the capture of the stash of secret information taken from the steamship only came to light 71 years later when a copy of the report emerged in Germany. What is clear is that in the hands of the Japanese, the summary information taken from the *S.S. Automedon* solidified the preparations being made by the Tokyo planners to bomb Pearl Harbor and strike south, safe in the knowledge that Britain did not have the means of defending its colonies. In the end, it was the capture of a vulnerable steamship that was to transform the European War into a Global War, and that, it seems, had been Churchill's goal from the beginning.

At war's end, the Union Jack flew again from the flagstaffs of the liberated colonies, and many of their pre-war administrators sailed back to resume their sworn duty to God and Country. To Churchill's relief, every one of Britain's colonies and outposts would resume their pink presence on the maps of the world, and just as it had been since the glorious days of Queen Victoria,

ASIA BETRAYED

the sun never set on the British Empire. Things had gone well, the plan to save England had worked. If the colonies had been inconvenienced, they could be thankful to Britain for their liberation. But while Churchill is commemorated and lionized, rejoiced as the man who helped save Western civilization, and voted by his countrymen as the greatest Briton, there are some, notably those who survived Japanese prison camps, who remember him for his perfidy, his prejudices and his stubborn imperialism.

But as it was, and as it would always be with Winston Spencer Churchill, it was never about the people, it was always about the place.

Casualties in the Pacific War numbered approximately 36 million, about half of the total casualties of World War II. Compare that with the total number of people living in Great Britain (48 million) or France (39 million) in 1941.

Number of civilian victims of the Japanese Holocaust:
China: 18,000,000 - 20,000,000
Indochina: 2,500,000
Indonesia: 375,000
Dutch East Indies: 4,000,000
Malaya and Singapore: 283,000 - 350,000
Thailand: 60,000
Philippines: 1,000,000 - 1,300,000
Burma: 170,000 - 200,000
Pacific Islands: 57,000
Timor: 70,000
Papua New Guinea: 15,000
United States: 1,536

Number of POW deaths in Japanese captivity:
United States: 13,381
Australians: 8,031
British: 12,433
Canada: 290
Dutch: 25,000
Netherlands: 8,500
Philippines: 23,000
New Zealand: 31

Of 60,000 Indian Army POWs taken at the fall of Singapore, 12,000 died in captivity.

Thirteen ships were sunk while transporting 15,712 POWs from Southeast Asia to Japan where they were to be auctioned off to industrialists and mine owners. An estimated 10,720 prisoners died in the sinking of those unmarked "Hell Ships".

A FINAL WORD
CONNECTIONS

IN MY INVESTIGATIONS leading to this work I was constantly thinking in terms of connections: one thing leading to another thing, which in turn leads to another.

Here's an example: I learned about the pro-fascist leanings of the British aristocracy from an ex-Nazi general living in the snow-covered village of Hinterthal, Austria. Herr General Reinhard Spitzy had been private secretary to Joachim von Ribbentrop, the pre-war German Ambassador to Great Britain. In June of 1940 he had been export advisor to a German weapons mission in Portugal, and the general told me of secret meetings he attended in Lisbon and Estoril between Hitler's representatives and the Duke and Duchess of Windsor. The Duke, he said, advised Hitler to drop bombs on London to bring England to the negotiating table. Some years later, I met one of the Nazi negotiators near Lisbon — then the owner of a respected real estate business — and General Spitzy's story about the Duke and Duchess was corroborated.

In Hong Kong, Malaysia and Singapore I heard stories from a number of people — ex-military and civilian — who had been brutally treated by the Japanese. They had spent nearly four years behind barbed wire being humiliated, starved and tortured, and their bitterness was profound. Many of them were unable to shake the notion that someone at the top had betrayed them. As an ex-POW was to say to me, "Treachery at the top, treason in the middle, and all hell to pay at the bottom."

Near Hiroshima, I spent a week in the home of an ex-Kempeitai warrant officer who had been a translator at the prisoner of war camp near Kanchanaburi on the Khwae Yai River. Due to the popularity of the fictional film *The Bridge Over The River Kwai*, in 1960 the name of the river was changed to the Kwai.

In our conversations, Nagase Takashi told of stumbling onto a secret file one night on his commander's desk indicating an unnamed Englishmen had provided the Japanese with military information prior to the invasion of Malaya and the bombing of Pearl Harbor.

He also told me of the night in the final days of the war when he was sitting alone at his commanding officers desk in Bangkok, and while moving papers around he saw the secret memo from General Terauchi instructing camp commanders in the Southern Region to kill all military POWs and civilian internees the moment the allies landed in Japanese-occupied territory.

In Hong Kong, a former intelligence officer in Chiang Kai-shek's Kuomintang army—my wife's father—told of Madame Sun Yat-sen's late-night departure from Hong Kong just before the Japanese troops stormed across the border. She and a number of dignitaries were hurried across the harbor to a plane sent by Chiang Kai-shek.

Almost to a man and woman, those who survived the Japanese Holocaust were reluctant to talk about their experiences, and when some of them eventually did, they discovered that the world had very little interest in 'that' war. The war in Europe had been the important one, and when Germany surrendered it was time to sort things out and move on. One particular illustration of that was the experience of Captain Ernest Gordon who had lived through the jungle battles of Malaya, the humiliation of torture at Changi Jail in Singapore, and was a survivor of the Kanchanaburi Death House at the River Kwai. The war was over, and after more than four years he stepped back on British soil at the Liverpool docks. His train to Scotland was the following day, so carrying a stained and battered suitcase that had been with him through the war and his years of captivity, he went to a hotel to get a room for the night. During check-in, the manager scowled and suggested that he remove his filthy bag from the lobby as quickly as possible "so it wouldn't disturb others."

The war was over, the world had indeed moved on.

However, a few people did tell their stories, some in privately printed books describing their years of captivity, some who wrote to complain about the world's indifference to the war in Asia, and frequently in conversations in which they expressed their belief that something happened, somewhere there had been a cover-up. I heard it as a drum roll: Something Happened…Something Happened…

I listened and took notes: a scrap of information here, another there—there were few government records to refer to, which always seems the case when officialdom has blundered. The missing military supplies to Hong Kong and Singapore, the transfer of trained solders away from the troubled areas, the sudden recall home of experienced colonial officials…

Like the shuffled pieces of a chaotic puzzle, I had a jumbled mix of times and places, personalities and events, but there was no picture on the box and no assembly instructions. It was obvious to me that something was amiss and someone was to blame, but the British Secrets Act had put the truth beyond reach for thirty years. And Churchill had taken additional measures to seal his papers until fifty years after his death.

Still, having spent many hours of research in various libraries and government archives—often, it seemed, in dank basements that smelled of wet concrete—and more often than not being given palpable run-arounds by civil servants and their cohorts who wished to slam shut all doors to the past, I managed to put together an article based on what facts I had unearthed, the underlying message being that the many failures and the astonishing lack of military preparation could not be attributed entirely to errors of judgment. In the back of my mind I continued hearing the words repeated: *something happened, somebody knew.* The entire Asian situation, I thought, had the earmarks of strategic ruthlessness on an unprecedented scale.

At one point, an international magazine with a Far East edition accepted an article in which I questioned the notion that the invasion of Hong Kong and Malaya, as well as the bombing of Pearl Harbor, had been a surprise to the British and the Americans. I also indicated that the Japanese had first-hand intelligence and knew that Hong Kong, Malaya, Burma and the Philippines were undermanned and indefensible. Someone was to blame, I wrote, leading to the unnecessary torture and death of millions. After looking at the proofs, the magazine's office in Japan declared that if the story went into print, every Japanese advertisement would be pulled from future issues of the magazine. That's the way it is in Japan: discussion of their war remains highly controversial.

It has been forty years since I began my quest, and helped by the passage of time, by a considerable number of biographies and autobiographies and, most importantly by the arrival of the internet, I have at last assembled the pieces. There had never been much doubt in my mind that the person responsible for the abandonment of the people of Asia was Winston Churchill. What I didn't have were the facts to confirm it, the information that would make it possible to make my connection. As George Orwell, one of Churchill's contemporaries, was to write *"In a time of deceit, telling the truth is a revolutionary act."* And after the war he wrote *"The very concept of objective truth is fading out of the world. Lies will pass into history."*

That's precisely what the major players in this wartime epoch were hoping for—lies passed forward to become history. Churchill wanted it, Roosevelt wanted it, and it would be another fifty or more years before we had the answer to the question asked by John Stericker in Hong Kong, by the Prisoners of War in Changi Jail, by the multitude of slave laborers who were building a railroad in the jungles of Thailand, and by the millions upon millions of human beings who would become victims in the Asian war. If—and this requires a stretch of the imagination—if John Stericker and the others had computers during those years, and if there had been such a thing as Wikileaks, this is what they would have discovered, and it would have answered the lingering question: *Who knew?*

Berlin, September 27, 1940. U.S. Embassy reports the signing of the Tripartite Pact, the mutual assistance treaty between Germany, Italy, and Japan: "It offers the possibility that Germany would declare war on America if America were to get into war with Japan, which may have significant implications for U.S. policy towards Japan."

Washington, October 7, 1940. Having considered the implications of the Tripartite Pact, Lt. Cdr. Arthur McCollum, USN, of the Office of Naval Intelligence (ONI), suggests a strategy for provoking Japan into attacking the U.S., thus bringing America into war in Europe. The proposal called for eight specific steps aimed at provoking Japan. Its centerpiece was keeping the U.S. Fleet in Hawaii as a lure for a Japanese attack, and imposing an oil embargo against Japan. "If by these means Japan could be led to commit an overt act of war, so much the better," the memo concludes.[72]

---

[72] http://www.findingdulcinea.com/news/on-this-day/September-October-08/On-this-Day--McCollum-Memo-Delivered.html

JOHN BELL SMITHBACK

Washington, June 23, 1941. One day after Hitler's attack on the Soviet Union, Secretary of the Interior and FDR's advisor Harold Ickes wrote a memo for the President, saying that "there might develop from the embargoing of oil to Japan such a situation as would make it not only possible but easy to get into this war in an effective way. And if we should thus indirectly be brought in, we would avoid the criticism that we had gone in as an ally of communistic Russia."

Washington, July 22, 1941. Admiral Richmond Turner's report states that "shutting off the American supply of petroleum to Japan will lead promptly to the invasion of Netherland East Indies: "[I]t seems certain [Japan] would also include military action against the Philippine Islands, which would immediately involve us in a Pacific war."

Washington, July 24, 1941. President Roosevelt says, "If we had cut off the oil, they probably would have gone down to the Dutch East Indies a year ago, and you would have had war." The following day he freezes Japanese assets in the U.S. and imposes an oil embargo against Japan.

London, August 14, 1941. After meeting the President at the Atlantic Conference, Churchill noted the "astonishing depth of Roosevelt's intense desire for war." PM is aware that FDR needs to overcome the isolationist resistance to "Europe's war" felt by most Americans and their elected representatives.

Washington, September 24, 1941. Having cracked the Japanese naval codes one year earlier, U.S. naval intelligence deciphers a message from the Naval Intelligence Headquarters in Tokyo to Japan's consul-general in Honolulu, requesting grid of exact locations of U.S. Navy ships in the harbor. Commanders in Hawaii are not warned.

Washington, October 18, 1941. FDR's friend and advisor Harold Ickes notes in his diary: "For a long time I have believed that our best entrance into the war would be by way of Japan."[73] Yet four days later opinion polls reveal that 74 percent of Americans opposed war with Japan, and only 13 percent supported it.

Washington, 25 November 1941. Secretary of War Stimson writes that FDR said an attack was likely within days, and wonders "how we should maneuver them into the position of firing the first shot without too much danger to ourselves... In spite of the risk involved, however, in letting the Japanese fire the first shot, we realized that in order to have the full support of the American people it was desirable to make sure that the Japanese be the ones to do this so that there should remain no doubt in anyone's mind as to who were the aggressors."

Washington, November 26, 1941. The US aircraft carriers *Enterprise* and *Lexington*, are ordered out of Pearl Harbor "as soon as possible". The same order included stripping Pearl of 50 planes, 40 percent of its already inadequate fighter protection.[74]

Washington, 26 November 1941. Secretary of State Hull demands the complete withdrawal of all Japanese troops from French Indochina and from China.

Tokyo, 27 November 1941. U.S. Ambassador to Japan Grew says this is "the document that touched the button that started the war." The Japanese react on cue: On December 1, final authorization is given by the Emperor, after a majority of Japanese leaders advised him the Hull Note would "destroy the fruits of the China incident, endanger Manchukuo and undermine Japanese control of Korea."[75]

San Francisco, December 1, 1941. Office of Naval Intelligence, ONI, 12th Naval District in San Francisco found the Japanese fleet by correlating reports from the four wireless news services and

---
73 http://voluntarysociety.org/conditioning/conspiracy/ww2.html
74 BBC Documentary: *Sacrifice at Pearl Harbor, Pearl Harbor, Mother Of All Conspiracies.* http://www.whatreallyhappened.com/WRHARTICLES/pearl.html
75 https://www.chroniclesmagazine.org/wikileaks-1941/

several shipping companies regarding signals west of Hawaii. There are numerous U.S. naval intelligence radio intercepts of Japanese transmissions.

Washington, 5 December 1941, 10 a.m. President Roosevelt writes to the Australian Prime Minister that "the next four or five days will decide the matters" with Japan.

Washington, 5 December 1941, 5 p.m. At a Cabinet meeting, Secretary of the Navy Frank Knox says, "Well, you know Mr. President, we know where the Japanese fleet is?" FDR replied, "Yes, I know … Well, you tell them what it is Frank." Just as Knox was about to speak Roosevelt appeared to have second thoughts and interrupted him saying, "We haven't got anything like perfect information as to their apparent destination."

Washington, 6 December 1941, 9 p.m. At a White House dinner Roosevelt was given the first thirteen parts of a fifteen-part decoded Japanese diplomatic declaration of war and said to Harry Hopkins, "This means war!" he said to Harry Hopkins, but did not interrupt the soiree and did not issue any orders to the military to prepare for an attack. [76]

My quest, from the neo-fascist British aristocracy, to the Royal House of Windsor, to William Forbes-Sempill, to Winston Spencer Churchill, to the *S.S. Automedon*, to Franklin Delano Roosevelt, to the invasion of Malaya, the bombing of Pearl Harbor, the fall of Hong Kong and Singapore…

Connections made. A story of ruthless political determination, subterfuge and treason at the highest level.

JBS

---

76 https://www.chroniclesmagazine.org/wikileaks-1941/

THEY SURVIVED

I was a Chinese male, tall, and the Japanese were going for people like me because Singapore had been the centre for the collection of ethnic Chinese donations to Chongqing to fight the Japanese. So they were out to punish us. They slaughtered 70,000 – perhaps as high as 90,000 but verifiable numbers would be about 70,000. But for a stroke of fortune, I would have been one of them. But they also showed a meanness and viciousness towards their enemies equal to the Huns. Genghis Khan and his hordes could not have been more merciless. I have no doubts about whether the two atom bombs dropped on Hiroshima and Nagasaki were necessary. Without them, hundreds of thousands of civilians in Malaya and Singapore, and millions in Japan itself, would have perished.

Lee Kuan Yew, The Singapore Story: Memoirs of Lee Kuan Yew,
Singapore Times
Publishing, 1998

Names of but a few of the Changi and Death Railway POWs

Sir Norman Alexander, New Zealand, Professor of Physics, Raffles College, Singapore, Vice-Chancellor, Dean of Science, University of Malaya, Professor of Physics and Vice-President, University College, Ibadan, Nigeria, Professor of Engineering Physics, Middle East Technical University, Ankara, Turkey, Vice

Chancellor, Ahmadu Bello University, Nigeria, University of the West Indies, Vice Chancellor University of the South Pacific, Laucala Bay. Helped build a salt evaporation plant at Changi and a small industrial plant that fermented surgical spirit and other products for prison hospital.

Sir Harold Atcherley, businessman, public figure and arts administrator. Served with Royal Dutch Shell in Egypt, Lebanon, Syria, Argentina, and Brazil until 1959 and was the RDS Group's Personnel co-ordinator from 1964 until 1970. He was Recruitment Advisor to the Ministry of Defence, 1970–1971, and Chairman of Tyzack & Partners, 1979–1985.

Geoffrey Bingham, AM, MM, Australian, wrote several books reflecting on his experiences, including his conversion to the Christian faith in *The Story of the Rice Cakes, Angel Wings*, and *Tall Grow the Tallow Woods*.

Freddy Bloom, journalist and campaigner for deaf children.

Russell Braddon, Australian writer. His chronicle of his four years as a prisoner of war, *The Naked Island*, sold over a million copies.

Sheila Bruhn (née Allan), who wrote *Diary of a Girl in Changi*, the story of her experiences in Singapore's Sime Road and Changi internment camps from 1941 to 1945.

Sir John Carrick, AC, KCMG. Australian. The impact of his experiences on his political thinking is described in his biography, *Carrick: Principles, Politics, and Policy*, written by Graeme Starr.

Anthony Chenevix-Trench, A classics scholar, he taught Classics at Shrewsbury School, and for a year at Christ Church. He was headmaster of Bradfield College. Appointed headmaster of Eton College in 1963.

James Clavell, Australian. Novelist and screenwriter best known for his Asian Saga series of novels and their televised adaptations. Author of *King Rat* (1962), *Tai-Pan* (1966), *Shōgun* (1975), *Noble*

House (1981), *Whirlwind* (1986), *Gai-Jin* (1993), *The Love Story from Whirlwind* (1994), short novel adapted from *Whirlwind* (1986).

Eugene Ernest Colman, British chess master. His name is attached to the Colman Variation of the Two Knights Defense, but the most remarkable thing about it is the circumstances under which it was first analyzed. Interned in Changi Civilian Internees Camp, his opening analysis helped take his (and his fellow prisoners') mind off the horrors of the prison.

John Coast, British, writer and music promoter. He wrote one of the earliest POW memoirs of Changi, *The Railroad of Death*, (1946). Coast admitted that he and his fellow officers regularly stole coconuts during the night to alleviate their hunger. Other works of Coast include *Dancers of Bali* (1953), and *Dancing Out of Bali* (1954).

Hugh Edward de Wardener, British, CBE, MBE, physician and professor of medicine at Charing Cross Hospital. He was a member of the Royal Army Medical Corps and operated a Cholera Ward at the prison hospital. He also treated British soldiers who were forced to build the Burma Railway, as fictionalized in the film *The Bridge on the River Kwai* (1957). He was a gifted renal research physician having made many breakthroughs in that area. Although he attained the advanced age of nearly 98, in his last months he suffered from peripheral neuropathy, a legacy of Changi. He died in the De Wardener Ward, the intensive care renal unit at Hammersmith Hospital, London.

Lieutenant Colonel Sir Ernest Edward "Weary" Dunlop, AC, CMG, OBE. Australian surgeon, courageous leader and compassionate doctor who restored morale in the prison camps and jungle hospitals at the River Kwai. Dunlop defied his captors, gave hope to the sick and eased the anguish of the dying. He became, in the words of one of his men, "a lighthouse of sanity in a universe of madness and suffering". His example was one of the reasons why Australian survival rates were the highest.

Carl Alexander Gibson-Hill, a British medical doctor, naturalist, ornithologist and curator of Singapore's Raffles Museum. His main area of expertise and legacy of published knowledge was the natural, geographical and cultural history of Malaya, Singapore and Christmas Island and Cocos (Keeling) Islands.

Ernest Gordon, Presbyterian Dean of the Chapel, Princeton University who wrote *Miracle On The River Kwai* (renamed *Through The Valley Of The Kwai*) which inspired the film *To End All Wars*.

John Hayter, Anglican priest who later wrote of his experiences in *Priest in Prison*.

Percy Herbert, actor. Beginning in the early 1950s, he made nearly seventy films, often playing soldiers, most notably in *The Cockleshell Heroes*, *The Bridge on the River Kwai* (for which he also worked as consultant), *Sea of Sand*, and *The Guns of Navarone*. But he was equally at home in comedies (*Barnacle Bill*, *Casino Royale*, two Carry On films), fantasy (*One Million Years B.C.*, *Mysterious Island*) and drama (*Becket*, *Bunny Lake is Missing*).

Ezekiel Saleh Manasseh, British rice and opium merchant, died in Changi Prison

Sir Percy McElwaine, Chief Justice of the Straits Settlements.

Jim Milner AM, Australian. Former chairman Washington H. Soul Pattinson and former President NRMA.

Sir Alexander Oppenheim, mathematician. In 1984, he published *The Prisoner's Walk: an exercise in number theory*, based in part on his experiences at Changi.

Lieutenant-General Arthur Ernest Percival, commander of Allied forces in Singapore, following his surrender to the Japanese he was moved to a camp in China in late 1942.

Sydney Piddington, postwar Australian mentalist entertainer with wife Leslie, "The Piddingtons" ABC and BBC radio and stage mindreading team, who developed his verbal code in Changi.

Rohan Deakin Rivett, Australian, writer and journalist with Malaya Broadcasting Corporation in Singapore. Formerly a soldier in the Australian Imperial Force. The British surrendered the island on February 15, 1942, but he was not captured until March 8, in Java. His harrowing experiences are chronicled in *Behind Bamboo* (1946). Reprinted eight times, it sold more than 100,000 copies.

Tjalie Robinson, Dutch Indo-European (Eurasian) author, activist, journalist.

Ronald Searle, CBE, RDI. was a British artist and satirical cartoonist. He is perhaps best remembered as the creator of St Trinian's School and for his collaboration with Geoffrey Willans on the Molesworth series.

Robert Skene, Polo player, and the first Australian to be classed as a 'ten goal' polo player, the highest rating that can be attained in the sport.

Julian Taylor, C.B.E., M.S., F.R.C.S., Hon.F.R.A.C.S, neurological surgeon, Senior Surgeon at University College Hospital, a former Vice-President of the Royal College of Surgeons and later Professor of Surgery at the University of Khartoum.

Ernest Tipson, linguist and gifted Chinese scholar. His *Pocket Dictionary of the Amoy Vernacular* (1935) is still referenced during the compilation of modern Chinese/English dictionaries. Another of his publications, *A Complete Chinese Character Course* (1949), was based on lectures he gave in Changi Prison during World War II.

Sir Michael Turner, Chief Manager of the Hongkong & Shanghai Bank (1953–1962).

Loet Velmans, Chief Executive Officer, Hill & Knowlton, America's largest public relations firm. Velmans put aside his horrific experiences as a POW, and worked on improving business relations with post-war Japan, becoming known for his efforts at closing the "communication gap".

Leo Vroman, Dutch poet. After the war, Vroman went to work in New York as a hematology researcher. He gained American citizenship and lived in Fort Worth until his death in 2014, aged 98. In 1946 he published his first poems in the Netherlands, and since then has won almost every Dutch literary poetry prize possible.

Stanley Warren, artist and art teacher; murals produced during his incarceration remain at the prison.

Ian Watt, literary critic, literary historian and professor of English at Stanford University. His *The Rise of the Novel: Studies in Defoe, Richardson and Fielding* (1957) is an important work in the genre.

Leonard Wilson, CMG, KCMG, Bishop of Singapore, Dean of Manchester, and later Bishop of Birmingham.

Sir Michael Woodruff, FRS, FRCS, an English surgeon and scientist principally remembered for his research into organ transplantation. While at Changi he devised an ingenious method of extracting nutrients from agricultural waste to prevent malnutrition among his fellow POWs. He performed the first kidney transplant in the United Kingdom and devised a method for implanting a transplanted ureter in the bladder that is still used today. He established a transplant unit in Edinburgh that remains one of the world's best.

BIBLIOGRAPHY

SOME OF THE information regarding the conversations which took place among the numbers of The Big Six in Tokyo in the first days of August, 1945, and especially those held during the final Imperial meeting when Emperor Hirohito ordered the ruling military to surrender, remained concealed for many years. At the conclusion of that critical meeting, all recorded minutes and proceedings were ordered destroyed at the request of the Emperor. However, Admiral Sadatoshi Tomioka, with the assistance of Admiral Yonai, felt it essential to history to preserve them for posterity. Those papers, along with a number of other documents pertaining to the final days of the war with Japan and the Allies, were subsequently hidden in the private library of Admiral Tomioka who, at the time, was the head of the Historical Research Institute in Tokyo.

The author wishes to express his personal gratitude to Nagase Takashi, a former warrant officer and English translator in the Japanese Imperial Army at various Prisoner of War camps at Kanchanaburi and along the River Kwai, for providing additional information concerning the wording of the secret directive from General Terauchi to POW camp commandants throughout Southeast Asia which ordered the execution of more than one million Allied military and civilian POWs in the final days of the war. He came upon the directive concealed among a number of papers on the desk of his commanding officer at a command post in Bangkok three days before Japan's surrender. His work seeking forgiveness from Allied prisoners of war at the River Kwai led to the making of several films, including *The Railway Man* and *To End All Wars*.[77][78]

Adams, Geoffrey Pharaoh. *An Illustrated History Of The Thailand To Burma Railway Of World War 2*. Published by author, Poole, England 1978

Adams, Geoffrey Pharaoh, with Hugh Popham. *No Time For Geishas*, Cooper, London 1973

Allen, Louis. *The End of the War in Asia*. London, Hart-Davis, MacGibbon, 1976

Baker, Alf. *What Price Bushido*. London, Torch Books, 1991

Baldwin, Hanson W. *Battles Lost and Won and Great Mistakes of the War*. New York, Harper and Row, 1966

Boyle, J.H. *China and Japan At War: 1937-1945*. Stanford California, Stanford University Press, 1972

Braddon, Russell. *The Naked Island*. London, Brian Adams Publishers, 1951

Brooks, Lester, *Behind Japan's Surrender*. McGraw Hill, New York, 1968

Butow, Robert J.C. *Japan's Decision To Surrender*. Stanford, California, Stanford University Press 1954; *Tojo And The Coming War;* Ibid. 1961

Chapman, F. Spencer. *The Jungle Is Neutral*, The Reprint Society, London 1949

Collier, Basil. *The War in the Far East, 1941 - 1945*. London, Sidgwick and Jackson, 1976

Cook, Haruko Taya & Theodore F., *Japan At War- An Oral History*. The New Press, New York, 1992

---

77 https://en.wikipedia.org/wiki/Takashi_Nagase
78 Takashi Nagase: *To End All Wars*. http://www.imdb.com/name/nm0619186/

Churchill, Winston S. *The Second World War: The Grand Alliance.* London, Cassel & Company. 1949

Churchill, Winston S. *Churchill's Secret Speeches: The Fall of Singapore.* London, Cassell & Company. 1946

Churchill, Winston S. *Winston Churchill's Secret Session Speeches*, New York, Simon and Schuster, 1946

Craig, William. *The Fall Of Japan*, New York, Dial, 1967

Donnison, F.S.V. *British Military Administration in the Far East.* London, HM Stationery Office, 1956

Endicott, G.B., and Birch, A. *The British Aid Group, Hong Kong Eclipse.* Hong Kong, Oxford University Press. 1978

Eyre, James K.: *The Roosevelt-MacArthur Conflict.* Chambersburg Pennsylvania, The Craft Press, 1950

Farago, Ladislas. *The Game of the Foxes.* London, Hodder and Stoughton, 1971

Frank, Richard B. (1999). *Downfall: the End of the Imperial Japanese Empire.* New York: Penguin

Gordon, Ernest. *Miracle On The River Kwai*, Quality Book Club, London 1963

Gray, Edwyn, *Operation Pacific: The Royal Navy War Against Japan, 1941-1945.* Naval Institute Press, Annapolis, Maryland, 1989

Guest, Captain Freddie. *Escape From The Bloodied Sun.* London, Jarrold Publisher, Peterborough, England, 1956

Gunther, John: *Roosevelt In Retrospect.* Hamish Hamilton, 1950 London.

Halifax, The Earl of. *Confidential Dispatches, An Analyses of America.* New University Press, 1973

Hong Kong During The Pacific War. [(H.K.P.) 940.5425 - C 45]

Ike, Nobutaka: *Japan's Decision For War: Records of the 1941 Policy Conference.* Stanford, California, Stanford University Press, 1967

Ike, Nobutaka: *Japan During the War: 1941 Policy Conference.*

Stanford, California, Stanford University Press, 1967
International Military Tribunal, Tokyo War Crimes Tribunal Report, 1946-48: See Wikipedia.
James, Dorris Clayton. *The Years of MacArthur, Triumph and Disaster,1945-1964*. New York, Houghton, Mifflin, 1985
Kazutoshi Hando, *Japan's Longest Day*. The Pacific War Research Society, Tokyo Kondansha International, Ltd., 1968. pp. 11-53
Kirby, S. Woodburn, *The War Against Japan, Vol. 5*. London, H.M. Stationery Office, 1969
Journal of Imperial and Commonwealth History, Vol II, No.1. October, 1973. London, HM Stationery Office, 1973
Leasor, James. *Singapore: The Battle That Changed The World*. Hodder & Stoughton, London. 1968
Lomax, Eric. *The Railway Man*, Vintage, New York 1995
Luff, John. *The Hidden Years*. Hong Kong, South China Morning Post Press (SCMP), 1967.
MacArthur, Douglas. *Reminiscences*. New York, McGraw Hill, 1964
Manchester, John. *American Caesar*. New York, Little, Brown & Company, 1964
Masanobu, Tsuji. *Singapore: The Japanese Version*. New York, St. Martin's Press, 1961
Masuo Kato, *The Lost War*. Knopf, New York 1946
Morrison, Ian. *Malayan Postscript*, Faber & Faber, London 1942
Masanori, Ito, *The End Of The Japanese Navy*. W.W. Norton, New York, 1962
Parkin, Ray. *Into the Smother*. London, Hogarth Press. 1963
Pavillard, Stanley S. *Bamboo Doctor*. St. Martin's Press, New York 1960
Rawlings, Leo. *And The Dawn Came Up Like Thunder*, Chapman Publishers, London 1962
Rovere, Richard H. and Schlesinger, Arthur N. *The General and*

the President and the Future of American Foreign Policy. New York, Farrar, Straus and Young, 1951

Russell, Braddon. *The Naked Island.* London, Werner Laurie, 1954

Simson, Ivan. *Singapore – Too Little, Too Late,* London, Leo Cooper, 1970

Smith, Michael. *The Emperor's Codes,* Arcade Publishing, New York, 2011

Snow, Philip, *The Fall of Hong Kong,* Yale University Press, New Haven and London, 2003

Stericker, John. *A Tear For The Dragon.* London, Arthur Baker, 1958

Tojo And The War, Hong Kong University, # 952.033- B98729

Time Life Books, *The Battle of Britain,* Time-Life Books Incorporated, New York, N.Y., 1978

Toland, John. *The Rising Sun: The Decline and Fall of the Japanese Empire, 1936 - 1945.* New York, Random House, 1970

Truman, H.S. *Memoirs, Volume 1: Years of Decision.* Garden City New York, Doubleday. 1956

van der Post, Laurens. *The Prisoner And The Bomb.* W.M Morrow. New York, 1971

Velmans, Loet. *Long Way Back To The River Kwai,* Arcade Publishing, New York 2013

The War Against Japan. H.M. Stationery Office. London. 1956

Ward, R.S. *Asia For The Asiatics? The Techniques of Japanese Occupation.* Chicago, Chicago University Press. 1945.

Whymant, Robert. *Stalin's Spy.* London, I.B. Tauris, 1996

The reference numbers below refer to papers available at Hong Kong University Library:
CHURCHILL'S SECRET SPEECHES LIBRARY #: 940.5342 - C 5
HONG KONG DURING THE PACIFIC WAR H.K.P.- #940.5425 - C 45

JOHN BELL SMITHBACK

ESCAPE FROM THE BLOODIED SUN H.K. - #940.5425 - G 93
TOJO AND THE WAR # 952.033- B98729
JAPAN DURING THE WAR: 1941 POLICY CONFERENCE #940.5352 - I 26

The remarks attributed to Major G.F. Eliot on Page 31 appeared in the *South China Morning Post*, Hong Kong, in an article entitled Japan Must Yield or Fight, and is dated the day of the Japanese attack, December 8, 1941.

The poem HONG KONG 1941 signed L. is from the *South China Morning Post* of November 17, 1941.

Some of the data relating to the amount of destruction and the number of deaths at Pearl Harbor are from *Life Magazine, Bicentennial Issue, 1975.*

The information that the Hongkong Bank had been authorized to move its Head Office from Hong Kong is contained in the *Hong Kong Government Gazette Extraordinary* dated December 3, 1941.

The Internet contains a great many sites containing information that until recently was not available or would have required a great deal of effort and research to uncover. Fortunately, today the interested reader can Google virtually any name mentioned in this study to uncover more information and, in several instances, find videos and photographs depicting all sides of the events.

A huge amount of information and an extensive list of books for further study can be found at www.cofepow.org.uk/pages/books.html

A summary of the surrender can be found here:
* https://en.wikipedia.org/wiki/Surrender_of_Japan

Two must-see films can be viewed at the following:
* hauntedchangi.blogspot.com/2010/01/och-japanese-invaion-of-singapore-ww2.html
* singaporeevacuation1942.blogspot.com/2010_10_01_archive.com

The Japanese Holocaust: Acts of Terrorism and Atrocity
* http://www.ww2pacific.com/atrocity.html

Japanese War Crimes:
* en.wikipedia.org/wiki/Japanese_war_crimes
* http://www.duhaime.org/LawMuseum/LawArticle-1625/1941-The-Japanese-Military-Field-Code.aspx
* www.forces-war-records.co.uk/prisoners-of-war-of-the-japanese-1939-1945
* www.google.com/search?q=japanese+pow+camps+punishments&sa=X&biw=1536&bih=866&tbm=isch&tbo=u&source=univ&ved=0ahUKEwie2LGMzsLNAhVFy2MKHShyAT4QsAQINg
* www.teraph.co.uk/history/world-war-two/10382906/Burma-Railway-British-POW-breaks-silence-over-horrors.html
* http://law2.umkc.edu/faculty/projects/ftrials/tokyo/tokyolinks.html

A song of reconciliation: The Railway Man - Nagase Takashi and Eric Lomax
* www.youtube.com/watch?v=ladeBDc8Ldk

About The Author

A newspaper columnist and former teacher, John Bell Smithback has published more than fifty books defining English idioms and proverbs for an international audience, with his wife as illustrator and translator, as well as *The Lonely Dark*, a novel about America in the age of the atomic bomb, and *Silent in the Dawn*, a collection of poems. For more than thirty years, their educational column has appeared in a number of Asian newspapers, including *Ming Pao* in Hong Kong and the *Star* in Malaysia. John's feature column WRITE ON appears in *Ming Pao*, his fiction in the European journal *Spotlight* and the Canadian literary magazine *Brick*. Describing themselves as "literary gypsies," they have lived in various places including Hong Kong, Portugal, Singapore, and France, all the while producing their books and daily newspaper column. Until recently, they resided in England where they lived close to Shakespeare's birthplace at Stratford-upon-Avon.